# Ordinary Literature Philosophy

Also available from Bloomsbury

*Metanoia: A Speculative Ontology of Language, Thinking, and the Brain* by Armen Avanessian and Anke Hennig
*Lacanian Realism: Political and Clinical Psychoanalysis* by Duane Rousselle
*Lacan Contra Foucault: Subjectivity, Sex, and Politics* ed. by Nadia Bou Ali and Rohit Goel
*Understanding Derrida, Understanding Modernism* ed. by Jean-Michel Rabaté

# Ordinary Literature Philosophy

*Lacanian Literary Performatives between Austin and Rancière*

Jernej Habjan

BLOOMSBURY ACADEMIC
LONDON • NEW YORK • OXFORD • NEW DELHI • SYDNEY

BLOOMSBURY ACADEMIC
Bloomsbury Publishing Plc
50 Bedford Square, London, WC1B 3DP, UK
1385 Broadway, New York, NY 10018, USA
29 Earlsfort Terrace, Dublin 2, Ireland

BLOOMSBURY, BLOOMSBURY ACADEMIC and the Diana logo are trademarks of
Bloomsbury Publishing Plc

First published in Great Britain 2020
This paperback edition published in 2021

Copyright © Jernej Habjan, 2020

Jernej Habjan has asserted his right under the Copyright, Designs and Patents Act, 1988,
to be identified as Author of this work.

For legal purposes the Acknowledgements on p. vi constitute an extension
of this copyright page.

Cover design by Simon Goggin
Cover image © ZUMA Press, Inc. / Alamy Stock Photo

All rights reserved. No part of this publication may be reproduced or transmitted
in any form or by any means, electronic or mechanical, including photocopying,
recording, or any information storage or retrieval system, without prior permission
in writing from the publishers.

Bloomsbury Publishing Plc does not have any control over, or responsibility for, any
third-party websites referred to or in this book. All internet addresses given in this
book were correct at the time of going to press. The author and publisher regret any
inconvenience caused if addresses have changed or sites have ceased to exist, but
can accept no responsibility for any such changes.

A catalogue record for this book is available from the British Library.

A catalog record for this book is available from the Library of Congress.

ISBN: HB: 978-1-3500-8607-4
PB: 978-1-3502-6740-4
ePDF: 978-1-3500-8606-7
eBook: 978-1-3500-8608-1

Typeset by Deanta Global Publishing Services, Chennai

To find out more about our authors and books visit www.bloomsbury.com
and sign up for our newsletters.

# Contents

Acknowledgements vi

Introduction: Literature and speech acts from Austin to
    Derrida to Butler 1

1: Literature as parasite: Austin excludes poetry as a parasite
    of speech acts 7
*Ad* 1: Austin's poetry in *Dead Poets Society* 31

2: Parasite as necessary possibility: Derrida elevates the parasite
    as the poetry of speech acts 49
*Ad* 2: Derrida's parasite in *Romeo and Juliet* 69

3: Necessary possibility as necessary actuality: Butler finds poetry
    in every parasite 91
*Ad* 3: Butler's poetry of parasites in *We Are All Jews and Germans* 111

Conclusion: Literature and political disagreement from Austin to
    Rancière to Ducrot 127

Notes 147
Index 181

# Acknowledgements

Ana, Gabriel, Anton, Ivana and Tone Habjan.

Alexander Beecroft, Rok Benčin, Lev Centrih, Grant Farred, Suman Gupta, Simon Hajdini, Daniel Hartley, Fabienne Imlinger, Alex Juffer, Jane Juffer, Marko Juvan, Jernej Kosi, Primož Krašovec, Marko Kržan, Juliet Flower MacCannell, Raoul Moati, Rastko Močnik, Benjamin Noys, Sowon S Park, Matthew Reynolds, Neus Rotger, Lidija Šumah, Hrvoje Tutek, Jan Völker and Jessica Whyte.

\* \* \*

This book was written at the Research Centre of the Slovenian Academy of Sciences and Arts in the framework of the research project 'The Structure and Genealogy of Indifference (J6-8263)' and the research programme 'Studies in Literary History, Literary Theory and Methodology (P6-0024)', both of which were financed by the Slovenian Research Agency.

Chapter *Ad* 2 is based on an article published in *(a): The Journal of Culture and the Unconscious* 8, no. 1 (2009–10): 35–46, by permission of the editor of *(a)*, Juliet Flower MacCannell; Chapter 3 is based on a chapter forthcoming in *Prismatic Translation*, ed. Matthew Reynolds (Oxford: Legenda), by permission of the volume's editor, Matthew Reynolds.

# Introduction: Literature and speech acts from Austin to Derrida to Butler

Literary criticism loves to accuse philosophy and, more recently, critical theory of exploiting literature for its own conceptual needs; sometimes, however, post-Kantian philosophy doesn't exploit literature enough. The first accusation is a commonplace both in literary criticism and in critical philosophy; the second one has been made sparingly and implicitly, notably in Jacques Derrida's critique of John L. Austin's exclusion of literature from the realm of speech acts. The first accusation results in a mutual misunderstanding between philosophy and literary criticism; the second one has the potential to start an actual debate (like the one started by Derrida). Such a debate can (again, like the one initiated by Derrida) go beyond the question of philosophy's ignorance of literature and, by extension, of literary studies, insofar as literature and literary studies are being increasingly ignored not only by philosophy and critical theory but also by contemporary societies as such, which, as so many late capitalist imagined communities, tend to imagine themselves in globalized entertainment rather than in national or any other kind of literature.

Austin's ordinary language philosophy is about ordinary language. It is not about canonical literature. It is even expressly not about that, insofar as Austin denies literature the status of a proper speech act. And yet literature and other improper speech acts have become the focus of one of the most noticed chapters of ordinary language philosophy, namely its reception in contemporary critical theory, particularly in its many attempts to deconstruct Austin. In short, once this so-called Oxford philosophy reaches the continent, ordinary language philosophy becomes ordinary literature philosophy.

*Ordinary Literature Philosophy* is the first book-length Lacanian reading of J. L. Austin's ordinary language philosophy as it has been received in the continental tradition by Jacques Derrida and Judith Butler as well as by Jacques Rancière and Oswald Ducrot. In this tradition, Austin's general theory of speech acts has been neglected on behalf of his special theory of the performative as well as upgraded with a new attention to the literary and the aesthetic. In *Ordinary Literature Philosophy*, I propose Lacanian readings of these thinkers and put each reading into action by a case study. In this way, I respectively read Austin, Derrida and Butler with a Hollywood blockbuster, a Shakespearean bestseller and a globally exhibited and reproduced May 1968 poster – texts preoccupied with the problem of subjectivity in early, high and post-modernity respectively. Hence, Austinian constatives with *Dead Poets Society*, Derridean naming with *Romeo and Juliet* and Butlerian aesthetic re-enactment with *We Are All German Jews*. All this leads me to Rancière and Ducrot, as they enable a final return to Austin beyond his continental reception. In this return, I valorize Austin with a theory as attractive, and as irreducible, to the continental tradition as his own thought, namely Jacques Lacan's theory of the signifier.

In the book, I trace the process that has led from Austin's constitutive exclusion of literary and other 'parasitic', 'etiolated', 'non-serious' performatives from his theory of the performative to Butler's grounding of her theory of performativity in just such 'etiolations'. I address this continental reception of Austin by applying his own procedure of 'bogging, by logical stages, down'. Ever since Derrida posited Austin's non-serious speech acts as the condition of (im)possibility of 'serious' speech acts, continental close readers have adhered to Austin's bogging down of his own theorization of speech acts, but only so as to reject all the more fundamentally his dismissal of etiolations. As a result, these critical theorists have themselves become liable to bogging down, that is, to the project of analysing how their blurring of the ordinary/aesthetic distinction rests on their blurring of the distinctions among Austin's, and even Derrida's, key categories. Hence, the bogging down continues and increases, leading to Butler's belief in the subversive force of etiolations. For Butler, every performative, even hate speech, is bound to be etiolated and hence subverted by the way in which the addressees receive it – which makes any social sanctioning of such performatives not only obsolete, but even reactionary, as it blocks their reception by the addressees. So, whereas Derrida recognizes etiolations without analysing the institutional conditions of their social recognition, Butler conditions their social recognition precisely on the destruction of their institutional conditions, as she develops an anti-statist argument against censoring hate speech and with it its subversive etiolation by the addressees themselves.

Adding a Lacanian perspective to the recent return of the continental debate on Austin in books by Raoul Moati and Toril Moi, and building on recent psychoanalytically informed readings of Austin in essays by Geoff Boucher, Moati and Constantine V. Nakassis, my book sketches a conception of etiolations as Lacanian signifiers without signifieds, empty signifiers that as such signify signification itself. Such master-signifiers can be subversively appropriated only beyond the horizon of Butler's atomized addressee – as suggested already by Austin's own substitution of his intersubjective model of communication for the logico-positivist opposition between subject and object.

In Chapter 1, I pose the following question: Why has Austin excluded literary performatives as etiolations from his speech act theory if literature has since Aristotle been placed beyond the ordinary/etiolated line, that is, precisely in the field that Austin entered when he refuted the presuppositions of logical positivism by treating utterances as acts? A possible answer seems to emerge once we notice that Austin explains away not only etiolated performatives but also what he calls 'half-way houses' between performatives and constatives, as well as constatives themselves. All these phenomena, I argue, function as Lacanian subjectivating signifiers: Austin excludes etiolated performatives because he excludes the subjectivating effect of speech acts. His readings of *Alice's Adventures in Wonderland*, Walt Whitman and 'The cat is on the mat', his canonical and even sole example of the constative, are analysed in this chapter from the perspective of the Lacanian theory of the signifier to test the proposed answer.

In *Ad* 1, I follow up on Chapter 1, where constatives are shown to be not mere performatives (*pace* Austin), but subjectivating signifiers. I take Austin's famous example of the constative, the phrase 'The cat is on the mat', and trace its use in Peter Weir's 1989 Hollywood blockbuster *Dead Poets Society*. To counter an interpretation of the film written by Alenka Zupančič at the time, I use her own then nascent but by now canonical Lacanian distinction between the categorical and the superego imperative. I employ Sigmund Freud's myth of the primal horde and Lacan's theory of the act to this end as well. The film's poetic topic and aesthetic structure allow me to introduce Chapter 2 and with it a discussion of Derrida's critique of the literary in Austin.

In Chapter 2, I attempt an intervention in Derrida's paradigmatic continental critique of Austin and of his chief advocate, J. R. Searle. As I demonstrate in

Chapter 1, Austin's dismissal of literary and other 'parasitic' speech acts, which has been criticized in the continental reception of speech act theory, is just one example of his ignorance of the subjectivating dimension of the signifier. On this basis, I concretize, in Chapter 2, Derrida's critique of Austin. Positing the possibility of parasites as a necessary possibility, Derrida does maintain that – like Edmund Husserl's 'senseless' expressions – non-serious speech acts can indeed signify, but he finds the source of this possibility in the signifying nature of the act as such. I, on the other hand, recognize this source rather in the concrete institutional, ideological valorization of non-serious speech acts as subjectivating empty signifiers. Furthermore, I analyse this valorization as it is produced by grammar, the institution that in Derrida remains a mere neutral battery of signifiers free of any master-signifier.

In *Ad* 2, I stage and continue Chapter 2 and its Lacanian preoccupations with Derrida's signification; I revisit Derrida's reading of the balcony scene in William Shakespeare's *Romeo and Juliet*. Interpreting the anthological stage dialogue as a monologue, I question not only Derrida's reading of *Romeo and Juliet* but also his implicit critique of Lacan's seminar on Edgar Allan Poe's *The Purloined Letter*. For insofar as Derrida's *Romeo and Juliet* is a return to his critique of Lacan's *The Purloined Letter*, my own *Romeo and Juliet* is a kind of reading that, had Lacan produced it, perhaps might have served as the implicit target of Derrida's *Romeo and Juliet*. I hence aim to provide, in *Ad* 2, a missing link in Lacan's and Derrida's thoughts on the question 'What's in a name?', a task both impossible and always already implicitly achieved by Derrida's allusion to Lacan's Poe. Finally, this may not be without consequences for Shakespeare studies itself, where both deconstructive critics and equally deconstructive advocates of the Bard's place in the Western canon reiterate the commonplaces of *Romeo and Juliet* as a 'bad tragedy' and a 'bad quarto', thus overcoming their methodological divisions in a merely negative way.

In Chapter 3, I focus on Butler's notion of cultural translation, the necessarily endless process of translating identities that are constitutively excluded from the legal notion of universality back into this notion, which is itself said to be retroactively universalized in the process. For Butler, in contemporary multicultural societies it is no longer possible to either universalize a particular culture or define a universal trait of cultures. Hence, the universalization of recognition depends, not on law and the state, but on cultural translation as a process in which excluded identities performatively reappropriate the identitary speech through which they have been excluded. In Chapter 3, I argue that this liberal, anti-statist reliance on the addressees' subversive translation of hate speech and other kinds of identitary speech rests on a misreading of Derrida's reading of Austin's speech act theory. If, in Derrida, the possibility of the speech act is conditioned by the necessary possibility of its etiolation, Butler reifies this possibility into an actuality. For only by treating hate speech as always already etiolated can she claim that it can be subverted by its addressees without their having to resort to institutional sanctions.

In *Ad* 3, I try to demonstrate the reservations I voice in Chapter 3 about Butler's Derridean Austin; to this end, I focus on a historical utterance that Butler could have seen as a paradigm of the performative reappropriation of identitary speech. This historical utterance is in fact seen as a paradigm of political subjectivation by Rancière, one of the two key figures of the following, concluding chapter. The utterance, 'Nous sommes tous des Juifs et des Allemands' ('We are all Jews and Germans'), was launched by a poster, and celebrated as a slogan, against the interdiction of the stay in France issued on 21 May 1968 against Daniel Cohn-Bendit, the student protester whom the entire French political class had identified as a Jewish German troublemaker. In *Ad* 3, I focus on the fact that the protesters reacted to both the pro-fascist *Minute* and the communist *l'Humanité*, instead of realizing that the other that is split between positions as divergent as *Minute* and *l'Humanité* is a barred Other that should be replaced in an institutional struggle rather than sustained as the subject of the hate speech that the poster and the slogan performatively reappropriate.

In the concluding chapter, I return to the Austin–Derrida–Butler sequence as it is analysed in the previous chapters. I address the sequence's limits as they are effectively shown in Ducrot's break with Austin's speech act theory, at one end of the sequence, and in Butlerian appropriations of Rancière's aesthetics, at the other. My 'Conclusion' rejects this Butlerian continuation of the Austin–Derrida–Butler sequence and critically adopts Ducrot's alternative to Austin. After criticizing the way in which certain Butlerians reduce Rancière's theory of the aesthetic regime to a pre-Austinian conception of non-heteronomous art, I trace the source of these appropriations of Rancière to Rancière himself, particularly to his neglect of the institutionalized field of the symbolic as a condition of political subjectivation. As a potential solution, I turn to Ducrot's polyphonic theory of enunciation and reread it with the Lacanian theory of the signifier. For Ducrot, the difference between the utterance and its enunciation is the source, not of the Austinian etiolation of sense, but of sense itself. I present Ducrot's key analysis of ironic negation and solve its contradictions by recognizing in ironic negation the structure of the Lacanian expletive *ne*, and in Ducrot's example of ironic negation a case of the Lacanian discourse of the university, the central ideological apparatus of the capitalist state, according to the classical definition by Louis Althusser.

# 1

# Literature as parasite: Austin excludes poetry as a parasite of speech acts

J. L. Austin is a key figure of Anglo-American analytic philosophy whose work crucially inspired such proponents of continental thought as Jacques Derrida and Judith Butler. The results, however, were quite unexpected, as the inspiration travelled across the epistemological sea. If Austin's speech act theory constitutively bracketed off literary and other etiolated performatives, Butler decided no less than to ground her theory of performativity in just such etiolations. In the process, literature was painstakingly expelled, by Austin's nomothetic (or, in Giambattista Vico's language, critical) science, from the notion of the performative, only to be equally painstakingly elevated to the level of the very notion of the performative by Butler's idiographic (or topical) philosophy. This begs the question of how something that started as a theoretical intervention in the nomothetic ideology of logical positivism could end up as an idiographic ideology of cultural performativity. In this book, I will try to answer this question by drawing, like Butler, from an eminently scientific research programme of the humanities themselves, anti-humanist structuralism.

I will address this continental reception of Austin by applying his own procedure of 'bogging, by logical stages, down,'[1] that is, of refining given concepts in order to develop their contradictions and thus to replace them with subtler concepts. Since Derrida, continental close readers and critical theorists have adhered to Austin's bogging down of his own theorization of speech acts, but only so as to reject all the more fundamentally his dismissal of aesthetic speech acts as etiolations. As a result, they have themselves become liable to bogging down: to a project of demonstrating how their blurring of the ordinary/aesthetic distinction rests on their blurring of the distinctions among Austin's, and even Derrida's, key concepts. Hence, the bogging down continues and increases, leading to Butler's belief in the subversive force of etiolations. Whereas Derrida recognizes etiolations without analysing the institutional conditions of their social recognition, Butler even conditions their social recognition on the destruction of their institutional conditions, arguing for atomistically reappropriated, etiolated performatives. I will propose a conception of etiolations as empty signifiers, or rigid designators, which can be subversively appropriated only beyond the horizon of Butler's atomized addressee. This beyond, far from any mysticism, was delineated by Austin himself when he forsook logical positivism's subject/object pair for an intersubjective model of communication.

But first we need to pose the following question: Why does Austin abstain from conceptualizing literature at all, if literature has since the famous Chapter 9 of Aristotle's *Poetics* figured beyond the true and the untrue, that is, precisely in the realm that Austin discovers as he rejects the presuppositions of logical positivism and develops the idea about utterances as acts? We can venture a reply once we notice that etiolated performatives are not the only thing that Austin expels from his theory of speech acts: besides etiolations, he explicitly excludes the subjectivating dimension of 'half-way houses' between constatives and performatives,[2] while also ignoring constatives themselves. And like the exclusion of etiolations, these two cases of exclusion persist through Austin's key step in his avowed bogging, by logical stages, down, namely the transition from the special theory of the performative to the general theory of speech acts. The problem is thus not just simply that of excluding literature, the exclusion condemned by the continental reception of Austin and ignored by the analytical one. The problem is much more interesting, and it begins with the question of the common ground for the three expulsions. An outline of this common ground, the trait that excludes all three speech phenomena, is something that, as I will argue, the Lacanian theory of the signifier can help us provide.

\* \* \*

As noticed by such thinkers working across the analytic/continental divide as Stanley Cavell and David Gorman, Austin rejects, not literature, but the metaphysics of logical positivism.[3] Indeed, in his famous Harvard lectures of 1955, which appeared posthumously as *How to Do Things with Words*, Austin proposes an alternative to logical positivism. He discovers a class of utterances that, far from reproducing the metaphysical gap between subject and object, produce relations between subjects. Where logical positivism sees only utterances that are true or untrue, Austin notices also utterances that act. Adding such performative utterances about subjects (like 'I am running') to constative utterances about objects (like 'I apologize') allows Austin to break with logical positivism.[4] But far from simply adding performatives to constatives, Austin discovers that, like performatives, constatives themselves can under certain conditions perform an act simply, and only, by saying something. Hence, he degrades his opposition between constatives and performatives into a 'special' theory of the performative within his 'general' theory of speech acts.[5] According to this 'general' theory, each utterance has the locutionary force of uttering a sentence, the illocutionary force of producing intersubjective relations by this utterance and the perlocutionary force of influencing subsequent utterances. Depending on the illocutionary force (which the special theory designated with the notion of the performative), Austin classifies speech acts as verdictives, exercitives, commissives, behabitives and expositives.[6]

The scope of views on Austin's theoretical practice can be said to be delimited by Austin himself, on the one hand, and J. Hillis Miller, on the other. Austin sees his work as the process of producing the special theory of the performative followed by the general theory of speech acts.[7] Miller, on the other hand, regards Austin's work as the process in which the constative/performative pair is undone by the locution/illocution/perlocution triplet, which in turn is undone by the verdictive/exercitive/commissive/behabitive/expositive quintuplet, which finally is itself undone by Austin's resignation.[8] The supplement of the general speech act theory is recognized by both the author and the authoritative commentator, but whereas for the former this supplement finishes a construction, for the latter it starts a deconstruction. But it seems that no matter how many shifts there really are, they all entail the expulsion of literary speech practices from the class of utterance in question; in Austin, a literary utterance can produce neither a performative nor an illocutionary speech act, even when such an act comprises as many as five classes.

Indeed, the exclusion of literary speech acts from all the classes of speech acts that make up ordinary language can be seen as Austin's theoretical practice at a zero-degree, as it persists both in his special theory of the performative and in his general speech act theory. This exclusion implies that Austin deems literary speech acts either superior or inferior to ordinary language, from which he excludes them. But this leads us to a dead end, as we can give arguments for both.

Inferiority seems to be implied by Austin when he treats literature as an etiolated use of ordinary language, language whose complexity is said to be underestimated by theory: 'In real life, as opposed to the simple situations envisaged in logical theory, one cannot always answer in a simple manner whether [a constative] is true or false.'[9] Yet all Austin says here is that ordinary language is complex, and that literature is a form of its etiolation – which is not to say that etiolated language is less complex than ordinary language. As for the hypothesis that, for Austin, literature is superior to ordinary language, there may be some support for it in a certain thesis and a certain testimony by Cavell: the thesis that the theory of those speech acts that Austin had dubbed 'etiolations' in 1955 was developed two years later in Austin's article 'Pretending', but inadequately; and the testimony that Austin himself was not satisfied with the article.[10] However, the empirical fact that Austin has conceptualized literature later and, by his own standards, less successfully than ordinary language cannot verify the superiority hypothesis.

Neither inferiority nor superiority of literary speech acts to ordinary language can be grounded theoretically; the dilemma is pre-theoretical. For the inferiority hypothesis forces upon us the question whether Austin excluded literature because he did not want to analyse it (since it did not present a worthy challenge) or because he was not able to analyse it (and with it ordinary language itself, since the hypothesis claims precisely that ordinary language is even more complex than literature). And the opposite hypothesis necessarily confronts us with the question whether the reason that Austin failed to refine his speech act theory with a theory of literature lies in his untimely death or perhaps in the theoretical inadequacy of speech act theory itself.

Hence, both hypotheses ultimately ask the same question: Is the absence of a theory of literary speech acts contingent or structurally necessary? In the first case, we get a theory of speech acts, but one that cannot serve as a theory of literary speech acts. In the second case, we accord Austin's expulsion of literary speech acts – the gesture that started the superiority/inferiority dilemma – the dignity of a necessary operation, but we derive this necessity from a fatal deficiency of speech act theory. The question raised by the two hypotheses is therefore a false alternative that forces us to choose between a diminished theory and a non-existent one – just like, for example, Lacan's armed robber forces us to choose between existence without money and non-existence when he greets us with 'Your money or your life!'[11] The question therefore has to be rejected, and Austin's line between ordinary and etiolated language moved. Only once we do this can we ask why literature is absent from speech act theory at all, given that literature has since Aristotle been placed beyond the ordinary/etiolated line, which is precisely in the field that Austin entered when he refuted the presuppositions of logical positivism and started to approach utterances as acts.[12]

Let us then see how Austin treated those rare cases of literary utterances that he did actually treat. For if we do this, we can finally articulate the initial forced choice in theoretical, rather than ideological, terms and thereby leave it behind. We can reject, not simply the presupposition that enforces the choice, but the presupposition that is enforced by the choice itself, the presupposition that Austin discards literature. In brief, lacking in Austin's object of knowledge is not literature, but signification. The problem of Austin's relation to literature is merely a special case of the general problem that speech act theory has with the signifying practice. A Lacanian analysis can trace a feature common to all three phenomena ignored by Austin, namely their status of subjectivating signifiers. The reason that Austin rejects etiolated performatives is that he rejects subjectivation, bracketing off the subjectivating effect of the performative and the constative as well as the 'absurd' 'half-way houses' that he finds lurking between them.

\* \* \*

The special case of this problem, namely Austin's bracketing off of literature, can be demonstrated by following Rastko Močnik's idea of projecting Austin's five illocutionary forces of speech acts onto Roman Jakobson's famous six functions of speech events: Austin's verdictives (such as 'I find') correspond to Jakobson's referential function (such as 'This is cold'), commissives ('I oppose') to the emotive function ('Huh?'), exercitives ('I urge') to the conative function ('Eat!'), behabitives ('I welcome') to the phatic function ('Here we are then'), and expositives ('I mean') to the metalingual function ('Do you know what I mean?') – but, as Močnik notices, there is no illocutionary act to match Jakobson's poetic function, the function of language that predominates precisely in literature.[13]

As for the general problem, namely Austin's ignorance of the signifying dimension of any speech act, not just those that we find in literature, this can be conceptualized only with a theory that is stronger than Jakobson's classification of the functions of language (where, as Močnik himself notes, the poetic function, the one function of language that has no match in Austin's classification of illocutionary acts, 'might be just a structuralist oversimplification on Jakobson's part').[14] This kind of theory will be sought, in what follows, in the direction of the Lacanian theory of the signifier (which was the main source of Močnik's analysis as well).

From this new perspective, we can see that Austin not only subsumes literary utterances under etiolations but also gives short shrift to 'absurd', or 'rude', utterances as well:

> Even if we take as half-way houses, say, 'I hold that …' as said by a nonjuryman, or 'I expect that …', it seems absurd to suppose that all they describe or state, so far as they do this or when they do, is something about the speaker's beliefs or expectations. To suppose this is rather the sort of Alice-in-Wonderland over-sharpness of taking 'I think that $p$' as a statement about yourself which could be answered: 'That is just a fact about you'. ('I don't think …' began Alice: 'then you should not talk' said the Caterpillar or whoever it was). And when we come to pure explicit performatives such as 'state' or 'maintain', surely the whole thing is true or false even though the uttering of it is the performing of the action of stating or maintaining. …
>
> … That is, to say 'I state that he did not' is to make the very same statement as to say 'He did not': it is not to make a different statement about what 'I' state (except in exceptional cases: the historic and habitual present, &c.). As notoriously, when I say even 'I think he did it' someone is being rude if he says 'That's a statement about you': and this *might* conceivably be about myself, whereas the statement could not. So that there is no necessary conflict between
>
> (a)  our issuing the utterance being the doing of something,
> (b)  our utterance being true or false.[15]

As our main problem with Austin will be his ignorance of the signifying dimension, and with it the context, of utterances, let us look at some of the text surrounding the 'absurd' retort to Alice:

'They were learning to draw,' the Dormouse went on, yawning and rubbing its eyes, for it was getting very sleepy; 'and they drew all manner of things – everything that begins with an M –'

'Why with an M?' said Alice.

'Why not?' said the March Hare.

Alice was silent.

The Dormouse had closed its eyes by this time, and was going off into a doze; but, on being pinched by the Hatter, it woke up again with a little shriek, and went on: '– that begins with an M, such as mouse-traps, and the moon, and memory, and muchness – you know you say things are "much of a muchness" – did you ever see such a thing as a drawing of a muchness!'

'Really, now you ask me,' said Alice, very much confused, 'I don't think –'

'Then you shouldn't talk,' said the Hatter.

This piece of rudeness was more than Alice could bear: she got up in great disgust, and walked off.[16]

These two passages – one written by an Oxford philosopher celebrated for the wittiest book of ordinary language philosophy, and the other by an Oxford mathematician celebrated for the most philosophical book of literary nonsense – share a strange keyword, namely 'rude': for Austin, it is 'rude' to meet the utterance 'I think he did it' with 'That's a statement about you'; for Lewis Carroll's narrator, whose free indirect speech clearly ventriloquizes Alice herself, the Hatter is being 'rude' when he reacts to her 'I don't think …' with 'Then you shouldn't talk.' In other words, Austin's denial of the 'necessary conflict' between the performative and the constative aspects of Alice's utterance 'I don't think …' is characteristic of Alice herself: Austin, without bothering to check who exactly cut Alice short so abruptly, shares the label 'rude' with none other than Carroll's narrator, the instance in *Alice's Adventures in Wonderland* that uses the word 'rude' to convey Alice's common-sense reaction to the Hatter's (and not the Caterpillar's) reply 'Then you shouldn't talk.' Moreover, 'absurd', the other term used by Austin to distance himself from the Hatter's reply to Alice, functions pre-theoretically as well, insofar as it fails to distinguish between Carroll's nonsense literature and the spontaneous, everyday notion of the absurd, a notion typical, again, for Alice's (but also the King of Hearts')[17] ideological use of the word 'nonsense'.[18] Austin's Saturday morning seminars at Oxford may well have occupied, with their 'learned jokes, donnish jokes, silly jokes, jokes that veered into the surreal', the 'fantastic territory of *Alice in Wonderland*';[19] but what he lectured during the week, either under the title 'Words and Deeds' at Oxford or as the 1955 William James Lectures at Harvard, failed to reach the realm created by Carroll in the actual *Alice's Adventures in Wonderland*.

Austin therefore merely uses the term 'rude', instead of analysing it like, for example, Robin Tolmach Lakoff. Lakoff shows that the inhabitants of Wonderland (but also the creatures from the other side of the looking-glass) seem rude to Alice because they disrespect her conversational implicatures and other 'normal rules of everyday conversation'.[20] As a result, Alice slowly learns that her Victorian ethics are not self-evident at all, as they have no power over the authority of the utterances of the Hatter & Co.; consequently, Alice herself behaves more and more rudely towards the Wonderlanders. These

> ignore or override rules of politeness and conversational implicature. The creatures are regularly intolerably rude to one another and Alice (even as they insist on playing by the rules of etiquette …); Alice is rude out of tactlessness on frequent occasions, with her violations generally emanating out of her awareness of a power discrepancy between herself (or her pet) and her addressees, thus moving from mere non-politeness to rudeness.[21]

Similarly, as we will see below, retorts like the Hatter's 'Then you shouldn't talk' remind Jean-Claude Milner of the tradition of negative protreptic, as he calls the rhetorical device aimed to catch the interlocutor off guard 'at the point of the imaginary where the moment has situated him … to dislodge him from this natural place through a violent motion which … takes the form of diatribe, if not invective: … monological and impolite dialogues'.[22] As Milner adds in a passing note,

> Lacan developed a technique which could be called 'negative protreptic': To incite the subject to wrench himself from *doxa* by scolding him. The technique is not new. The Cynics, for example, practiced it, and one finds it in Lewis Carroll where the excellent Alice, lovable but dull holder of the most Victorian views, is continually insulted by the representatives of nonsense …, a symptom of the real. Finally, one also finds it in the surrealists and Groucho Marx.[23]

It seems, moreover, that Austin's own notion of literature fails to break free from the common sense and to add anything less exclusive on the topic than the following:

> As *utterances* our performatives are ... heir to certain ... kinds of ill which infect *all* utterances. ... A performative utterance will, for example, be *in a peculiar way* hollow or void if said by an actor on the stage, or if introduced in a poem, or spoken in soliloquy. ... Language in such circumstances is in special ways – intelligibly – used not seriously, but in ways *parasitic* upon its normal use – ways which fall under the doctrine of the *etiolations* of language. All this we are *excluding* from consideration. Our performative utterances, felicitous or not, are to be understood as issued in ordinary circumstances.
>
> ... Let us be quite clear that the expression 'use of language' can cover other matters even more diverse than the illocutionary and perlocutionary acts. For example, we may speak of the 'use of language' for something, e.g. for joking; and we may use 'in' in a way different from the illocutionary 'in', as when we say 'in saying "p" I was joking' or 'acting a part' or 'writing poetry'; or again we may speak of 'a poetical use of language' as distinct from 'the use of language in poetry'. These references to 'use of language' have nothing to do with the illocutionary act. ... There are parasitic uses of language, which are 'not serious', not the 'full normal use'. The normal conditions of reference may be suspended, or no attempt made at a standard perlocutionary act, no attempt to make you do anything, as Walt Whitman does not seriously incite the eagle of liberty to soar.[24]

When Austin labels Hatter-like retorts 'absurd' and 'rude', he, as we have seen, assumes the representational view of the nonsensical reduction of performative prefixes to constatives. In the same way, when he regards literature as a type of etiolation of ordinary speech acts, as in this passage about Whitman, the implication is that poetry is about representation; 'non-serious' representation – representation of speech acts – but representation no less.[25] He reads literature spontaneously, as a so-called naive reader, even as a native of language, insofar as the view that language is a vehicle of representation is held and reproduced by language itself: as Oswald Ducrot has shown, the spontaneous self-image of language is the image of a representation, as language speaks of itself using words such as *meaning, expressing, conveying*.[26] So when Austin assumes that literature does the work of representation, that is, of meaning, expressing, conveying something, he unwittingly adopts what language says of itself – and of literature, one could add. But language is the very object of both literary refraction and Austin's theorization: it is what literature estranges and what speech act theory attempts to think as it precisely abandons language's own representational viewpoint for the idea of language as action. And as for the Austinian representational view of the Hatter's nonsense, it is, as we have seen, characteristic of Alice. But, again, Alice is the very object of both the Hatter's ripostes and Austin's inquiry; Austin's reduction of nonsense to non-sense is then the result of his adoption of Alice's common sense, his inability to bracket off his object's spontaneous ideology and to analyse it.

Whereas the Hatter interprets Alice's use of the phrase 'I don't think …' as if it were not a phrase, Austin approaches Whitman's poetry as if it were not poetry. The form of the literary text itself seems accidental to him, as he feels no need to actually cite the Whitman text in question.[27] He has to disregard literature because he reads it solely for its referential function, thereby inevitably recognizing in it an etiolated reference and hence a non-serious perlocution. So, if we want to conceptualize Whitman's appeal to the eagle of liberty, or the Hatter's reduction of Alice's performative–constative half-way house to its performative opening, we have to first introduce an epistemological break and put an end to Austin's common sense.

What is truly common to 'absurdly' 'rude' retorts à la the Hatter's and performatives etiolated in literature (or in jokes, citations, recitations)? What is their zero-degree, the dimension that Austin evacuates from his theory first and foremost? We can begin to answer this question without having to leave the Austinian tradition, where all these types of utterances can be gathered under the notion of pretending as developed by J. R. Searle (even though he himself noticed pretending only in etiolations).[28]

The reason that the Hatter pretends that Alice's 'I don't think …' is a self-sufficient constative, rather than a performative prefix to a constative, is that he wants to reject both this utterance and the illocutionary act itself, namely Alice's rejection of the Dormouse's belief in the existence of muchness. The Hatter pretends that her half-way house is a pure constative, just like a stage actor, a joker, a reciter pretend that they are serious. Pretending is what bothers Austin here as much as in the case of literary or theatrical etiolations. Austin has to exclude the Hatter's 'over-sharpness' because he insists (as does Searle after him)[29] on the 'split'[30] between illocutionary force and propositional content. And on this split of the half-way house between the performative opening and the constative that-clause Austin insists in both Lecture VII and

Lecture XI, that is, both before and after the transition (better, the tendency to transition) from the 'special' theory of the performative to the 'general' theory of speech acts.

\* \* \*

Our generalization of 'pretending' may enable us a kind of leftism in theory, a negative critique of Austin's ideological approach to Whitman and the Hatter, but it cannot show us a positive entrance into a theoretical discussion of these two phenomena. So let us leave behind the external perspective of speech act theory in favour of a structural, relational approach. For Austin's point of view is indeed merely one of exteriority: assuming the position of the naive reader who reads literature with no regard to its intrinsic features and goes straight for the representation that it seems to offer, Austin treats Whitman's literature as a vehicle of representation; and sharing the viewpoint with Alice as she judges Wonderland from the outside world of Victorian Britain, he charges the Hatter with 'rudeness' and 'absurdity'. Hence non-serious nonsense, the purely negative result of Austin's external approach to literature, be it the pathos of Whitman or the bathos of Carroll. The exclusive exteriority of Austin's observations results in his borrowing from the most spontaneous interiority of what he observes: the part of interiority that itself embodies the external perspective, as Alice does when she speaks about the Hatter's nonsense ('rude'), or as language itself does when it speaks about itself and its refraction in poetry (*meaning, expressing, conveying*).

What seems to be missing here is a view of language as what Claude Lévi-Strauss, following Marcel Mauss, terms a 'total social fact': an object as both a 'thing' observed from the outside and a 'representation' created by the object itself in self-observation; to grasp an object as a 'total social fact', writes Lévi-Strauss, 'any valid interpretation must bring together the objectivity of historical or comparative analysis and the subjectivity of lived experience'.[31] Or, in the words of a scholar of pragmatics, 'in social life, *conceptualizations* and *practices* are inseparable', which means that 'there is no way of understanding forms of social behaviour without gaining insight into the way in which the social actors themselves habitually conceptualize what it is they are doing'.[32]

Incidentally, as I hope to show, this forsaking of Austin's approach on behalf of a more Lacanian theorization is not dependent on a focus on the phenomena that Austin chose to exclude from the domain of speech act theory. A Lacanian apparatus will be needed also in the case of Austin's notion of the constative itself, namely the *p* in performative–constative half-way houses of the type *I don't think that* p; the *p* that, as the second half of every half-way house, survives Austin's transition from the theory of the performative to speech act theory.

So, when Austin's external viewpoint is supplemented with the internal one it becomes evident that the Hatter's utterance is a confrontation between two enunciators (to anticipate a term by Ducrot that we will encounter more thoroughly in the 'Conclusion'). The 'rude' inhabitant of Wonderland starts by anticipating Alice's rejection of Dormouse's presupposition that it is possible to draw a muchness. This then enables the 'rude' Hatter to reject Alice's *doxa*: the Hatter interprets her phrase 'I don't think …' in a literal way, turning it in a constative, a statement by Alice about the absence of thought in her mind. With this literalization and constativization, Alice's idiomatic phrase is no longer a statement about the non-existence of muchness, but a statement about the non-existence of her own thought. In other words, the Hatter knows very well – the locution of 'I don't think …' alone tells him, with its rising intonation – that Alice intends to go on and use the prefix 'I don't think …' as just an idiomatic form of negating the proposition that Dormouse uttered before 'I don't think …'. The reason that the Hatter pretends that (he thinks that) Alice is saying that she doesn't think is that he knows that Alice really doesn't think and that, as such, she would indeed reject the possibility of drawing a muchness if he let her finish. Condemned to the eternity of the mad tea-party, the mad Hatter knows what Alice wants to say; but due to her previous utterances (and their surplus, the element in them that reveals her Victorian position of enunciation) he also knows what she really thinks. He literalizes the prefix 'I don't think …' as the statement 'I don't think' precisely because he knows that she really doesn't think. The Hatter doesn't think that Alice wishes to say that she doesn't think; on the contrary, he knows that she wants to say that she thinks (nay, knows) that it is impossible to draw a muchness. The Hatter pretends that Alice doesn't think because he knows that she doesn't think.

As mentioned above, the Hatter's utterance is an exchange between two enunciators, or two perspectives enacted in the utterance. The first enunciator, the one with which Alice identifies, excludes the possibility of abstract painting, as it were, and the second enunciator (here, the Dormouse) allows for it, and this is the enunciator with which the utterer of 'Then you shouldn't talk' identifies, that is, the Hatter. This is one possible way, at least, to formalize the Hatter's reply as a case of Milner's negative protreptic.[33]

Hence, when Austin disregards this ad hominem retort as something impertinent – that is, both rude and, as such, not pertinent for his theory of speech acts – he disregards a dialogic speech strategy. And it seems that when he insists on the half-way house's split between the performative and the constative this is because he wants to avoid treating it along the lines of Lacanian empty signifiers, or, to keep closer to Austinian philosophy, Kripkean rigid designators,[34] linguistic elements that refer in every possible world because they refer merely to the subject of enunciation (in our case, the Victorian point of view of Alice's half-way house, which, without the Hatter's interference, would sound something like *I don't think that there even is such a thing as muchness*).

\* \* \*

But what about Whitman? No different from the Hatter, the speaker who is said to incite the eagle of liberty to soar does that in order to respond dialogically to a previous utterance. Austin, as mentioned above, fails to cite the passage in question, so let us limit ourselves to considering Harold Bloom's take on Whitman's poetry. According to Bloom, modern poetry is the result of the poets' struggle with the anxiety of the influence of their predecessors, and Whitman's strategy in this struggle is sublimation:

> Poetic sublimation is an *askesis*, a way of purgation intending a state of solitude as its proximate goal. Intoxicated by the fresh repressive force of a personalized Counter-Sublime, the strong poet in his daemonic elevation is empowered to turn his energy upon himself, and achieves, at terrible cost, his clearest victory in wrestling with the mighty dead.
> 
> … Every post-enlightenment master moves, not towards a sharing-with-others as Dante does …, but towards a being-with-oneself. *Askesis* in Wordsworth, Keats, Browning, Whitman, Yeats, and Stevens, to examine a half-dozen representative modern figures, is necessarily a revisionary ratio that concludes on the border of solipsism.[35]

Bloom chooses to analyse these figures 'by pairs – Wordsworth and Keats, Browning and Yeats, Whitman and Stevens, for in each case the earlier figure is both a precursor and a sharer in a common precursor: respectively Milton,

Shelley, Emerson'.[36] And his thematic analysis of Whitman's poem *Crossing Brooklyn Ferry* concludes as follows:

> Whitman ... is comforted that others coming after him will see as and what he does. But his majestic poem ... is centered only on his isolated self, and on Emersonian seeing, which is not far from shamanistic practice, and has little to do with external observation. In Whitman, the Emersonian isolation deepens, the eye becomes even more tyrannical, and as the eye's power identifies with the sun, an immense *askesis* is accomplished. ...
> 
> ... Whitman's incarnation as the sun is an Emersonian great Defeat, a flowing-in that contains an ebbing-out, an *askesis* of the Emersonian prophecy of the Central Bard who shall come.[37]

For Bloom, Whitman is not only the victim of Ralph Waldo Emerson's anxiety-provoking influence, but in turn becomes himself the new centre of the American canon and as such the chief source of anxiety for new generations of American poets. In short, Bloom's 'Antithetical Criticism'[38] sees the history of modern literature as a history of antagonistic dialogue 'with the mighty dead'.

But besides this intertextual anxiety there is in Whitman also intratextual anxiety; besides poets, Whitman's use of the English language fills with the uncanny affect also readers who don't become poets. Franco Moretti has called Whitman's poetry 'democratic monologism'.[39] Whitman's style of unstoppable epic cataloguing registers, according to Moretti, not the social and political polyphony of America, but the monologue of this poetry's own formal monotony: the anaphoras of *Leaves of Grass* ('I', 'and', 'the', 'for me', 'what', 'where' ...), tirelessly repeated, acquire 'a hypnotic force'[40] that makes the reader 'forget the things listed' and 'remember, instead, the *form* that holds them together and gives them meaning'.[41] Repetition drains meaning and produces 'a voice, or more precisely a grid – a *gaze*', since '"I see" or "I look" are the most common locutions used to establish the list': the egalitarianism of what is listed gives way to control and surveillance ('Bentham's Panopticon, and Polanyi's "total inspectability"'),[42] the motor of which is repetition itself. And the same is true of the other omnipresent device in *Leaves of Grass*, the rhetorical question; this, too, results in an overdetermination of the dialogic content by a monologic form, as 'the orator puts a second voice on the stage, rather than allowing a second orator to speak'.[43]

Harold Bloom is right, Whitman really does control the American canon by provoking anxiety with his 'tyrannical eye'. But we can now also see that the real, the non-symbolizable element of the voice and the gaze from which the anxiety is coming is produced by an operation that is strictly symbolic, a form of compulsion to repeat. (And although Bloom never moves beyond the levels of motifs and themes, in Whitman's case he cannot ignore the repetition that metaphors and argumentation create as if to set a limit on Whitman's free verse.)[44] Whitman's refraction of the specifically American ideology of liberty is a strictly rhetorical feat; the poetic form itself is the source of anxiety, which is the effective equivalent precisely of the opposite of liberty. It really is irrelevant whether the 'eagle of liberty' is an actual citation or a mere imputation by Austin; Whitman's poetry controls and surveils its readership not so much with its motifs and themes as it does with its form, with itself as poetry. Whitman's poetry itself is what makes his American revolution resemble the state grasped by the following classic example of a somewhat different kind of free verse: 'Freedom, Equality, *Property* and *Bentham*'.[45]

\* \* \*

As we have seen, both literary etiolations of performatives and performatives combined with constatives are observed by Austin only in terms of representation, terms he borrows directly from the objects that he wants to observe. In the case of the specifically literary refraction of language, this would be the spontaneous perspective of language itself and with it the naive reader; in the case of the Hatter's negative protreptic, it would be the Victorian viewpoint adopted by Alice. It comes as no surprise, then, that the same holds for the remaining half of the performative–constative half-way house, the constative.

It must be said at this point that our Lacanian analysis of Whitman and the Hatter can only supplement Austin, insofar as its ambition is to conceptualize phenomena that hold no interest for Austin beyond the appearance of their impure performativity. But we can allow this supplement to help us reformulate Austin's horizon itself if we add to our analyses of 'I don't think …' and 'the eagle of liberty' an account of 'The cat is on the mat', which is Austin's favourite, or better, only example of the constative.[46] And whereas even a half-way house is, precisely as a half-way house between a constative and a performative, still connected to the performative, a constative is of course the opposite of the performative, according to Austin. Which is why it can also easily appear to be the genuine opposite of the subjectivating empty signifier.

In Austin, the constative is a means of representation rather than, for example, a means of manipulation with the representational ideology (which, as I will argue below, is what it actually is). Granted, Austin upgrades his special theory of non-constative, performative utterances with a general theory of speech acts precisely in order to surpass the logico-positivist notion of language as representation. In this general theory, statements become illocutionary acts of stating. But this suggests that here the illocutionary act is a metaphor rather than a concept, insofar as the theory merely takes common-sense notions of acts (a promise, a warning … a statement) and renames them to complicated terms (*an illocutionary act of promising, an illocutionary act of warning … an illocutionary act of stating*). This dialectic of the special and the general is therefore not without a certain twist. When it seems that the last vestige of representation has been overcome, the general theory unwittingly shows its representational presuppositions; at the point where the constative is forsaken for the illocutionary act of stating, the general theory becomes saturated, immune to falsification – and hence ideological, pre-theoretic, reduced to a simple classification of common-sense notions of acts using fancy terms. The absence of a theoretical disintegration of the constative/performative distinction is supplemented with the fetish of 'more general *families* of related and overlapping speech acts'[47] that include the act of stating.

But we don't even have to evacuate the act of stating to the class of illocutionary acts like Austin. We can grasp this kind of act also as the act at a zero-degree, an empty signifier that represents nothing but the subject. 'The cat is on the mat', Austin's sole example of the constative, is a case in point. Well before the utterance 'The cat is on the mat' is a constative, it is a case of iambic trimeter (U – | U – | U – |) with an internal rhyme ('cat' – 'mat') as well as a case of the idiomatic phrase *to be on the mat* ('to face rebuke', 'to be under discussion'). As a rhetic act (defined by Austin as the act of uttering words as voices codified by dictionary and grammar), 'The cat is on the mat' is a iambic trimeter that features an internal rhyme; and as a rhetic act (the act of uttering words as bearers of sense), it is an idiom.[48] Far from representing some extradiscursive reality, 'The cat is on the mat' refers to itself alone, that is, its rhyme, rhythm and idiomaticity. The utterance refers, therefore, to poetic devices that, as Roman Jakobson might add, suspend its referential function.[49] Moreover, if one really wanted to utter the proposition *The cat is on the mat*, one would precisely avoid any structured rhythm and rhyme as well as any literal use of idioms. By uttering 'The cat is on the mat', one can, at best, respond to one's addressee's statement, or non-stated but implied knowledge, that the cat is on the mat (the first word alone, the definite article 'the', tells us that the utterer shares the situation of enunciation with someone, namely someone who knows which cat the utterance refers to). So, knowing that the addressee knows that the cat is on the mat, the utterer could say that this would be a nice opportunity to say: 'The cat is on the mat.' He or she would therefore say: 'Are you trying to say: "The cat is on the mat"?'; or: 'Well what do you know, the cat is on the mat!'; or anything else that would communicate the propositional content *I am hereby saying: 'The cat is on the mat'*, that is, anything that would subjectivate the proposition *The cat is on the mat*, appropriating (and at once alienating) it by citing it.

'The cat is on the mat' is an idiomatic utterance. As such, far from referring to anything – least of all to a cat on a mat – it subjectivates in the Lacanian sense: it represents, not something for someone, but its own utterer for the linguistic system, the machine through which the addressee decodes the meaning of the utterance but also the utterer's position in relation to him or her.[50] 'The cat is on the mat' is not a sign that represents the referent for a receiver, it is a signifier that represents, in Lacan's scandalously circular definition of the signifier, 'a subject … for another signifier'.[51] The modality of the utterance can of course vary; and to some extent, the idiom is dependent on reference, since the conversation must nevertheless involve a cat. But all this must indeed always already exist if the phrase is to be possible at all. And vice versa, if the referent *cat* would first have to be introduced (and especially introduced, as opposed to commented on), a more prosaic utterance would be needed, as its dominant function would have to be the referential one.

Here, the utterer is displaying to the addressee the ability to utter the latter's original observation (that the cat is on the mat) or intention (to report on the cat and the mat) in an unoriginal, conventional manner (by using an idiom, a meter and a rhyme) – while also using this convention in an original, intentional way (literally, prosaically). The utterer is reminding the addressee that the matter of the latter's originality is decided by someone else, the utterer, and that he or she is able to use the convention in an original way only because the other, the addressee, has already made his or her observation or intention known. 'The cat is on the mat' can indeed be used as a constative – as a statement that the cat is on the mat (and not as a statement that the cat is facing rebuke, and/or as a poem) – but only if somebody (maybe even the utterer in a past now) has already constated that the cat is on the mat. And every constative has to presuppose somebody, refer to his or her – refer, hence, to the situation of enunciation itself; every constative has to include an empty, non-referential signifier, something like the 'the' here, that constates nothing but the split between the utterance and the intersubjective situation of its enunciation. If 'The cat is on the mat' constates anything it all, it constates symbolic castration, the irreducibility of the subject's entrapment – and at once liberation – between enunciation and the enunciated, between intention and convention.

The reason that Austin has to 'pretend' that the utterer's intention with 'The cat is on the mat' is to describe the extradiscursive reality is that, if he wants to totalize his theory, he has to limit the constative to what Ducrot talks about as a surface structure where declarative utterances assume the appearance of statements, as opposed to their deep structure, where every utterance is an argument directed at an actual or presupposed other. According to Ducrot, constatives are declarations habitually used as statements in ordinary language, where their regular use tends to create the appearance that they refer to a given property, rather than serving as declarative arguments in the process of (re)producing intersubjective relations. Following Émile Benveniste, Ducrot calls this procedure delocutive derivation. In Benveniste's classic example, the verb *to okay* is derived not from *okay* the noun, but from 'Okay!' the locution; hence, the verb *to okay* simply means 'to say: "Okay!"'.[52] Similarly, the adjective *intelligent* is derived simply from speakers saying that someone is or is not intelligent in their attempts to make arguments that have no basis in any clearly defined concept called *intelligence*:

> On the deep level, the utterance 'P is intelligent' is not a statement – that is, basically it doesn't serve the assertion that a certain proposition (in the logical sense of the term) is in accordance with reality. At this deep level, the description of such an utterance can be purely argumentative ... : one only has to show the type of conclusions in favour of which the utterance can be presented. At a later stage, however, delocutive derivation produces a second meaning for the adjective, where it designates a property that is supposed to belong to the objects X about which one makes arguments by saying: 'X is intelligent'. ... Once this kind of derivation is accomplished, the declarative utterance 'P is intelligent' can be reread, reinterpreted, as a

statement attributing to P a quality that precisely justifies the argumentation that basically is carried by this very utterance. ...

... To my mind, the existence of a property called 'intelligence' is one of the mirages that delocutive derivation produces as it does things with discourses.[53]

Austin's presupposition that the utterance 'The cat is on the mat' is a constative is therefore refutable already from the standpoint of Ducrot's theory of argumentation, according to which declarative utterances are arguments in their deep structure and become statements only if, at a later stage, they undergo delocutive derivation. But our aim should not be to simply replace Austin's undertaking with a different one. The signifying aspect that we found in literary performatives, in the 'absurd' and 'rude' constativization of performative–constative half-way houses, as well as in the constative itself – this dimension of dialogue or argument with the other ought to be introduced back to the theory from which Austin ejected it, and in a way that this theory itself becomes capable of conceptualizing the practice of signification.

In the case of literature as etiolation, this can be achieved with the help of those literary theories that, such as Bakhtin Circle's or Althusser Circle's, show that the specific literary refraction of language is a refraction of ordinary language, the language composed precisely of Austinian speech acts. In this sense, literature is neither etiolation of performativity nor, as Derridean and Butlerian critiques of Austin would have it, the pinnacle of performativity. Instead, it is a 'refraction' or 'interruption' of the spontaneity of ordinary language (to use the terms conceptualized respectively by Pavel Medvedev in the late 1920s and Pierre Macherey in the mid-1960s).[54] The same holds for 'rudeness' and 'absurdity' (which, like 'etiolations', signal with their very names the conceptual problems Austin was unable to solve). The Hatter's 'rude' utterance is up to the task of negative protreptic: 'Then you shouldn't talk' works precisely because it remains within the horizon delineated by the constative and the performative, as it chooses to reinterpret the performative prefix as a fully uttered constative. And the polemical effect of 'The cat is on the mat' is immanent to the utterance itself, rather than being a mere potential outcome of reception.

With the help of Ducrot's Benvenistian delocutive analysis, we could hence show that, in ordinary language, the utterance 'The cat is on the mat' argues instead of constating. Declarative utterances, such as 'The cat is on the mat', are constatives only on their surface, while their deep, non-derived structure is the structure of an argument for a conclusion. But if this is so, all Ducrot could say to Austin on the topic of the constative is that he is being superficial and ignorant of the deep structure – and even this he could say only to the Austin of the first, performativist theory. 'The cat is on the mat', however, refers on no level, including its surface: a delocutive derivation of a constative statement from this utterance would succeed only if it first prosaised the utterance's verse and everything else that promotes its poetic function above the referential one – but this would, of course, no longer be a delocutive derivation of this utterance. In the case of 'The cat is on the mat', no delocutive derivation is needed to demonstrate that we are not dealing with a statement.

But even the fact that Austin insists on illustrating the constative with an utterance that doesn't refer to anything does nothing to refute his concept of the performative; it says a lot only about his firm belief in the existence of the constative, a belief he betrays himself once he changes the theory. Instead, the strength of this kind of critique of Austin's 'The cat is on the mat' lies in showing us what is wrong with his notions of etiolation and absurd, notions to which he is faithful to the end. The reason that Austin needs these notions is that his approach remains limited to a view from the outside, a perspective based on the presupposition that the truth is hidden behind appearance.

If anything, Austin is not being superficial enough. Since he observes the Hatter's nonsense from the outside, through Alice's Victorian eyes, he fails to see that there is nothing beneath the surface, that Alice's prefix 'I don't think …' can be followed only by a proposition that retroactively confirms the prefix, grants it the self-sufficiency of a statement that Alice doesn't think; unlike the Hatter, Austin fails to see that 'I don't think …' really is simply 'I don't think.' But Austin views from the outside Whitman's verse as well, as he borrows the point of view of the naive reader and sees in literature something that primarily refers to something other than itself (albeit in an etiolated fashion), without noticing that the form that is supposed to do the work of referring is utterly self-referential, merely an utterance about the utterer's modality, that is, about itself. Finally, Austin measures from the outside even his beloved example of the constative: he assumes the perspective of dictionary and grammar to decode 'The cat is on the mat' as an utterance with a referent rather than an empty signifier whose sense one would seek in vain in a dictionary.

But what about the performative, the concept that sets Austin's entire theoretical practice in motion? In the performative, Austin recognizes a 'masquerader' that tends to 'masquerade as a statement of fact, descriptive or constative', exactly 'when it assumes its most explicit form'.[55] This means that, if he is right, a performative can have both a form and a mask; moreover, it is when it assumes the form of an explicit performative (such as 'I name this ship the *Mr. Stalin*',[56] to cite an example that Austin chose to give in 1955 at Harvard) that it puts on the mask of a constative (a statement about the act of ship christening). The constative is therefore, if nothing else, the surface of a constative, according to Austin. This is so not only when a statement like 'There's a draft in here' implies a performative ('Please close the door!') but also, and primarily, when a performative has the explicit form and wears the mask of a statement about an act (that is, an order) performed by the utterer in the time of the enunciation of the utterance (that is, the time of the giving of the order).

However, as Igor Ž. Žagar suggests in his Ducrotian polyphonic approach to speech acts, even the performative may very well be 'merely constative, at least in the explanatory sense, which means that it explains the force of the utterance of which it is the sequel'.[57] For example, in the dialogue

'Are you coming?'
'I promise to come.'

the promise may simply be making explicit the constative reply to the question in the following presupposed dialogue:

*Are you coming?*
*Yes. I am coming.*
*That would be a surprise. You never come.*
*I promise to come.*[58]

If this is so, the constative is not only the surface of the performative but also the truth of the performative. Instead of uncovering the face of something other than itself – perhaps even the face of its opposite, the unspeakable depth of the I that is uttering a promise or a plea – the performative merely makes explicit what is always already presupposed, thereby uncovering the face of the subject (but here, there is nothing to uncover, strictly speaking, as the subject is already on the surface, and faceless). The whole thing is reminiscent of the legend of Zeuxis and Parrhasius, ancient Greek painters who decided to stage a contest: the battle was won by Zeuxis, whose painting of grapes made birds fly down to peck at them, but the war was won by Parrhasius, who hid his supposed painting under a veil that turned out to be the real painting when Zeuxis tried to uncover it. In short, 'if one wishes to deceive a man, what one presents to him is the painting of a veil, that is to say, something that incites him to ask what is behind it'.[59]

If then Austin looks for the performative beyond its 'masquerade', beyond the screen that is the constative, Žagar and the Greek legend seem to suggest that the screen is all there is – and that this is less evident than the invisible beyond. Granted, Žagar can no longer have in mind the constative from Austin's first theory; the constative here is closer to what we have seen in the case of 'The cat is on the mat': a promise does refer like a constative, but not to anything outside itself, insofar as it refers to its own dividedness between the utterance (that is, itself) and its enunciation. In the role of the answer to 'Are you coming?', the utterance 'I promise to come' is characterized by the same kind of surplus as the utterance 'The cat is on the mat' when it merely answers a question about a cat and/or a mat: 'I promise to come' represents the subject for the addressee's presupposed reproach – *That would be a surprise. You never come.*

Conversely, if Žagar's invitee were aware that he or she is making, not a promise, but – as we will see now – a declaration, which includes proving (or referring to) his or her constancy, he or she would avoid precisely answering with: 'I promise to come.' For this answer gives the interlocutor the chance to reply along these lines: *No one is asking you to promise anything – and why this overcompensation anyway: are you perhaps thinking of not coming?* In short, the invitee's answer 'I promise to come' retroactively actualizes the potential objection presupposed by the invitee him/herself (and perhaps no one else): *That would be a surprise. You never come.*

In Žagar's own assessment, his analysis is fully compatible with the delocutive approach. Indeed, Ducrot has shown that speech act theory borrows, rather than theorizes, the notions of ordinary speakers not only in the case of the constative (such as 'P is intelligent' above) but also in the case of the performative, the theory's founding ambition. 'The man in the street'[60] and, with him, 'the linguist' use the utterance 'I promise' as a screen onto which they project their 'performative illusion'.[61] In 'I promise', the man in the street and the linguist see a sign of a promise, that is, the promise itself, since a promise is but its own sign. Hence, they think that they can dispose of the utterance and focus on the promise, the thing itself, just as, as we have seen, Zeuxis wanted to move away the screen thinking it is but a sign of Parrhasius's painting. It is because, not in spite of, the fact that the man in the street and the linguist see a non-ambiguous sign in the utterance, and even a self-referential sign in the performative utterance, that they go straight for the referent. Consequently, the former, the ordinary speaker, has no concept of what he is doing, while the latter, the linguist, grants the speaker's spontaneous notion of the promise the dignity of a theoretical concept, equating ordinary language with linguistic metalanguage: 'On his own behalf and without being conscious of it, [the linguist] *did* what speaking subjects do – instead of *describing* what they do and allowing them to become conscious of it.'[62]

This is what Ducrot undertakes when he shows the promise to be no more than the result of a delocutive derivation of a declaration. If Benveniste has shown, as we have seen, that the verb *to okay* means 'to say: "Okay!"', a locution whose use in time derived the verb *to okay*, then Ducrot sees this kind of derivation from a locution at work in any performative, not just 'Okay!'[63] For example, a performative like 'I promise to come' may very well be an act of promise in the eyes of the man in the street, but Ducrot's linguist should be able to describe it as a derivation from a declaration like 'I am saying: "I promise to come."' Which, incidentally, is no different, in its subjective dimension, from a declaration like '*I am thinking: "therefore I am"*' (to use Lacan's derivation of *cogito ergo sum*).[64]

So, just as 'P is intelligent' is, as Ducrot has shown, an argument produced by the utterer that with time acquires the meaning of a statement about P, so too 'I promise to come' is a declaration conventionally understood as a speech act; it is, first and foremost, an attempt to reach a conclusion that the addressee can accept, not an attempt to specify the level of one's attachment to his or her potential coming. One's promise is about the other before it is about oneself; it is an utterance about the other's relation to the utterer's coming that ordinary language treats as a much more monologic, much less antagonistic utterance about the utterer's own relation to his or her coming. Ducrot's question is not whether the utterer of 'I promise' is going to fulfil the promise; the starting point of his theory is the opposite question of why the promise is made at all.

As the result of this kind of delocutive derivation, the promise constates that its utterer is constant; its aim is to confirm what was already uttered. Shoshana Felman talks about this constancy very influentially,[65] much more so than Ducrot or Žagar, but with no less debt to the theory of the signifier. There is much more charity of interpretation in her account, though, as she attributes this valorization of the constative surface, or 'masquerade', of the performative to Austin himself. But as we have seen above, Austin does insist on the referentiality of the constative, and he does rationalize etiolations and the half-way houses between constatives and performatives, precisely because he fails to see that the surface is not at all the surface of something, but the thing itself.

As we have also seen, the constative 'The cat is on the mat' turns out to be a mere dialogic commentary of the proposition *The cat is on the mat*. We can therefore close by returning to the beginning of speech act theory, the constative, and supplementing Žagar's question whether the performative should not be viewed as just a complex constative with the question whether the constative itself should not be grasped as just a complex constative, or, in other words, whether Austin's constative is in fact not just Žagar's constative, a weapon in an argument? It is not enough to recognize in the constative a performative; the constative is something more than that, something beyond Austin's constitutive opposition between the constative and the performative. The constative, this supposedly monologic statement about extradiscursive reality, is, as this opening chapter tried to show, a subjectivating reply to a statement that was already presupposed by the utterer, if not uttered by his or her other.

# *Ad* 1: Austin's poetry in *Dead Poets Society*

The previous chapter suggested that the 'ordinary' context of 'The cat is on the mat', Austin's sole example of what he dubs 'the constative', is one of those extremely complicated contexts that Oswald Ducrot denies pertinence for the analysis of ordinary language.[1] This chapter will be an attempt to disentangle that complicated context. This will take place at three levels. At the first two levels, most of the work will be done by this chapter's object itself as a specific example of artistic texture. This example can help us in two ways: as an artistic text, it always already offers an interpretation of its own realization; and as a Hollywood film, it does this especially clearly, insofar as, in the words of an already cited co-founder of the Ljubljana Lacanian School, 'in American movies, there is always the "coincidence" between narration and representation, which we tend to regard as "idiocy" and say that Americans have to be told everything twice and are hence told everything both in images and in words'.[2] Finally, at the third level, the context of 'The cat is on the mat' will be disentangled by this chapter's own interpretation of this Hollywood film.

\* \* \*

The plot of Peter Weir's film *Dead Poets Society*, released in 1989 (and novelized in the same year by N. H. Kleinbaum), is set in the late 1950s at a fictional New England boarding prep school for boys.[3] The first day of school offers predictable scenes of bidding farewell to the parents, and of reuniting with the classmates, amid the ritual parading of the school banners. Nothing in the comportment of the students or the teachers suggests a coming tragedy, let alone an Oedipal one; the sole exception may be the film itself, which has to show things like the lighting of a fresh candle to tell us that this is but the beginning, not the end, and that the tragic – if not the uncannily comic – hero is yet to arrive. The transition from parental to academic control is smooth even for the youngest of students, perhaps because parental control was itself exercised by the symbolic father rather than the biological one.

The students' public chanting of the 'four pillars' of the school, 'Tradition! Honour! Discipline! Excellence!', is no more conventional than their private reiterations as travesty, horror, decadence and excrement;[4] the same holds for their habitual renaming of the school from Welton to 'Hellton'.[5] No excess in sight, the Oedipus is resolved.

But the film does begin, and the protagonist does enter. The students meet Professor Keating, their new teacher of English Literature – and of how to become a hero. Keating starts by returning to them their object-cause of desire after these well-adjusted adolescents seemed to have already successfully got rid of. This he does in a genuinely artistic fashion: this lover of Whitman takes his students out of the classroom to show them the photographs of their predecessors on the corridor walls: 'If you get very close, boys, you can hear them whisper ... Go on. Hear it? ... Carpe Diem.'[6] Keating needs all these dead semblables plus a dead poet in Latin just to be able to channel a dead poet who wrote in English, namely Robert Herrick and his verse 'Gather ye rosebuds while ye may':

> 'Mister ... Pitts. ... An unfortunate name. Stand up, Mister Pitts. ... Open your text, Pitts, to page 542 and read for us the first stanza of the poem' ...
> ... '"To the Virgins, to Make Much of Time"?' ...
> 'That's the one' ...
> ...
> '*Gather ye rosebuds while ye may,*
> *Old time is still a flying:*
> *And this same flower that smiles today,*
> *Tomorrow will be dying.*'
> ... '"Gather ye rosebuds while ye may" ... The Latin term for that sentiment is *Carpe Diem*. ... Seize the day.'[7]

Having offered his students this translation, Keating takes them out to the corridor and invites them to look at old school photographs and carefully peruse the faces that he is sure they have walked past many times without noticing them:

> They're not that different than any of you, are they? ... Did most of them not wait until it was too late before making their lives even one iota of what they were capable? ... Most of these gentlemen are fertilizing daffodils now! However, if you get very close, boys, you can hear them whisper. ... Go on. Hear it? Can you? ... Seize the day. Make your lives extraordinary.[8]

Here, the English Lit teacher seems to be dabbling in painting: he takes the cue from the visual arts, which (to return to the essay cited at the beginning of this chapter) depict 'that which is missing from them ... by alluding to that which is always missing from a spatial, momentary representation, namely its past, its future'.[9] He teaches his students to recognize in their predecessors their own past and to grab on to the object in the future while they may. As such, Keating's picture seems to come from the Baroque: the commonplaces of *vanitas* and *Carpe diem!* – of the poetics of ruins and of hedonism – are two dimensions of the same Baroque landscape.

But Keating is even more than that, he is almost an author of a total work of art, a cineaste who adds the voice to the gaze to evoke the lost object audibly as well: he whispers 'Carpe Diem' behind his students' backs, while they look at the photographs of their dead predecessors. In this genuinely filmic combination, the voice behind their backs becomes back-stabbing, as it were, as it enables their dead predecessors to borrow Keating's living voice to return to the students their own gaze.[10]

An acousmatic voice and a reverse perspective: obedience guaranteed. Here, no answer to Keating's 'Hear it? Carpe Diem' is needed.[11] After Herrick was resurrected together with Freud's two objects of desire, the breasts and the faeces, Horace and old Weltonians were brought back to life along with the two objects added by Lacan, the voice and the gaze.[12] The murder of the symbolic father, the instance that keeps the object-cause of desire hidden behind a symbolic veil of knowledge, is now just a formality: the students return to the classroom, but only to follow Keating's order and rip the pages of *Understanding Poetry* by Dr. J. Evans Pritchard, PhD,[13] the nomothetic textbook that Keating excludes as 'garbage'[14] and replaces with this idiographic lesson: 'One reads poetry because he is a member of the human race, and the human race is filled with passion! Medicine, law, banking – these are necessary to sustain life. But poetry, romance, love, beauty? These are what we stay alive for! ... What will *your* verse be?'[15]

In one quick lesson, poetry's symmetry is replaced with poets' and readers' membership in the human race; sustaining life is replaced with staying alive; reading 'Dr. J. Evan[s] Pritchard, Phd'[16] is replaced with listening to 'either Mr. Keating or "O Captain! My Captain!"';[17] and, as a result, learning from the Pritchard textbook that 'to fully understand poetry, we must first be fluent with its meter, rhyme, and figures of speech'[18] is replaced with compulsory creative writing. The dichotomy can be expressed 'in terms of the symbolic father, the symbolic authority sustaining the army and the church, and the rule of the superego, the dark underside of the Name of the Father, sustaining the mass', to borrow Mladen Dolar's formulation of Freud's distinction between artificial and primary masses. Moreover, as Dolar adds in a brilliant twist of this distinction's valences, 'one could see in that not a regression to an archaic stage, but rather a clue to modernity, ... something to be tied up with the demise of the symbolic father and the new rule of the superego, celebrated as a feat of democracy'.[19] So, by dissolving the authority of the textbook, Keating in effect introduces 'the regime of the brother' (to cite the title of a Lacanian reading of Freud's primal-horde myth that appeared two years after *Dead Poets Society*).[20]

Along with jokes about the school whose rules he just suspended, Keating, a former Weltonian himself, shares with his new brothers his own past as well, including his membership in Dead Poets Society, a clandestine group of Welton students who used to 'meet at the old cave, and ... take turns reading Shelley, Thoreau, Whitman'.[21] After the resurrection of the students from the photographs but also of Horace and Herrick, it is time that Keating himself and his beloved Whitman provide an alternative to Pritchard's graph of perfection ('If the poem's score for perfection is plotted on the horizontal of a graph and its importance is plotted on the vertical, then calculating the total area of the poem yields the measure of its greatness'),[22] just as Vico's idiographic method itself once provided an alternative to 'the geometral relation', the 'constructed relation, the object on which the philosopher lingers',[23] namely the nomothetic philosopher René Descartes, who 'means, and says, ... that if two and two make four it is, quite simply, because God wishes it so'.[24]

But this God was ripped apart together with the textbook. The toppling of 'the four pillars', a ritual limited, under the rule of the symbolic father, to the reverse, obscene side of the institution, is now itself erected as the new pillar. The official version of the four pillars of Welton had been chanted in the chapel, and the unofficial version had been whispered in the dorm rooms. But far from being a mere external opposition to Welton, the carnivalesque profanation of the pillars was reproduced by the institution as a tradition handed down from generation to generation, not least by students who, like Keating, returned to Welton as teachers. This alone suggests that Keating merely embodies the obscenity of the official rules themselves. So when his teaching becomes the new law, the result is no less institutional than the situation before his arrival. The fall of the old rules is followed by the rise of the injunction to be spontaneous, and spontaneity is understood, in Keating's 'liberal humanism',[25] along the lines of the ideology of sincerity and authenticity. The dethroning of Pritchard's nomothetic formalization of poetry is followed by the crowning of Keating's idiographic empathy for, or *Einfühlung* in, poetry; instead of symbolic alienation from poetry, the students get imaginary identification with Keating and his dead poets.

As such, the students are eager to comply when their teacher-cum-brother asks of each of them to take a walk in the courtyard as spontaneously and originally as possible, kick the football while reciting a verse as authentically as they can (a verse selected by Keating, that is), look at the classroom from a new perspective high up on the desk. The tautology of this last exercise was pointed at already by Henry A. Giroux, who noted that, once these students graduate, they will assume the highest positions in business and politics anyway.[26] The dialectic of walking seems to bring this tautology to its highest point, the contradiction. When the first three students begin to walk more and more conventionally, Keating starts clapping along like a drill sergeant; when the others begin to clap along, he reminds them that they are no better; and when one of them decides to exercise his right not to walk, Keating uses him as the illustration of the whole point, namely to swim against the stream. Keating starts by guaranteeing to the students that his intention is, not to ridicule them, but to liberate them from the shackles of conformity. But this only enables him to enchain them even more by showing them that any manner of walking can be accompanied by army-like clapping, which in turn can reveal the uniformity of the audience – which, finally, can unwittingly achieve the aim even (if not only) if it does nothing but exercise the right not to walk. So, when that one student exercises this right by neither walking nor clapping to the walking of the others, Keating can turn this negativity into an internal limit, an endpoint of the positive freedom administered to the students by Keating himself. The big brother replaces the prohibition of transgression with the injunction to transgress, demanding even of walking, gression, to be trans, above itself, original. But when the students are demanded to walk in an original way, they, of course, inevitably end up mimicking the various ways of walking they know from the movies or the circus; sincere and authentic exploration of the depths of self discovers only repetition of others.

Let us see how this clan of brothers, this reincarnation of the Dead Poets Society, transgresses the rules of poetry itself. Besides their ways of walking, the students have to show also their poetry to Keating and his Whitmanesque 'tyrannical eye' or 'gaze' (to borrow two notions of Whitman cited in Chapter 1), the 'evil eye' looking less for objects than for their very '*showing*' (to add Lacan on the gaze as object of desire).[27] After the original walks across the courtyard whose non-originality Keating is quick to expose with the kind of impersonations one expects from the actor playing him, Robin Williams, the students are tasked with writing their own poems. The outcome seems to be varied: while Neil falls in love with poetry almost without the help of the big brother, his schoolmate Todd is not lured in by Keating. But this variety of responses to the homework is just the empirical face of a certain speculative identity between Neil and Todd, as these classmates can easily exchange their respective positions at this stage of the plot. Connected with an invisible thread that only death can cut, Neil and Todd all too easily exchange their respective roles of poetry lover and poetry hater, and *Dead Poets Society* shows this exchange as a story, *muthos*, that the film basically is. Todd starts out as the only student who doesn't have a poem of his own to recite, but Keating, using the method of free association, manages to evoke in him the image of Whitman as, in Todd's own mumbling words, 'a sweaty-toothed madman … with a stare that pounds my brain',[28] a creature 'mumbling' through Todd's mumbling voice this little poem:

> Truth … Truth is like a blanket that always leaves your feet cold! … Stretch it, pull it, it will never cover any of us. … Kick at it, beat at it, it will never be enough. … From the moment we enter crying … to the moment we leave dying, it will cover just your head as you wail and cry and scream![29]

This is the result of Keating using free associations to activate Todd's desire and make him do the homework right there in the classroom: a poem whose spontaneity is matched, and belied, only be the fact that Todd, caught in his associations, has to accredit it to Walt Whitman himself. But that is no problem for Keating, as he is less interested in producing original verbal art than in activating his students' desire. Which, in turn, is no problem for poetry itself: if Keating's channelling of the students' dead predecessors enabled us to return to that co-founder of the Ljubljana School from the beginning of this chapter and cite him on the visual arts, Keating's student Todd's channelling of what he imagines could be Whitman can only be met with the passage in full:

> The visual arts are the arts of representation; that which is missing from them they depict by alluding to that which is always missing from a spatial, momentary representation, namely its past, its future. This lack of representation is the object, and a good work of art evokes it in the representation itself. Literature, on the other hand, is the art of the signifier; the object falls out of it at the outset. But literature nevertheless evokes the object through the affect, that is, indirectly, as the signifier induces the affect in the reader. So, in painting, *the object is evoked*, whereas in literature, the *affect* aroused by the object *is induced*.[30]

'Don't you forget this.' When Todd mumbles the last verse of his free associations and opens his eyes to a class of mates who suddenly start to clap and cheer, Keating puts his hand on the back of the new poet's head and whispers: 'Don't you forget this.'[31] At the end of the scene, Todd Anderson should not forget the beginning, when he admitted that he hadn't wrote a poem, to which Keating said this in front of the entire class: 'Mr. Anderson believes that everything he has inside of him is worthless and embarrassing. Correct, Todd? Isn't that your fear? ... Then today we will see that what is inside of you is worth a great deal.'[32] Between his obscene ridicule of whatever the students do to meet his own expectations, on the one hand, and, on the other, his patronising grand finales à la 'Don't you forget this', Keating seems to be following the motto of the concluding session of Lacan's *Seminar XI*: '*I love you, but, because inexplicably I love in you something more than you – the* objet petit a *– I mutilate you.*'[33] No wonder, then, that the scene in which Todd is born as a poet, even a dead poet, is followed by an almost homoerotic scene of football scored to Ludwig van Beethoven's *Ode to Joy*, a monument to humanity notoriously loved by authoritarians left and right.[34]

\* \* \*

This turmoil in the fictional Welton Academy is set in late 1950s New England, I said at the beginning of this chapter. In fact, the year is 1959, and the film location is St. Andrew's School in Middletown, Delaware, which is one of the Middle States, not a state in New England. Ever since *The New York Times* review,[35] though, the film has been associated with New England (most often the state of Vermont), and understandably so: Welton is designed as if it wanted to become a new England. The only thing locating Welton in the United States is the national flag, but even this is only a detail of a fresco on a corridor wall. The only thing locating the school in the 1950s is the car it features to take students to pre-approved dinners with alumni families. Everything else that this prep school has pretends to be shifting the students from the core of the world-system at the time, the post-war United States for which it is supposed to prepare them, to the previous core, Great Britain: the football I mentioned at the end of the previous section is association football, and there is no American football in sight, nor is there any jazz or rock and roll – radio is prohibited – but (as Giroux notices) also no beat poetry;[36] there is, however, no lack of mist, rowing, Scottish pipes or professors' Oxford English. The school offers all this academic kitsch, and yet it takes a former Weltonian coming back from London and freeing his students from 'Hellton' to turn Welton into a hellishly claustrophobic primal horde. Only Keating takes the ritual folklore literally, realizing the metaphoricity of British Romanticism and establishing a law of enjoyment whose implementation he obstructs by, paradoxically, following it with the excessive commitment of the superego.

Keating's sadistic comments about the insufficient sincerity and authenticity of the students' enjoyment effectively prevent that which they proscribe. We already touched on the contradiction of walking the school courtyard sincerely and authentically, so let us just briefly mention some of the other examples before focusing on the one that can lead us to the source of Keating's law of enjoyment.

In matters of sport, this law is, not simply Romantic, but overtly neoliberal: in the scene where Keating encourages his students to kick the football while reciting an uplifting verse, he, as already mentioned, provides the verses himself – and even introduces this exercise in spontaneity with the following spontaneity-crushing lesson: 'In … sport … other human beings can push us to excel.'[37] When it comes to more explicit bodily pleasures, the coexistence of enjoyment's injunction and prohibition is more explicit as well: when Charlie, a member of the Dead Poets Society, publishes his anonymous demand that girls be admitted to Welton and then uses the resulting school assembly to act out, Andy Warhol-like, a phone call from God asking for the same thing, Keating warns him that he should be less audacious in his spontaneity – only to mock him for not being audacious enough to make the phone call from

God collect.[38] Similarly, when Keating tells the students about the society, he warns them that school authorities would never allow them to bring the society back to life – but also leaves for Neil to find the protocols of the original society. Finally, when the desperate Neil confides to his mentor that his stern father forbade him to pursue an acting career or even to play Puck in a local production of *A Midsummer Night's Dream*, Keating suddenly forgets his own lessons and tells his closest devotee that he should either convince his parent or postpone everything until he reaches financial independence.

Which brings us to the liminal example announced above, the meeting point of the two ends of the Möbius strip that the students walk even when they don't walk the courtyard – the band that takes them from the paternal prohibition of enjoyment to Keating's brotherly law of enjoyment, and back. The coexistence of both kinds of law forces Neil to choose between his father and his new big brother. He is the only member of the society whose empirical father had to actually work to be able to pay for Welton. Neil is therefore not allowed to take up any career that doesn't justify all the sacrifices the father made (and made his wife and their son make).[39] But Neil's chances on the job market are limited from the start, compared to those of his classmates, while the other, libidinal economy (the only economy that his father truly cares about) never works out without a certain remainder anyway. That which is forbidden is therefore the impossible; the prohibition is a prohibition of the impossible, in other words, a taboo. But this finally turns the impossible into the object of desire; his father's prohibition of enjoyment is what makes Neil so susceptible to Keating's injunction to enjoy, which, as such, can only lead to a prohibition, the forbidding of enjoyment that lurks behind Keating's brotherly advice to Neil to act according to the circumstances and adapt the aim to the means – in other words, to act pathologically, unethically.

At this consultation with Keating, Neil seems to have learned that the big brother, as someone who is satisfied by no object, no poem, no disobedience of authority and no style of walking, embodies only the truth of his father's prohibition; Neil appears to have realized that the injunction to enjoy is a mere explication of its opposite as his big brother's laughter obscenely supplements his father's sternness. This is at least the realization Neil displays in practice when he rejects the respective desires of both the father and the new brother, barring the desire of the Other and being faithful only to the desire in its pure form, the death drive. When the night before the premiere of *A Midsummer*

*Night's Dream* Keating asks him if he followed his advice, Neil lies and says that, in the end, his father did allow him to play the role he auditioned for but won't be able to see the play due to a business trip he has to make.[40] This lie – potentially, in the symbolic register, but nevertheless – bars the Other, giving up on the father and the big brother at the same time. And when this lie is no longer sufficient, and the father drags his son from the post-premiere party (while Keating, the other side of the Other, merely calms the other students down when they try to help their friend), Neil does something that Jacques-Alain Miller might, and Alenka Zupančič actually does, call the act, the only act that a subject can actually do, the act of trespassing the field of the Other, of mere relationality, of the non-all nature of the symbolic order: Neil commits suicide.[41]

Suicide is needed to free Neil from the gaze he had presupposed on both sides, the father's and the brother's. Suicide is Neil's way out of a life without acting – a life in which he would only be playing the part of the dutiful son, as Keating reminds him[42] – as well as a way out of a life of trying and failing to please Keating's own superego demands. When Neil lets go of theatre, he betrays Keating without yielding to his father, whose desire he betrays as well, as he lets go of theatre in a way that his father would never wish for, a way that addresses his father's demand that he quit acting and Welton for a military school and then Harvard's medical school and retroactively turns it into his last demand, his father's last will, as it were. The Other is exposed in its idiosyncrasy, its idiocy, its ignorance about Neil's desire: Keating sees through Neil's lie, but doesn't show it because he realizes that Neil has already left the conversation, given up on the consultation and with it the realm of the symbolic (so that, by pretending that he believes Neil, the mentor pretends that he himself hasn't lost yet); and once Neil exits this symbolic realm of intersubjectivity for good, his big brother, like his father, can only cry. When Neil, as the subject born out of the suicide of the subject, forces his mentor and his father to face his act and its utter inexplicability, he demasks both theatre masks, his father's weeping and his mentor's laughter. Theatre – whose consumption would sooner or later turn it into an abject just as surely as its prohibition had turned it into an object of desire – Neil's suicide replaces with the object of desire in its purest, that is, nothing, the absence of any object.

'For the first time in my whole life I know what I want, and for the first time I'm gonna do it whether my father wants me to or not! Carpe diem …!'[43] This is how Neil declared to Todd his decision to become a stage actor. But this was his father speaking through him – using, moreover, the words of Keating (which, in turn, were always already the words of his own Other, Horace). Neil's act therefore frees his desire from the desire of both his father and his teacher: both the one who moved theatre from the dimension of pleasure to the realm of enjoyment when he prohibited it and the one who presented this realm as something one can actually reach of one's own free will. Neil's act of suicide exposes the Other to the traumatic object, but, unlike Keating, it provides no fantasy, no set of instructions for the taming of that object. This challenges all those who stayed behind in their fidelity to the real, a test that most of them fail, as they disavow the event and turn to the institution for meaning, which the institution in question, the school, is all too keen to provide. On his part, the father demands an investigation into the circumstances of the suicide, and the school loses no time to blame Keating for having lured the student into disobedience, and terminates his appointment. But Keating has no fidelity to Neil's act either: just as he had allowed Neil's father to take the son away from the post-premiere party, he now peacefully leaves the school, even if, as he had told the boy at that consultation, he doesn't want to be anywhere else. Even the students begin to feel guilty, after Neil's suicide, for the initial parricide they committed fuelled by Keating's preaching of freedom; in the terms of Freud's myth of the primal horde, they begin to manifest 'deferred obedience' to the dead father,[44] the school that they had already seen through as members of the society.

In myth as well as in fact, though, the deceased wields a power greater than anything he had when he was alive; a power that could save his life if only it weren't attainable only in death. When Keating destroyed his students' coordinates of desire – the frame connecting the four public pillars and their private profanation – he not only made the students question their true desire but also offered his own desire by way of answer. Yet the question of what the Other really wants as it invites me to enjoy remained unanswered as the declaration of the Dead Poets Society turned out to be an insatiable, frameless superego imperative of a dead letter (taken from Horace, Herrick, Whitman or any other dead poet). The only answer the students could offer Keating was themselves, their transference love. And when it becomes clear to them that the big brother cannot be satisfied, that his every love message is accompanied by sadistic ridicule, they try to return to the old frame in 'deferred obedience'. But there is no turning back anymore: deferral is always already retroactivity, the students can obey only an absent yet presupposed father. The transgressive flip side of the pillars implodes and the motto that even most of the schoolteachers repeat as a senseless ritual becomes law to most of the students, who break one by one and sign a statement blaming Keating for the events that have led to Neil's suicide (as if this act can be reduced to a pathological result of prior events), returning to school without ever again thinking of the society. The frame is thus narrowed down to a single point: only one student remains faithful to Neil's fidelity to the real, non-symbolizable remainder of the Other.

Todd, the mumbler, steals the final scene of the film by stepping on his desk like Keating taught him to and bidding farewell to the now abandoned teacher, as if to remind him that he has given ground relative his desire and abandoned himself.[45] When Keating interrupts the class taught by his own substitute teacher, the headmaster, collects his personal belongings under close scrutiny by his former overseer and looks at Todd for the last time, the hystericized student still seeks and then avoids his uncanny gaze. But when Keating reaches the door to remove from the classroom the traumatic object that he has become, Todd reminds him of his own imperative in its pure form, and of the fact that it is imperative to him first and foremost, and cheers for the first and last time: 'O Captain! My Captain!'[46] Unlike most of the students, who had welcomed Keating's self-given nickname with enthusiasm, Todd accepts it only at the moment he can in effect use it to summon an absent man, as if to make explicit the functioning of any name and the metaphoricity of this particular name. For 'O Captain! My Captain!' is Keating's citation from Whitman's appeal to the dead Abraham Lincoln. Just as Whitman calls on the assassinated president, his 'father', to 'rise up', the students, having torn their textbook, their symbolic father, had recognized in brother Keating a new father who, however, all too quickly revealed himself as a dark double of the textbook father, a doppelgänger impossible to awaken with one's love cries, a father who, like Lincoln, 'has no pulse nor will'.[47] Whereas Keating introduced 'O Captain! My Captain!' to deliberately name himself in an informal and spontaneous way, Todd takes up the name (giving it its very last reiteration) to unwittingly call Keating to account at the moment this big brother disowns his name to escape the consequences of Neil's suicide and to effectively follow the headmaster himself in reducing this act to a pathological acting out for his own gaze. Todd therefore assumes Keating's desire only when it is cleansed of the pathology of the big brother and when 'Carpe Diem' is emptied of all content.

But our interpretation should not end with this fidelity to the act. For the uncanny object that Todd brings back after everyone from Neil's father and school administration to Keating and the students tried to substantialize and embody in Keating is substantialized on their behalf by the film itself. Calling Keating by the name 'O Captain! My Captain!', Todd looks at the camera – yet this is no gaze as *objet petit a*, the viewer is not returned his or her own gaze, because the perspective from which the viewer sees Todd looking at the camera is simply the point of view of Keating, the addressee of 'O Captain! My Captain!' Todd's gaze is framed in Keating's perspective, and, for the first time, the viewer sees what Keating sees. But as Keating has already abandoned his fidelity to the object, he can now also limit Todd's gaze to the nomothetic geometral relation that he once made the students tear apart together with the textbook: Keating sees Todd looking at him and, with him, at the camera through the spread legs of a student in the forefront who also mounted his desk, the student's trouser legs framing Todd's gaze with a shape reminiscent of the upper half of a losange.[48] At first glance, this dark frame seems to throw an eerie heavenly light on Todd, but, at a second, final glance (at once Keating's and the viewer's), it merely separates Keating and, with him, the viewer from the unmediated traumatic gaze. The heavenly light becomes the light in an earthly classroom, and the darkness in the room becomes a detail of the uniform worn by a random student; Todd's non-human, 'saintly' position of an outcast loses its inexplicability as it dissolves into an expression of human warmth of a future representative of the bourgeoisie, a 'priest' in this or that institution.[49] The viewer sees (Keating's) fantasy that the object can be schooled – which makes it possible for the viewer to see anything at all. The film does show Todd's gaze, but through Keating's eyes, as if it were unable to resist quilting the *objet*, the absence of objectivity, into an empirical object, the dark edge of a ray into a slit.

As such, *Dead Poets Society* betrays the potential of its own story and reproduces the conservative nature of its genre. By victimizing Neil and indicating that his suicide served a purpose after all, endowing Todd with a human face, the film misses the chance to suggest that this humanity, the inner freedom preached already by Keating, will enable Todd to thrive precisely under the external coercive laws of the society for which Welton was built to prepare him. Sincerity and authenticity as capitalism with a human face.

*  *  *

The end. The only thing left to do is to say how any of this can help us on our way to ordinary literature philosophy. To do this, we have to return to the scene of poetry recitation, where the film unwittingly interprets itself. The handful of youngsters who, unpersuaded by Keating, are reluctant to compose poetry include a certain Hopkins, who does no more to fulfil Keating's task than uttering, very rhythmically: 'The cat sat on the mat.' Not exactly 'The cat is on the mat', the only example of the constative Austin chose to give at Harvard in 1955, but 'The cat sat on the mat.' Now, if a fictional character placed in a prep school for Harvard in the year 1959 thinks that 'The cat sat on the mat' is a poem, it has to be a ready-made; it becomes a lot more, though, if read against the backdrop of the clan of brothers delineated in the sections above. Keating has presented Hopkins and his classmates with the following alternative: either the Shakespearean unity of content and form demanded by the Pritchard textbook or his own Romantic law of sincerity and authenticity; either 'medicine, law, banking' or '*O me! O life*', as he likes to cite from Whitman.[50] An alternative as alienating as 'Your money or your life!' (Lacan's example of a forced alternative that we already met in Chapter 1), this is nevertheless exactly what Keating offers to his students – before sadistically demanding both options at once, that is, the impossible: his advice to Neil is that he postpone his acting career until he reaches financial independence, and his advice to everyone is that their 'poetry, romance, love, beauty' merely supplement 'medicine, law, banking' and all the other pursuits that 'sustain life'. And Hopkins does choose the impossible point of intersection itself: just like Neil's lie, Hopkins's 'The cat sat on the mat' rejects both the society and the textbook.

Needless to say, 'The cat sat on the mat' is hardly the sort of poem the brotherly clan would appreciate. Indeed, Keating's review is predictable: for him, 'The cat sat on the mat' is the first poem to have a negative score on the Pritchard scale. He does, however, reassure Hopkins that the class is laughing near him, not at him, and that a poem can indeed have a simple theme, like a cat, a flower or rain, as long as it is not 'ordinary'.[51]

A devastating critique, albeit more topical than critical, to use Vico's terms for the idiographic and the nomothetic approaches. Keating begins critically, nomothetically: borrowing from the very textbook he made Hopkins and his classmates tear to pieces, he says that Hopkins's poem would make the textbook project the graph over its origin. But this is just to ridicule the textbook one more time, not the poem, as Keating shifts into the topical, idiographic mode, patronisingly saving the poem with the topos of simple themes such as cats, flowers or rain (all of which are topoi themselves). Neither the critical approach nor its topical alternative can save Hopkins's little poem, then. In turn, however, his poem marks the zero-degree of these approaches and with it the truth of verbal art as, once again, 'the art of the signifier' from which 'the object falls out ... at the outset' but which 'nevertheless evokes the object through the affect': 'The cat sat on the mat' is a chain of signifiers as well as an idiom irreducible to its lexical components, that is, an icon, a picture. Hopkins in effect manages to merge literary narration and visual representation, thereby reaching the intersection between poetry and painting, the impossible intersection sought by both poetry and painting, according to Gotthold Ephraim Lessing (and Rastko Močnik, who in the passages cited above formalizes Lessing's aesthetic in terms of signifiers and objects). As a spatial poem and at once a temporal painting, 'The cat sat on the mat' induces the affect aroused by the object that is structurally absent from the signifying chain and evokes this object in the same breath. It induces laughter while evoking 'that which is always missing from a spatial, momentary representation, namely its past, its future'. This enables the poem to locate the brotherly clan in its context and make visible its insincerity and inauthenticity. Together with his poem, Hopkins recites to Keating's little brothers their truth: the uncanny proximity of the object from which they fled straight into the poetry workshop where they only ran into Keating, the figure they were in fact running away from as they were trying to escape the object of desire aroused by none other than Keating. With his little poem, Hopkins returns into Keating's symbolic universe the empty signifier, 'The cat sat on the mat', as precisely an empty signifier, a symptomatic embodiment of the repressed relationality and arbitrariness of the clan. Hence laughter – the affect of anxious laughter – as the effect, even the *Verfremdungseffekt*, of Hopkins's self-authorization. This is why Keating feels the need to criticize the poem and its object – the poem as its object – within the textbook aesthetic as well as within the aesthetic he conjured up to replace the textbook; and this is why, between the two criticisms, he has to try to neutralize his students' involuntary, automatic laughter as a kind of carnivalesque laughter by reassuring Hopkins that the class is laughing near him, not at him.

What is it that makes his brothers laugh even before Hopkins finishes reciting his little poem? Why does everyone know intuitively, without delay, that, as René Magritte might say, this is not a poem? We can quickly rule out the usual suspects: the fact that 'The cat sat on the mat' doesn't refer to anything can't be the problem, since no artwork is about reference (the irrelevance of any original context to be referred to is even the condition of possibility for a work of art); there can't be any problem with the formal side either, because, after all, Hopkins does offer his audience a perfect iambic trimeter with an internal rhyme; and even the ordinary motif is fine, given that even Keating says that sometimes the most beautiful poetry can be about simple things, like a cat, a flower or rain. All that remains are the poem's overt insincerity and inauthenticity, and, indeed, Keating's idiographic encouragement is directly followed by his critical prohibition of those, and only those, poems that are ordinary. The problem is that the whole syntagm, not only its individual parts, is literally taken from ordinary language as a kind of ready-made that the audience automatically recognizes, thereby saving what Freud would call the psychic energy needed for recognition and discharging that energy by laughter.[52]

'The cat sat on the mat' is no laughing matter, though. One of the ways Welton's headmaster prepares his students for entrance into the ruling class is by personally administering corporal punishment; as for Keating, he merely supplements the existing class divisions with his humanism. Between spanking and suicide – between nomothetic formalization and idiographic empathy, Pritchard's Shakespeare and Keating's Whitman, the old and the enlightened Bard,[53] money and life, representation and narration, the Cartesian subject and the Lacanian object – Hopkins chooses their intersection, a third voice, the voice as object. Yet this choice is, of course, impossible and as such made in an impossible manner, by uttering something that is neither scientific nor artistic, neither constative nor performative, and yet intervenes in all these fields to reject the forced choice itself.

Since his is a poem with a predominant poetic function (albeit in its negativity, its zero-degree of literary narration and visual representation),

Hopkins is able to negate the forced alternative between Pritchard's textbook and Keating's poetry without having to give up poetic language as such. In this sense, 'The cat sat on the mat' is not an act of a truant, an act of exiting the school field, but an act of prefiguring the field as a whole, which is what an act basically is. 'This is battle … War!',[54] sounds Keating's accompaniment to the tearing of the Pritchard textbook. Hopkins's war, on the other hand, is a struggle against both the school property and the one who destroys it – as if Hopkins knew that the final price for answering (or, indeed, for refusing to answer) Keating's draft would really be his 'soul',[55] as well as some of the more textbook, but also more vital organs.

In the terms of Chapter 1 above, Hopkins's utterance is an argumentative strategy:

Enunciator 1 (the symbolic father): *Money!*
Enunciator 2 (the clan brother): *Life!* (better, *Life with money!*)
Enunciator 3 (Hopkins): *You are wrong both individually and as a team (that is, as Keating himself): the dilemma is a false choice.*

But let us return to Austin. His presupposition that the utterance 'The cat is on the mat' is a constative utterance can, as we have seen in Chapter 1, be questioned even without this detour through *Dead Poets Society*. To this end, it suffices, for example, to refer to Ducrot's theory of argumentation, where declarative utterances are shown to be arguments used as statements only after they undergo delocutive derivation. However, as Chapter 1 has also made clear, we shouldn't aim to simply replace Austin's project with a different one; that which Austin feels the need to exclude from his theory ought to be integrated back into it, possibly in a way that makes this theory itself susceptible to what we see as the logic of the signifier.

In the case of literature, we can achieve this goal if, as also mentioned in the previous chapter, we realize that the specific literary refraction of language is a refraction of none other than Austinian ordinary language. And we can see something similar for rudeness and absurdity: the Hatter's 'rude' utterance 'Then you shouldn't talk' functions precisely because it remains within the realm of constatives and performatives as it chooses to reinterpret the performative prefix as a complete constative. So too, the polemical effect of 'The cat is on the mat', far from being a mere potential effect of the utterance's reception, is inherent in the utterance, as its use in *Dead Poets Society* makes so clear.

Even after a detour through Weir's film, however, 'The cat sat on the mat' only seems to make sense in ordinary language as an utterance that subjectivates instead of constating. In ordinary language – language unchecked by the kind of self-explanation that characterizes *Dead Poets Society* – 'The cat sat on the mat' really seems to function only in those extremely complicated contexts that Ducrot, as we have seen at the beginning of this chapter, deems nonpertinent for a proper ordinary language philosophy. But as we know already from Chapter 1, a proper ordinary language philosophy is an ordinary literature philosophy anyway, and nothing suggests this as strongly as the ordinary poetry of 'The cat sat on the mat'.

2

# Parasite as necessary possibility: Derrida elevates the parasite as the poetry of speech acts

In a single jump, speech act theory crossed both the sea dividing analytic and continental philosophy and the walls separating philosophy and philology when Jacques Derrida launched his critique of Austin's disregard for literature, jokes, citations and other non-serious speech acts. Derrida chose to deconstruct Austin's expulsion of literary etiolations of speech acts in the year that Richard Ohmann ventured the first major application of Austin in literary theory.[1] Derrida did this six years before Mary Louise Pratt would offer the first influential critique of Austin (and Ohmann) within literary theory, and another decade before she would reframe her critique from the then emerging perspective of gender performativity.[2] This perspective is still a Derridean one, though, and nowhere more so than in the work of its most visible representative, Judith Butler (as we will see in Chapter 3).

In 1971, Derrida spoke at a Montreal conference on communication with a paper on the non-existence of communication, particularly communication in the sense that follows from Austin's speech act theory. Titled 'Signature événement contexte', the paper appeared a year later in Derrida's book *Marges: de la philosophie*. By 1977, the first issue of the journal *Glyph* featured the English translation of the paper, titled 'Signature Event Context', along with a reply by Austin's student John R. Searle titled 'Reiterating the Differences: A Reply to Derrida'. Derrida's own reply, 'Limited Inc a b c …', followed in *Glyph*'s second issue. In 1988, Gerald Graff, Samuel Weber and the editors at Northwestern University Press wanted to collect all these interventions, but failed to secure Searle's permission to republish; Derrida, on the other hand, contributed a lengthy 'Afterword' subtitled 'Toward an Ethic of Discussion'.

Thus came about Derrida's book *Limited Inc*, with the French edition following two years later.

Derrida includes Austin in his basic project of reformulating communication in terms of writing. A written sign is written in order to be able to function outside its original context and even after the death of the writer and the addressee. The possibility of such functioning is hence a necessary possibility, in the case of a written sign. As a consequence, the possibility of further citation of a written sign outside that original context is a necessary possibility as well. A written sign is thus repeatable beyond the addressee's and even the writer's original intentions, and to this degree a written sign is also alterable; both repeatable and alterable, the written sign is, in a word, iterable. The possibility of a citation that is unfaithful to the original intentions or the original context in general is hence not external to a written sign, but immanent to it; it is a necessary possibility. And if the possibility of iteration is not external to a written sign, neither is a written sign itself merely external to a spoken sign, because a spoken sign, too, is vulnerable to citations outside its original context. Every sign is hence necessarily iterable and as such unable to express any original, idiosyncratic intention, which in turn means that communication cannot be a means of exchange of such intentions.

Not unlike deconstruction, Austin is said to have reduced intention and reference to so many effects of illocutionary formulas themselves. But this similarity between Austin and deconstruction is, according to Derrida, just a backdrop for the fundamental difference, Derrida's own *différance*.[3] If in the logocentric philosophical tradition, with which Austin 'would like to have so few ties',[4] the absence of the addressee is 'merely a distant presence', Derrida claims that 'this distance, divergence, delay, this deferral [*différance*] must be capable of being carried to a certain absoluteness of absence if the structure of writing, assuming that writing exists, is to constitute itself'.[5] This weight of the metaphysical tradition is supposed to force Austin's deconstruction of communication to remain logocentric and unsusceptible to the movement of *différance*. More precisely, Austin is said to regard locution as a mere contingent expression of the illocutionary formula, and not as its necessary and potentially altering embodiment. To escape the precariousness of locution, Austin clings to monosemy, according to Derrida, stable meaning guaranteed by the conventionality of context, particularly the seriousness of intention.

Hence, finally, Austin's infamous dismissal of jokes, citations and literature as non-serious, parasitic, etiolated speech acts.

For Derrida, the possibility of this etiolation is a necessary possibility, one that makes any speech act precarious and hence meaningful, non-redundant. In Derrida's Austin, however, etiolations are still a mere possibility external to serious illocutions; the citation is not a necessary possibility in the fate of any sign. As a result, Derrida can reproach Austin for making the illocutionary act dependent once again precisely on that which Derrida's own grammatology freed the sign from as it subordinated the sign to iterability and thus enabled it to function beyond its empirical and semantic source. This exclusion of etiolations enabled Derrida to integrate his critique of speech act theory into his by then classic early critique of Edmund Husserl's expulsion of meaningless or senseless (*bedeutungsloss* or *sinnlos*) utterances as utterances that are unable to formalize an intentional relation to a presupposed object. Derrida based his deconstruction of both Husserl and Austin in his wager that the iterability of the sign is a positive condition of the sign's possibility and at once impossibility.

In his retort to Derrida's deconstruction of Austin, Searle rejects Derrida's fundamental gesture of subordinating the entirety of communication to the graphematicity of all signs, not just those that happen to be written (graphemes). Searle agrees that the repeatability of a sign is a condition of possibility for any communication, but he seems to derive repeatability, not from the materiality, the unavoidable staging of the sign, but, on the contrary, from the virtuality of the code. For Searle refuses to relate repeatability with alterability and to admit that the necessary staging of the sign historicizes and hence potentially subverts that which is being staged; instead, he reduces this iterability to common-sense iterativity as repeatability of the sign's meaning. This allows Searle to equate the written and the spoken like Derrida, but with opposite predicates: Searle's reiteration knows of no alteration in repetition, as stability is guaranteed by the virtual, non-material code; the code is absent from the illocutionary act and as such the guarantor of the conventional relation between an utterance, its intention and its context; those utterances that break this convention are etiolated speech acts; as a result, the status of being alienated into the code is what makes intention possible, not invalid. To all this, Derrida responds at length and more than once, but always with the conviction that, in communication, the presence, rather than the absence, of the addressee is coincidental at best.

* * *

The most elegant entry into the debate seems to be the point where Derrida's and Searle's respective positions nevertheless align for a brief moment and the former grants his opponent a certain concession without noticing it (so that the concession in effect goes to the lack in Derrida's own theory, a point where his theory sinks to the level of that which it is supposed to deconstruct, namely Searle's image of Austin).

One of the things Searle tackles especially fiercely is Derrida's analysis of the agrammaticality of the sequence 'le vert est ou',[6] as Derrida translates 'Grün ist oder',[7] Husserl's example of sequences to be excluded from his pure logical grammar, which Derrida finds analogous to the way in which Austin expels etiolations from his speech act theory. Husserl writes:

> It is part of the notion of an expression to have a meaning: this precisely differentiates an expression from the other signs mentioned above. A meaningless expression is, therefore, properly speaking, no expression at all; it is at best something that claims or seems to be an expression, though, more closely considered, it is not one at all. Here belong articulate, word-like sound-patterns such as 'Abracadabra', and also combinations of genuine expressions to which no unified meaning corresponds, though their outer form seems to pretend to such a meaning, e.g. 'Green is or'.[8]

Derrida's reply is as follows:

> It is solely in a context determined by a will to know, by an epistemic intention, by a conscious relation to the object as cognitive object within a horizon of truth, solely in this oriented contextual field is 'the green is either' unacceptable. But as 'the green is either' or 'abracadabra' do not constitute their context by themselves, nothing prevents them from functioning in another context as signifying marks. ... Not only in contingent cases such as a translation from German into French, which would endow 'the green is either' with grammaticality, since 'either' (*oder*) becomes for the ear 'where' [*où*] (a spatial mark): 'Where has the green gone (of the lawn: the green is where),' 'Where is the glass gone in which I wanted to give you something to drink?' ['*Où est passé le verre dans lequel je voulais vous donner à boire?*'] But even 'the green is either' itself still signifies an *example of agrammaticality*.[9]

Finally, Derrida's subversion of Husserl is in turn subverted by Searle:

> [Derrida] says the meaningless example of ungrammatical French, 'le vert est ou,' means (*signifie*) one thing anyhow, it means an example of ungrammaticality. But this is a simple confusion. The sequence 'le vert est ou' does not MEAN an example of ungrammaticality, it does not mean anything, rather it IS an example of ungrammaticality. The relation of meaning is not to be confused with instantiation. This mistake is important because it is part of his generally mistaken account of the nature of quotation, and his failure to understand the distinction between use and mention. The sequence 'le vert est ou' can indeed be *mentioned* as an example of ungrammaticality, but to mention it is not the same as to *use* it. In this example it is not used to mean anything; indeed it is not used at all.[10]

We can feel a certain affinity for both opposing interpretations. But if this is so, the feeling is a pre-theoretical one and so are the interpretations themselves. As such, they should first be scrutinized. Instead of deciding between Searle's Austinian thesis that *'le vert est ou' is an example of agrammaticality* and Derrida's anti-Austinian thesis that *'le vert est ou' means an example of agrammaticality*, it seems more productive to ask what makes possible the very passage from one to the other. What is the condition of this shift from *is* to *means* (the shift that empirically took the opposite direction, but should be turned around for theoretical reasons that hopefully will soon become clear)? The wager of this chapter is that the shift is possible due to subjectivation. An utterer interpellated into the norm of the French language is the one who can 'mention' the sequence 'le vert est ou' as an example of agrammaticality, thereby already 'using' it to designate an example of agrammaticality. The sequence thus represents the utterer for the norm of the French language, acquiring against the backdrop of this norm a meaning, a zero-degree of meaning: 'le vert est ou' now means 'an example of agrammaticality', that is, it means itself. Once the utterer no longer uses the linguistic norm as a means of Husserlian expression of his or her intention, he or she stops using the sequence 'le vert est ou' in a spontaneous fashion, stops breaking the norm, and sees that this is a logically agrammatical sequence that can no longer formalize an intentional relation to an object. The utterer can now mention the sequence, wrapping it in quotation marks and distancing him/herself from it, for the sequence no longer represents his or her intention for an addressee (which is him or her first and foremost), but his or her alienation into the norm for the norm itself. And once this kind of interpellation into the linguistic norm is achieved, the subject can also spontaneously use the sequence 'le vert est ou' to cite an example of agrammaticality.

The transition from Searle's thesis to Derrida's therefore can be justified, and Derrida can be defended from the perspective of the theory of subjectivation. The only problem is that this perspective also enables an objection against Derrida that could not be raised by Searle. A sequence like 'le vert est ou' can indeed become grammatical, it can signify, but this doesn't mean that it is not exceptional, for it signifies precisely any grammatical sequence. Derrida is right, but he doesn't demonstrate why he is right, which leaves his thesis undertheorized: he seems perfectly satisfied with his initial insight that every sign is citable, separable from its original context, and as such capable of engendering 'an infinity of new contexts'.[11] But we can subvert the two arguments that he illustrates with the sequence 'le vert est ou' if we can show that he is forced to insist on the citability of a sign because he cannot conceptualize this citability.

First, Derrida's argument that Husserl's 'Grün ist oder' becomes grammatical if orally translated into French hinges on the presupposition that the sentence stress falls on the last word of the translation and that, as a consequence, this word is given a new meaning. This presupposition is wrong: such sentence stress changes, not one meaning of the word into another, but the word itself ('ou') into a different word ('où'). The sequence 'le vert est ou' becomes, not grammatical, but a different sequence altogether. The words *ou* and *où* are indeed homophones at their own level (phonetically, the grave accent does not discriminate between them), but not at the sentence level: as the analytical abstraction from the utterance, the sentence itself presupposes either that the sentence stress falls on the word *où*, or that the word *ou* is not stressed. These are two words, not two contextualizations and hence two meanings of one word: there is no word in the French languages that means both 'or' and 'where'. Hence, a translator of 'Grün ist oder' (rather than 'Grün ist wo', 'green is where') would refrain from placing the sentence stress on *ou* in the first place. The uptake of the translation 'le vert est ou' as 'le vert est où?' is therefore impossible, as much as Derrida would like to imagine it. (Which also takes away the pertinence of his example of *vert* and *verre* as homophones: 'Où est passé le verre dans lequel je voulais vous donner à boire?'; at best, this relation of homophones enables the uptake 'le verre est ou', that is, 'the glass is or', which, however, remains agrammatical.) Derrida's argument would be more convincing if he imagined the uptake of the oral translation of 'the green is either' to be, say, 'le vert est août' or 'le verre est août', that is, 'the green is August' or 'the glass is August'. This would move 'the green is either' from the class of agrammatical, *sinnlos* utterances, where it belongs according to Husserl, to the class of utterances that are merely 'false or contradictory (*widersinnig* and not *sinnlos*, Husserl says)'.[12] But even here, Derrida would be compelled to ignore the fact that the dictionary allows for two different pronunciations of the word *août*, which means that an oral translation of 'Grün ist oder' would avoid the uptake with 'août' by simply choosing the pronunciation that is homophonous with the dictionary pronunciation of the word *ou*.

An oral French translation of 'Grün ist oder' would therefore be uptaken as 'le vert est ou' by anyone subjectivated in the French language. And vice versa, without the stress on the last word, 'le vert est ou' could be uptaken as 'le vert est où' only by an unsubjectivated listener. But since an unsubjectivated listener is by definition unable to uptake anything, it is better to say that an oral translation of 'Grün ist oder' would be uptaken as 'le vert est où' by an individual who would become a subject with this very uptake. For this individual would stress the word 'ou' on the basis of the presupposition that the translation, the utterance addressed to him or her, cannot be senseless. This would make him or her take on the agrammaticality of the translation and move the sentence stress to the last word – thereby inscribing him/herself in the norm. This listener would thus save the translation from senselessness by supplementing it with a new sentence stress that, like an empty signifier, would change everything at the level of phonemes without altering anything at the level of sounds.[13] So, it is the normative Other that grants the sequence 'le vert est ou' grammaticality, in Derrida's 'contingent' case of the French translation of 'Grün ist oder', by replacing the sign *ou* with the sign *où*. The case is thus neither contingent nor a case of disseminating the meaning of a single sign: sanctioned by the Other, the agrammatical sign *ou* returns to its utterer as a different sign, the grammatical *où*. The condition of possibility of the sign's grammaticality is subjectivation, not dissemination. And this exceptional, liminal status of his 'contingent' case could be discerned by Derrida himself if only he were to return to his own conceptualization of the supplement and use it in the way in which it was just used in this paragraph.[14]

Second, Derrida's argument that 'le vert est ou' itself, that is, without being uptaken as 'le vert est où', can mean an example of agrammaticality is pre-theoretical as well. 'Le vert est ou' can indeed mean, rather than just be, that; however, like in the case of the French translation of 'Grün ist oder', this has to be corroborated by grammar. Derrida's argument does presuppose that it is grammar that can give the sequence 'le vert est ou' the meaning 'an example of agrammaticality'; yet this remains just that, a mere presupposition that remains unanalysed. If Derrida analysed it, he could develop the concept of grammar as an ideological apparatus of the nation-state. Instead, he spontaneously reproduces a gesture typical for ideological apparatuses themselves as he fetishistically disavows subjectivation by, as we will see below, substantializing it via his abstract category of iterability. With this category, Derrida recognizes that any signifier can be cited and subjectivated, but then refrains from analysing the discursive antagonisms at play in a given case that place one signifier in the exceptional position of the subjectivating signifier. Like his imagined addressee of the utterance 'le vert est ou', and like a grammarian, Derrida omits subjectivation as the condition of possibility of the utterance's grammaticality. The addressee and the grammarian make this omission to be able to grant the utterance grammaticality, and he seems to make it to be able to end the matter with his category of iterability.

Here, we could turn to phenomenology to reproach Derrida for stretching the Husserlian claim that the possibility of a sign to be grammatical despite the absence of its utterer, addressee and context is a necessary possibility. For Derrida concludes that this necessary possibility is inscribed in the sign itself and that the Husserlian opposition between grammaticality and agrammaticality is thus metaphysical – but he doesn't develop this conclusion by analysing this inscription.[15] To this objection we could add that this inscription of the sign's iterability into the sign itself is a reified category, an epistemological obstacle, that prevents Derrida from conceptualizing the conditions of the inscription, in this case, the institution of grammar.

\* \* \*

To be sure, the author of 'Limited Inc a b c …' does show quite concretely which of the potentially endless contextualizations can grant the sequence 'le vert est ou' grammaticality. Countering Searle's take on things, Derrida returns to the above passage from 'Signature Event Context' to say the following:

> I should perhaps have multiplied the quotation marks and written: 'the green is either' indeed signifies nothing (to the extent, at least, to which signification or meaning is bound to discursive grammaticality, something that is by no means obligatory), but the citation of the (mentioning) phrase '... "the green is either" ...' can also, as a citational reference, signify *in addition* (*encore*): 'this is an example of agrammaticality,' this example of agrammaticality ' ' 'the green is either' ' ' proving unmistakably, by virtue of its functioning, that a graft is always possible; just as every phrase endowed with grammaticality that is cited in a certain context, for example in a grammar book, can *also* signify (*encore*): I am an example of grammar.[16]

The 'example' of 'a grammar book' is not just any example here: it is the context in which, as Derrida claims, a grammatical phrase can signify an example of grammaticality – but it should be said here that a citation of an agrammatical utterance as an example of agrammaticality demands the context of grammar as well; moreover, such a citation itself produces the context of judgement the institutional version of which is grammar. Derrida doesn't seem to recognize that his grammar book is not just an 'example', since he doesn't pose the question about the institutional conditions that need to be fulfilled if an utterer is to make 'the green is either' signify 'this is an example of agrammaticality' and thus ultimately render it inscribable into a grammar book. Derrida seems to have no interest in the conditions necessary to quilt 'the green is either' onto the symbolic order and within it to grammaticality. If we were to ask the question of these conditions ourselves, we would do well to stay with Derrida's Husserl for a moment. The difference between single and multiplied quotation marks (more precisely, between the absence and presence of quotation marks), this gulf between use and mention is the difference between pure psychological experience and transcendental consciousness,

> a difference which in fact distinguishes nothing, a difference which separates no being, no lived-experience, no determinate signification. This is a difference however which, without altering anything, changes all the signs, and it is a difference in which alone the possibility of a transcendental question holds, that is, the possibility of freedom itself. This is, therefore, the fundamental difference without which no other difference in the world would make sense or even have a chance of appearing *as such*.[17]

In this passage, Derrida does ask the question of conditions, of course, but seems to carry on as if he did not.

But how exactly can quotation marks give an utterance its meaning without 'altering' it in any way? Following the Lacanian distinction between a sign and a signifier, we could say that quotation marks change the utterance's role of a sign into the role of a signifier; they transform that which represents something for somebody (or, in the case of 'le vert est ou', nothing for nobody) into that which represents the utterer for all other utterances. Quotation marks represent the grammarian for grammar, as the grammarian's utterance "'le vert est ou'" is symptomatically inscribed directly into grammar, which is the grammarian's presupposed Other. Grammar endows the utterance with meaning, namely 'example of agrammaticality', and the utterance in turn gives meaning to grammar as it supplements it with a signifier devoid of a signified, a signifier that precisely as a paradoxical sign without meaning signifies the field of signification itself, including, of course, grammar. As a citation of the other, the *objet petit a*, of grammar, "'le vert est ou'" is the Freudian ideational representative of the primordially repressed binary signifier in the signifying chain of grammar, where this binary signifier would function as a mythical unity of thought and being, an intersection between grammaticality and its *objet petit a*, its *a*(grammaticality). As such, "'le vert est ou'" saturates the non-all knowledge of grammar and at the same quilts onto grammar the utterer of "'le vert est ou'" as the grammar's author. Grammar allows for agrammaticality insofar as the grammarian takes agrammaticality onto him/herself. And vice versa, once the grammarian catches agrammaticality into quotation marks, that is, into him/herself as a self-referential subject of enunciation, he or she bestows agrammaticality onto grammar, thus enabling the latter to symbolize the former.

The agrammatical sequence is thus contextualized in a chain of signifiers that materialize the knowledge of grammar once the utterer, the grammarian, subjectivates him/herself in the sequence. But since this knowledge is merely relational, non-all, ignorant of its object, silent on the matter of being, the grammarian totalizes it with the signifier of this being, namely with quotation marks. For the grammarian supplements grammatic knowledge with him/herself as an uttering being emptied out of any objectivity, an utterer who can access being only in the form of a self-referential utterance. In short, the lack of grammatic knowledge about agrammaticality is masked by the grammarian with the lack of his or her being beyond the field of utterance. In the words of Milner's unsurpassed Lacanian analysis of the institution of grammar,

> Falling outside of science, grammar does not have to be noncontradictory or homogenous. Consequently, the completeness that it works toward can be obtained by any kind of tinkering. Similarly, the not-all which marks its domain hardly presents it with any difficulties. It is enough for it to make up for the lack with any kind of patchwork. The feeling for language on which, implicitly or not, all grammarians worthy of the name depend thus guarantees them that, whatever their own insufficiency may be, the completeness of language is there, present in each of the subjects who speak it.[18]

In this oscillation between the alienation of being, I, into grammar and the separation from grammar into 'being', 'I', emerges the subject (of grammar). This subject subjectivates its agrammatical being, the imaginary identity that supposedly cannot be subsumed under the Other, by grammaticizing it with the addition of quotation marks, the frame that gives the subject's agrammatical being a symbolic identity. The subject – the nothing that emerges between the empty signifier '"le vert est ou"' and all the other signifiers of grammar – can take care of two lacks once it is armed with quotation marks: its own agrammaticality, which kept it away from grammar, and its own self-referentiality, which kept grammar away from it as a subject. The subject gets rid of the traumatic proximity of limitless agrammaticality by citing it in grammar as an example of agrammaticality – but this supplementation of grammar is what produces agrammaticality in the first place, namely agrammaticality as both the lack and the surplus of grammar.

Grammar therefore achieves its self-consciousness in devouring its other by way of citation, like in Derrida's example of '"le vert est ou"'. This kind of citation belongs to the 'subterfuges'[19] that, as Milner writes, 'from time to time suffice to include … [the forbidden construction] within language', most typically by way of none other than 'quotation: if the sentence $P$ is incorrect, it is always permissible to write the sentence P': "it is incorrect to say that $P$".[20] Or, to apply Derrida's own terms, this kind of mention of agrammaticality is a necessary addition that, far from being an innocent appendix to grammar, both totalizes and compromises it. Quotation marks do not make sense of the real, the *objet*, of grammar, but they do at least evacuate it to the internal margin of grammar, thereby compensating with subjective sense for the absence of objective meaning. Quotation marks are the cut that, 'without altering anything, changes all the signs'. The grammar that the grammarian uses to grammaticize agrammaticality is illusory knowledge.

Illusory, but necessary. For, as implied in Ducrot's analysis of the actions of 'the man in the street' and the linguist (which we introduced in Chapter 1), the subject of grammar comes into being through the same operation as the subject of speech itself. And vice versa, when grammar coils itself up into a signifier of the signifier, it subjectivates itself through the same gesture as its user: when grammar not only mentions but also uses an agrammatical sequence, it merely signifies, 'multiplies' the quotation marks that a native speaker always already spontaneously uses (which is why Derrida's multiplication of quotation marks is redundant: the opposition between the presence and the absence of quotation marks suffices). In this respect, grammar approaches its object from a native's point of view – and is hence incapable of formalizing subjectivation. Its illusion is the same as the illusion of its user, which makes it a necessary illusion in the sense that, without it, there would be no speech, let alone grammar.

\* \* \*

Both Derrida and Searle are right, 'le vert est ou' both 'signifies' and 'is' an example of agrammaticality. But if this is so, they are right only together, which means that each of them is wrong. Indeed, they are both wrong, they both fail to inquire into the conditions that need to be met for the sequence 'le vert est ou' to 'signify' anything and to 'be' anything more than a non-symptomatic, theoretically nonpertinent mistake in enunciation. Granted, Derrida does respond to Searle that use and mention do not exclude each other, but then characteristically evades the problem by stating that the boundary between use and mention is unclear.[21] This, however, avoids the problem of the split between the utterance and its enunciation, the difference between use and mention, the boundary between 'is' ('le vert est ou') and 'signifies' ('"le vert est ou"'). This boundary may be undecidable, but only for the utterer, insofar as – together with Derrida – he or she disavows his or her split between the utterance and its enunciation and fosters the illusion that he or she has appropriated the utterance without any remainder and fully controls its enunciation. In this sense, the one is indeed inseparable from the other, Derrida is right about that (nor does he differ from Searle on the matter as much as he would like to) – but the boundary is determinable analytically, and Derrida could offer such an analysis if he surpassed the utterer's native point of view and traversed his own fantasy of undecidability and iterability.

Derrida could have shown that the boundary between use and mention is drawn along the line separating the sign from the signifier. At the level of the enunciated, 'le vert est ou' doesn't signify anything; moreover, as Husserl shows, it cannot signify anything. At the level of enunciation, however, the sequence signifies this nothing itself as it represents the nothing that is the subject of enunciation for any utterance that signifies anything for its addressee. And once the sequence is mentioned at the level of enunciation it can indeed also be used to signify an example of agrammaticality.

But for this kind of analysis, Derrida would need the concept of the subject. He deconstructs the 'external', empirical context as well as the 'internal', structural context[22] to demystify the 'empirically determined subject'[23] that he believes is presupposed in Austin. But having attended to the empirical and the structural context as well as to the empirical subject, he fails to consider the subject that is to the structural context what the empirical subject is to the empirical context. Derrida neglects the subject that is the split of the utterer between the utterance and its enunciation. Instead, he fetishizes the citability of a sign into 'infinity'. He is right to claim that all Austin's problems have 'a common root',[24] but he is wrong to locate that root in Austin's inability to see that even a simple locution always already subordinates its utterer to the rules of writing – rather than, as shown in Chapter 1, in Austin's failure to acknowledge that even such a locution can subjectivate, that is, subordinate its utterer to him/herself as a subject. Derrida's agrammatic sign can indeed obtain grammaticality due to the fact that the possibility of its limitless citability is a necessary possibility; but this iterability must first be institutionalized, sanctioned by the Other, the series of other signs for which the agrammatic sign represents its institutionalized utterer, the grammarian.

The choice between Searle's disavowal and Derrida's fetishization of the parasitic nature of intention ought to be rejected as a forced choice reminiscent of Lacan's robber who, as we have seen in the previous chapters, demands 'Your money or your life!'[25] Only then can we analyse subjectivation in the sign and leave the notion of the sign for the concept of the signifier. Only beyond both Searle's idea of the givenness of context and Derrida's endless game of contextualization can we hope to reconstruct the context in which a given signifier inscribes itself as the representative of the utterer for that context.

The forced choice between Derrida and Searle can be rejected even within their own respective horizons. We have already encountered the productivity of Derrida's conceptualization of the subjectivating effect of the supplement, where 'a possibility produces by delay that to which it is said to be added'.[26] No less productive is Searle's discussion of intention and convention, insofar as Searle reminds Derrida that intentional communication is enabled rather than precluded by iterativity.[27] This implies that speakers can express their intentions thanks to a set of conventions (words, syntactic rules) that regulate the expression of intentions. And if this thesis, with which Searle defends Austin against Derrida's deconstruction, is combined with his claim that intentions, far from preceding enunciation, emerge together with it,[28] a latent thesis emerges according to which our intentions are in fact intentions of others, more precisely, of the Other. For the simultaneous emergence of an intention and an utterance suggests that we have no original intentions at our disposal that we could express using repeatable conventional forms of others, or, in other words, that an original intention is just a repetition of someone else's utterance, a mere mention of a use.

None of this is made explicit by Searle, though; the relation between the code and intention remains a simple opposition for him. But we can't follow Derrida's alternative path either. He misses subjectivation in speech as well, albeit by way of deferring it to 'infinity'. He is right to insist that speech conforms to the same rule as writing, but this rule is governed by difference, not *différance*, such as the difference between the signifiers *ou* and *où*, or, in the case of oral speech, the difference between the presence and the absence of stress on the vowel *u*.

While there can be no doubt that any sign is citable, it should be added that this implies that no sign can be placed in just any context. Speech is indeed neither a game of intentions nor a game of contexts, but this does not prove that it is a game of *différance*. Speech can just as well be approached as the medium of subjectivation, where the intention is an unconscious contextualization, a quilting of the speaking being's own spontaneity to the symbolic network that is the ultimate addressee of speech. So, despite denying that deconstruction necessarily leads to neutralization,[29] Derrida in effect neutralizes the sign as he frees it from its context and allows for any contextualization. If there are no structurally overdetermined readings, all readings are idiosyncratic, or, in short, idiotic. As Derrida frees himself from Husserl's and Austin's paternal prohibition of agrammaticality, he is left with the superego injunction of idiosyncratic agrammaticality, a law that can only remain unsatisfied in the 'infinity' of contextualizations.

*Différance* is a fetish covering up the difference. Derrida's 'leftism in theory'[30] does manage to deconstruct the early Husserl, but fails to provide an alternative. Instead, it offers compulsive reassurance to itself and to others that it is the legitimate result of theoretical practice, rather than its point of departure.

\* \* \*

Husserl, for his part, remains faithful to the cut introduced by Descartes, the initial self-reduction to *cogito*, insofar as he resists the temptation to deduce logical agrammaticality from his logical grammar and treat grammar as the universal source of knowledge on (a)grammaticality. Delimiting logical grammar along the line separating contradictory, absurd, *widersinnig* expressions (such as 'square circle', which has no object attainable to intuition, yet possesses the intention to say something) from senseless, *sinnlos* expressions (such as 'Green is or', which is senseless precisely because it has no intention), he hollows speech out and introduces in it a certain difference. And emptying speech of senselessness, he posits speech as a non-all phenomenon, which by itself allows for a theory of subjectivation in the signifier, insofar as a signifier is a sign that is *widersinnig*, since it designates no referent, but not *sinnlos*, since it represents the subject of enunciation for logical grammar. The expression 'square circle' is not senseless, since it retains a minimal logical relation to the object, even if this object is not a referent, but rather a Lacanian *objet*, object as the cause of the subject's desire. The minimal distance from *objet* introduced by the fantasmatic formalization of the contradiction between the 'square' and the 'circle' as 'square circle' is enough for the entry of this expression in logical grammar. And vice versa, the sequence 'Green is or' is senseless and unacceptable to logical grammar precisely because it does not shield the subject from the traumatic object that is unacceptability to logical grammar itself.

While showing that quotation marks can guard against this unlocalizable object, Derrida disavows the price that the subject has to pay for this protection: by acknowledging too eagerly the originary absence of the object of expression, Derrida bypasses the practical necessity of the illusion of the object for the constitution of the subject and grammar itself. It is Husserlian reduction, and not Derridean deconstruction, of logical grammaticality that paradoxically enables us to analyse the subsumption of agrammatic sequences under grammar. As Močnik writes in one of the most rigorous Lacanian readings of Derrida's Husserl,

> Derrida asserts that Husserl values logical formalism only insofar as it is teleologically directed towards fulfilment with the presence of sense, and critically remarks that Husserl uses this 'capacity to express' as an implicit criterion for the formal logical accuracy of sequences. However, these analyses developed by Derrida ought to be understood as assertions describing Husserl's *dispositif* – not as critical points. By styling these assertions as 'anti-metaphysical' critiques, Derrida is unable to see that this is Husserl's way of thinking a fundamental theoretical problem (a problem that, incidentally, is fully absent from Derrida's theorisation): the problem posed by the fact that a bio-physio-etc. being can actually *subjectivate itself in the machine of a 'rule'*.[31]

Indeed,

> the 'rule' of the signifier subjectivates precisely with its incompleteness or, in Husserlian terms, indicativity. All the potentially 'full' expressions begin to function, to produce effects of presence etc., when someone (an individual, a speaker) 'takes on' these signs, signs that are necessarily, constitutively incomplete, that is, indicative: the speaker completes these indications with his or her *idiosyncratic* intuition, for example, the intuition of 'I' – and the rest starts to 'express'. In his dry manner, Husserl is right: if nothing else, he senses that idiosyncrasy immanent to subjectivation does not contradict intersubjectivity, but carries it.[32]

Elevating the structuralist theoretical concept of difference into a philosophical category of *différance*, Derrida makes it impossible for himself to analyse subjectivation in the differential signifier, that is, in the order of the symbolic, the institution that legitimizes a linguistic sequence as either grammatical or agrammatical in the first place. He sees in iterability merely the condition of possibility and of impossibility of intentional communication because he disavows the fact that that which is conditioned in its possibility here is irreducible to that which (more precisely, the one who) is conditioned in its (his or her) impossibility. Iterability conditions the possibility of the subject and the impossibility of the I; the possibility of intersubjectivity and the impossibility of the monologue of the soul; the possibility of desire and the impossibility of intention. The paradox lies not in the fact that any reiteration is always already a potential subversion, but in the subject whose possibility is conditioned by this iterability; the paradox lies in the fact that original subjectivity emerges in the Other, that is, in the iterable rule, the grammatical, conventional illocutionary utterance. Fixated on the quotation marks that surround an agrammatical sequence, Derrida neglects the entire institution of grammar behind them, the necessary link between a mention and grammaticality. Determined to prove, *contra* Austin, the dependence of serious, happy performatives on the possibility of their etiolation, he fails to see that etiolation itself is dependent on something even more serious than serious performatives, namely the Other that is institutionalized in grammar. Granted, etiolation is never merely etiolation, as any misfired speech act can hope to reach its addressee one way or another; however, this addressee is not the infinity of contexts, but the nothingness, the non-all nature of the Other, of grammar itself: the opposition between the serious and the etiolated is overdetermined by the Other.

We can now return to Derrida's 'contingent' case of grammaticization, where 'Grün ist oder' is translated as 'le vert est où', and question its contingency and the argument that Derrida builds on it. If anything, the transition from 'ou' (for 'oder') to 'où' suggests that communication is possible only once the utterer subordinates him/herself to grammar, and that this subordination (and not iterability) is the condition of possibility for meaning to emerge. A sign has meaning if it is sanctioned by grammar, and it is sanctioned by grammar if grammar separates the sign from agrammaticality by intervening in their imaginary, pre-symbolic unity. The scope of this kind of institutional intervention can be delimited precisely by Derrida's contingent and non-contingent cases: at one extreme, the Other can be satisfied by simply equipping the sign with barely visible quotation marks (the non-contingent case); at the other extreme, the Other can have the sign replaced with one of the already sanctioned signs (the contingent case).

Like in 'The cat is on the mat' from Chapter 1, in Derrida's non-contingent case the act of citation suspends logical ungroundedness with a certain illusion. As soon as quotation marks intervene to grammaticize the agrammatic sequence – or as soon as they personalize the impersonal idiom 'The cat is on the mat' – the new citation becomes a grammatic sequence that at least means itself, a sequence chosen by the utterer exactly for its grammaticality. In Derrida's contingent case, on the other hand, the Other adds to 'ou' a stress or, in case of writing, a diacritic: rather than merely recontextualizing 'le vert est ou' along the line suggested by Derrida, the Other locates this sequence, not in a new syntagm such as Derrida's grammar book, but in a new paradigm, namely the French language as such. Thus, the contingent case by itself, even before Derrida will introduce its non-contingent counterpart, suggests that there is at least one example where meaning is guaranteed by a change, not of context, but of text itself. The owner of 'the ear' to which the French translation of 'Grün ist oder' sounds like 'le vert est où' – 'in contingent cases such as a translation from German into French, which would endow "the green is either" with grammaticality, since "either" (*oder*) becomes for the ear "where" [*où*] (a spatial mark)', writes Derrida – the curious owner of that ear finds the solution to the riddle of 'le vert est ou' in him/herself, more precisely, in the intuition with which he or she recognizes in this agrammatic sequence a question for him or her concerning 'the green'. As 'Grün ist oder' requests of the French language to make sense of it and the machine replies with silence, so that 'the ear' faces the idiosyncrasy of the system of linguistic rules itself (in short, the idiocy of the Other as such), and the question of the desire of the other who speaks in a foreign tongue escalates into the question of the desire of the Other that is a foreign tongue – all that can be done is to take a guess. The only way to unveil the secret of the desire of the Other is to consider all its signifiers, all the ordinary, merely relational, equally (un)distinguished signifiers, and use one's own idiosyncratic intuition to select the exception, the signifier that might substitute for 'ou'. Indeed, his or her demand of sense returns to the owner of 'the ear' as its own unconscious desire. The barred desire of the Other, the agrammaticality of 'le vert est ou', is what 'the ear' gets rid of with the help of the illusion that he or she is the actual addressee of the sequence, that he or she is the real desire of the Other, and that he or she is able to return this love and complete the Other by giving an answer to the question concerning 'the green'. The illusion that the French rendition of 'Grün ist oder' is grammatical, and that communication is symmetric, is possible as soon as 'the ear' subjectivates him/herself in the French language, returning to it reciprocally the presupposed message in its own language (i.e. in the language that it, the French language, is) by quilting the message using one of its own signifiers.

Paradoxically, when Derrida links his contingent and non-contingent grammaticizations of 'le vert est ou' – 'not only in contingent cases such as a translation ... into French ... but even "the green is either" itself still signifies an *example of agrammaticality*' – the gesture is legitimate, but used to prove a false thesis. The two cases do demonstrate that the effect of meaning rests on the necessary possibility of contextualization, but this contextualization itself rests on the utterer's subjectivation in grammar. This is not to say that Derrida simply doesn't know this. Judging by the form of his linkage of the contingent and the non-contingent, it is better to say that he disavows it. For his linkage follows Octave Mannoni's formula of fetishistic disavowal, 'I know well, but all the same ...':[33] *I know well that the transition from 'ou' to 'où' is a transition between texts, not contexts, but all the same this is merely a coincidental transition, whereas my non-contingent transition, from 'le vert est ou' to '"le vert est ou"', proves precisely that text is subordinated to context.* In both cases, deconstruction disavows the fact that the possibility of an intervention by an exceptional, empty signifier – which is an institutional intervention first and foremost – is a necessary possibility. It disavows the fact that meaning is conditioned by symbolic castration – the kind of castration that, in psychoanalysis, is the ultimate object of disavowal. The other of the grammatic and of the serious is dispersed by deconstruction in the infinity of contexts, which allows deconstruction to dispose itself of the real that logical grammar and speech act theory at least acknowledge by respectively remaining faithful to the agrammatic and the etiolated. For in the horizon in which this chapter has unfolded, and into which Derrida could elevate Husserl and Austin more elegantly than anyone else if he didn't choose to deconstruct them, the agrammatic and the etiolated can be approached in terms of the return of the real that is repressed in grammar and seriousness. Derrida's defence of literature and other discourses that Austin reduces to etiolations, discourses which, as Derrida shows, Husserl potentially reduces to 'non-sense (*Unsinn*),'[34] is marked by the same metaphysical tradition to which Derrida reduces logical grammar and speech act theory.[35]

Derrida shows that the possibility of etiolated speech acts – which Austin admits, but only to deny its pertinence for his theory of speech acts – is a necessary possibility, a positive condition of the possibility of serious speech acts – and at the same time a condition of the impossibility of such acts, insofar as seriousness is conditioned here by its possible negation. This contradiction, where etiolations condition both the possibility and the impossibility of their other, can be solved, though: as the act of symbolic castration, writing conditions the possibility of subjectivation and the impossibility of identification, insofar as identification suspends the pulsating subjectivity of *cogito*. In our reading, Austin's opposition between the serious and the etiolated is barred rather than deconstructed, which has the advantage of opening the path to acknowledging speech as an act in which the real is both rejected and reintroduced.

# *Ad* 2: Derrida's parasite in *Romeo and Juliet*

The possibility that an utterance will be etiolated in its uptake is a necessary possibility: 'le vert est ou' can be uptaken as 'le vert est où' or even as '"even le vert est où"'; the danger that a diacritic, or even just quotation marks, will be added to the utterance on its path to the addressee is a necessary possibility. But this does not mean that any quotation mark, let alone any diacritic, can always interfere in the uptake of any utterance. On the contrary, as we have seen in the previous chapter, all interference is sanctioned by what Lacan calls the Other, the symbolic field of intersubjectivity that Derrida seems to disavow as he adds diacritics or quotation marks to utterances like 'le vert est ou' in order to reject Austin's notion of etiolation.

The possibility that a letter will not arrive at its destination is then a necessary possibility, to use the terms of Derrida's most influential critique of Lacan. But every letter nonetheless arrives at its destination, as every letter is ultimately addressed to the Other. After and following Lacan, Barbara Johnson showed this most influentially in an essay already cited in the previous chapter for its idea that diacritics can act as empty signifiers. In this chapter, we will see how Derrida returns to his critique of Lacan in a later text where the letter in question is no longer *The Purloined Letter* like in Lacan and in Derrida's original critique, but the letter in *Romeo and Juliet*. Shakespeare and the theme of suicide will thus be used to illustrate a problem in Derrida's Austin after they have already been used, in Chapter *Ad* 1, to illustrate a problem in Austin himself.

\* \* \*

In 'Aphorism Countertime', Derrida's 1986 essay on *Romeo and Juliet*, aphorism 12 begins as follows:

> Romeo *and* Juliet, the conjunction of two desires which are aphoristic but held together, maintained in the dislocated now of a love or a promise.

A promise in their name, but across and beyond their given name, the promise of *another name*, its request rather: 'O be some other name …' (II, ii, 42). The *and* of this conjunction, the theater of this 'and,' has often been presented, represented as the scene of fortuitous contretemps, of aleatory anachrony: the failed rendezvous, the unfortunate accident, the letter which does not arrive at its destination, the time of the detour prolonged for a *purloined letter*, the remedy which transforms itself into poison when the stratagem of a third party, a brother, Friar Laurence, proposes simultaneously the remedy and the letter ('And if thou dar'st, I'll give thee remedy. … In the meantime, against thou shalt awake, / Shall Romeo by my letters know our drift, / And hither shall he come …' (IV, i, 76, 113–5)). This representation is not false. But if this drama has thus been imprinted, superimprinted on the memory of Europe, text upon text, this is because the anachronous accident comes to illustrate an essential possibility.[1]

Besides the basic motif of Derrida's critique of Lacan, the passage also features a phrase, in English in the original, that, strictly speaking, signifies nothing but another series of phrases, the chain of signifiers that make up Derrida's original critique of Lacan: in aphorism 12, the phrase '*purloined letter*' signifies not only the title of Edgar Allan Poe's canonical short story but also, as Nicholas Royle observes in a translator's note,[2] the title of Lacan's take on Poe's story and of Derrida's own reply to Lacan. With Juliet's '*purloined letter*' to Romeo, Derrida's *Romeo and Juliet* becomes a reiteration of his (critique of Lacan's) 'Purloined Letter'.

According to Lacan's 1955 'Seminar on "The Purloined Letter"', the opening chapter of his 1966 book *Écrits*, the plot of 'The Purloined Letter' demonstrates that a letter, though it may miss the addressee who was the intended recipient, always reaches the addressee that is the Other, the intersubjective field of communication itself. For as pertaining to the field of the imaginary, the sender's intention is overdetermined by his or her symbolic relation to the Other, the symbolic instance to which the letter is addressed as a symptomatic signifier that represents the sender (the subject) for the signifying field (the Other). It is in this precise sense that, as the 1955 seminar concludes, 'a letter always arrives at its destination'.[3]

To summarize the famous short story in one long sentence, the Queen of France receives a compromising letter addressed to her at a moment when she is forced to hide it from the King by simply leaving it on the table in front of him – thus allowing Minister D–, who is also present, to see the letter as precisely an intervention in the relation between his two superiors, and to replace it with a letter he happens to have, purloin it, turn it inside out and address it to himself, and leave it in plain sight in his apartment to hide it (like the Queen hid it from the King) from the Queen's policemen, who know he took it – thus allowing amateur detective Dupin to see (like Minister D– saw in the Queen's chambers) in D–'s apartment in plain sight that which the policemen search behind the surface, and to return the letter to its addressee, but not without disclosing himself vengefully to D– by replacing the letter with a letter of his own – thus allowing Lacan to see in this final letter (like D– and then Dupin saw in the original letter) an intervention in a certain intersubjective relation, this time the relation that binds together Dupin, D– and the Queen.

This relation is mediated by Dupin as well as D–; while D–'s actions obviously prompt Dupin to serve the Queen, Dupin has an agenda of his own. By purloining the purloined letter, Dupin is able not only to subtly negotiate the value of the award offered by the Queen's Prefect – thus receiving yet another letter, the award cheque – but also to have his revenge on D–, his doppelgänger. Both these points, that the award cheque is a letter binding the Queen's Prefect, the narrator and Dupin in the same way that the first letter bound the Queen, the King and D–, and that, for this reason but also for many others, D– is Dupin's evil twin, is shown in an essay that Jean-Claude Milner published a year before Derrida wrote his 'Aphorism Countertime'.[4] Both points are made by Milner in the spirit of Lacan to supplement Lacan's reading of 'The Purloined Letter', and they both seem much more productive than Derrida's so-called deconstruction of Lacan's Poe, to which Derrida alludes in 'Aphorism Countertime'.

By reminding us that the award cheque is a letter written in advance for anyone that may deserve it, Milner provides us with a perfect example of a letter that always arrives at its destination simply because the destination is wherever it arrives. This is Johnson's reading of Lacan's formula,[5] and the reading that Slavoj Žižek uses as the starting point of his three additional readings, the final one of which can again be exemplified by Milner's reading of 'The Purloined Letter', namely his final point that, by sealing D–'s fate, Dupin's seals the fate of his double and hence of himself. Žižek, without referencing Milner, concludes with a similar idea, namely that it is everyone's fate to sooner or later receive the letter that spells out his or her finitude, which, as Žižek points out, is precisely the motif one would expect to find in Derrida.[6]

But there is an even more obvious reason why the letter always reaches its addressee, in Poe; a reason that, not unlike the locations of the letters in Poe's story themselves, is so obvious that it can be overlooked only by someone who, like Derrida, can never be satisfied with the obvious. The letters in Poe's short story arrive at their destinations simply because they are delivered to the door. The letter D– uses to replace the letter he took from the Queen's table is a letter he himself brought into her boudoir; the letter he produces by turning the stolen letter inside out and writing a letter to himself is a letter he not only brought into his apartment but also created; the award cheque the Queen's Prefect signs and addresses to Dupin is, again, something he himself brought with him on his visit to Dupin; the letter Dupin uses to replace the letter he took from D–'s apartment is also something that entered the apartment together with the visitor; finally, all these deliveries result in the Queen's Prefect's successful delivery of the original purloined letter to the Queen, its original addressee. The letters need not be sent at all: they are not only addressed to the Other but also sent from the position of the Other.

This is what Derrida misses when he insists that 'The Purloined Letter' but also Lacan's reading of the story demonstrate that a letter can always miss its destination. 'Not that the letter never arrives at its destination', as he writes, 'but that it belongs to the structure of the letter to be capable, always, of not arriving'.[7] He insists on this point in his reading of Poe, in 1975; he insists on it in his reading of Lacan himself, in 1992, despite, incidentally, declaring that 'it is out of the question for me to open once again, even for a second, the dossier of the argument I have attempted elsewhere';[8] and he alludes to the same argument in his reading of *Romeo and Juliet*, in 1986, where, as Royle writes in the already mentioned translator's note, Derrida 'follows Shakespeare's text in focusing on the (tragic, comic, ironic, and above all *necessary*) possibility that a letter can always *not* reach its destination'.[9]

In his own book on Derrida, Royle claims that the balcony scene 'isn't the same again after Derrida'.[10] This, however, should be read against the backdrop of Derrida's own assurance that 'everything is in Shakespeare: everything and the rest'.[11] As we will see, however, 'the rest' ought to be recognized in Juliet's final fidelity to a certain lack as well as surplus. And insofar as Shakespeareans are ignorant of this fidelity, the lack that is 'the rest' of everything ('the rest' that Prince Hamlet calls 'silence') becomes their lack, their contradiction. In the rest of this chapter, we will therefore proceed from the lack of *Romeo and*

*Juliet* in Derridean Shakespeare studies, to the surplus of *Romeo and Juliet* in Derrida, to the lack-as-surplus in *Romeo and Juliet*.

\* \* \*

Jacques Derrida stands at one pole of deconstructive Shakespeare studies; Harold Bloom occupies the other. At one extreme, Bloom effectively sees Shakespeare's universality as a sum of particularities, or particular selves (from Hamlet to Falstaff); at the other, Derrida seems to regard the universality of Shakespeare as a particular universality among other universalities (from Plato's to Paul Celan's).[12] Whereas Bloom ascribes the lovers' missed encounter – the problematic of the play – to 'time's ironies', Derrida traces it to the 'irony of the proper name'.[13] And, incidentally, whereas Bloom writes on Shakespeare extensively, but refuses to identify himself as 'a Shakespeare scholar', Derrida wanted to become 'a "Shakespeare expert"', but wrote only 'Aphorism Countertime'.[14] Now, Bloom's relation to this relationship between deconstruction and his criticism is precisely a relation of criticism: ever since the 1979 collection *Deconstruction and Criticism*, which he co-authored with Paul de Man, Derrida, Geoffrey Hartman and J. Hillis Miller, Bloom has been cynically critical of deconstruction: 'The title was my personal joke, which no one can ever understand: I meant that those four were deconstruction, and I was criticism', he told an interviewer in 1985.[15] Conversely, a deconstructive relation to the relationship between deconstruction and Shakespeare criticism, Bloomian or otherwise, can only be a relation of deconstruction, given Derrida's 1989 deconstruction of the traditional criticism's insistence on the singularity of a literary work (where Derrida's sole example is precisely *Romeo and Juliet*).[16]

Bloom's issue with deconstruction is part of his animosity towards contemporary French theory in general. Under the influence of 'a few French naysayers',[17] as he labels it, multiculturalist Shakespeareans are becoming 'apostles of Resentment'[18] and 'power-and-gender freaks'.[19] In the case of *Romeo and Juliet* studies, scholars whom Blooms describes as multiculturalist Shakespeareans can arguably be identified by their focus on the topic of naming. Within this topic, two opposing approaches can be noted: the extrinsic approach, where naming in *Romeo and Juliet* is external to, yet constitutive of, the self;[20] and the intrinsic approach, where this dualism is projected into the self as ambivalent love-hatred.[21] Both approaches, however, unwittingly regard the lovers as victims of a certain constraint, be it the external constraint of naming itself or the internal state of love-hatred that results from the external constraint. As such, they tend to pass into each other.[22] But this victimization of the lovers is at work also in Bloom himself as well as in many other major figures outside the multiculturalist camp: scholars like Bloom, René Girard or Northrop Frye merely naturalize the constraint of the multiculturalists and present it as eternal 'time's ironies', 'mimetic desire' of 'generalized hysteria' and 'the tragic heroic' respectively.[23]

Passing into each other, the extrinsic and the intrinsic approaches to naming unwittingly enact their own relationship to their antagonist: reducible to each other, they can also be reduced to Bloom's essentialist position. That is, by seeing in Romeo and Juliet victims of particular naming, the multiculturalist readings repeat the other camp's subsumptions of the character's action under universal fate.[24] Moreover, these multiculturalist interpretations reproduce the even more traditional exclusion of the play from the corpus of mature tragedies as well as the text-critical dilemma between 'any other name' and 'any other word'. Thus, they unknowingly collaborate with their conservative opponents in maintaining the clichés of *Romeo and Juliet* as a bad tragedy and of its first quarto edition as a 'bad' quarto.[25]

Regarding the 'bad' tragedy, the multiculturalists seem to agree with the standard judgement that the play is unable to meet the criterion of 'character as destiny – the "great man" undone from within either by an innate weakness or a fallible moral decision'.[26] And as for the 'bad' quarto, it is the sole version of the play among five quarto and four folio editions published between 1597 and 1685 that reads 'What's in a name? That which we call a rose / By any other name would smell as sweet', rather than 'What's in a name? That which we call a rose / By any other word would smell as sweet'.[27] The editor of the 1980 Arden *Romeo and Juliet*, Brian Gibbons, glosses the second line as follows: 'Shakespeare calls a name, as a thing apart from a person, a *word* ... Q2 makes sense and should stand, despite the irrational pressure of proverbial familiarity attaching to *name* as the choice in many earlier editions.'[28]

This rendition has since prevailed, with editions by Arden, Riverside, Cambridge and, for example, the 2007 Royal Shakespeare Company edition choosing 'any other word' over 'any other name'. It is worth noting that among conservative exceptions there is Bloom again, this time as the author of the afterword to the 2004 Yale edition. It probably wouldn't do much good to take sides here and try to solve a mystery that may as well have been a mystery to the Bard himself (insofar as, for example, David Farley-Hills,[29] in his refutation of the commonplace that the first quarto is a memorial reconstruction of the play and that it was published by the printer, John Danter, without the authority of its owners, maintains that Q1 derives from Shakespeare's own working drafts, known as his foul papers, and entertains even Jay L. Halio's idea that Q1 is not a reported text, but an abridged version of Shakespeare's original). It seems much more productive to stress that what has also prevailed besides the privileging of 'word' over 'name' is the notion that Gibbons's 'thing apart from a person', be it 'name' or 'word', victimizes the lovers and thereby makes the play a bad tragedy devoid of the '"great man" undone from within'.

In this respect, particularist multiculturalism fails to refute the universalist humanism of Bloom's Bardolatry. It reproduces the humanist choices regarding genre criticism, character analysis and textual criticism. Bloom defines the centre of the entire Western literary canon as '*Lear, Hamlet, Othello, Macbeth*',[30] and instead of critically theorizing this choice, multiculturalist Shakespeareans tend to merely supplement it with the Jew or the Moor of Venice. Due to this supplementary operation, one should assert, not an opposition but a speculative identity between Bloomian and Derridean (or otherwise 'French') Shakespeare scholarship. Within Shakespeare studies, this surprising symbiosis of universalism and anti-universalism has been analysed by Julia Reinhard Lupton;[31] within critical studies of contemporary ruling ideology as such, it has been tackled by theorists as divergent as Alain Badiou and Immanuel Wallerstein.[32]

As a result, the play itself is victimized, absent from both Bloom's centre of the Western canon – *King Lear, Hamlet, Othello, Macbeth* – and the multiculturalist Shakespeare of *The Tempest, The Merchant of Venice* and, again, *Othello*.[33] In order to negate this false choice, we should forsake the institutional antinomy for a theoretical debate: we should return to that which is excluded by the very alternative between multiculturalist contextualism and essentialist non-contextualism, namely the text.

* * *

This is precisely what Derrida attempts to do in 'Aphorism Countertime'. His aim in focusing on the naming in *Romeo and Juliet* is not to victimize the lovers in either essentialist or multiculturalist ways but to come closer to a feature of the text, even of any text. In fact, in Derrida's account, a name and a text depend for their symbolic efficacy on the same necessary possibility that he attributes to a letter, namely the necessary possibility that they fail to reach their addressees. The actual letter in the play, the letter with which Friar Laurence tries to inform Romeo that Juliet's death is staged and that he should use that to elope with her, misses Romeo, with tragic consequences known to almost anyone who attended school. To Derrida, this missed encounter is in effect merely the necessary outcome of the way in which naming works in the play.

Derrida rightly claims that the balcony scene is overdetermined by the symbolic instance of the name of the father:

> Romeo and Juliet love each other across their name, despite their name, they die on account of their name, they live on in their name. ... From this name which separates them but which will at the same time have tightened their desire with all its aphoristic force, they would like to separate themselves. But the most vibrant declaration of their love still calls for the name that it denounces.[34]

Juliet

> is speaking, here, in the night, and there is nothing to assure her that she is addressing Romeo himself, present in person. In order to ask Romeo to refuse his name, she can only, in his absence, address his name or his shadow. Romeo – himself – is in the shadow and he wonders if it is time to take her at her word or if he should wait a little.[35]

Juliet wants to save Romeo by killing his name, but ends up killing Romeo because his name cannot be killed and dissociated from the Montagues (and the Capulets); aphorism 21 reads:

> She wants the death of Romeo. She will have it. The death of his name ("'Tis but thy name that is my enemy'), certainly, the death of 'Romeo,' but they will not be able to get free from their name, they know this without knowing it. ... She declares war on 'Romeo,' on his name, in his name, she will win this war only on the death of Romeo himself. Himself? Who? Romeo. But 'Romeo' is not Romeo. Precisely. She wants the death of 'Romeo.' Romeo dies, 'Romeo' lives on. She keeps him dead in his name. Who? Juliet, Romeo.[36]

The play therefore subjects the imaginary to the symbolic, showing that Juliet can reach 'Romeo himself' only by calling out his name and thereby always already missing Romeo himself. But a Lacanian reading can show that the play goes on to interrelate the symbolic and the imaginary alike with the uncanny sphere of the real, which is introduced in the play by the subject's suicide. Juliet's attempts to symbolize the real, the object-cause of her desire, by borrowing the signifiers from the Other are eventually suspended by her suicide; the impossibility of symbolically designating Romeo himself without destroying him in the process is subjectivated in her *passage à l'acte*, which, as we have seen in the chapter on *Dead Poets Society*, is Lacan's name for the only possible passage from signification to action. Her entrapment in the pulsation between the Other's signifiers, the pulsating drive in which she can consummate her love for Romeo only by annihilating him, is ended only when she is reduced to a mute body uncannily pulsating in its very stillness, a real stillness symbolizable only by a fetish such as the statues of Romeo and Juliet that the lovers' fathers will retroactively erect.[37]

As we will see later, in the balcony scene as it can be read precisely after Derrida, the name cannot but reach its addressee, since the addressee is in effect Juliet's father, not Romeo. There, Juliet reduces Romeo not only to his name but also to the name of the Capulets. The name of the father is Juliet's Freudian ego-ideal, the Other that receives all her utterances long before they reach Romeo. And as she is still interpellated by the name of the father in the balcony scene, her messages to Romeo make for a monologue, the addressee of her utterances being but herself. This is why the only way to break with her name is to break with the field of the symbolic itself, which is what she will do when she will acknowledge the merely monologic nature of her messages to Romeo.

So, *pace* Derrida, Juliet kills Romeo because his name but also her letter do precisely reach their addressee, Juliet's father. And second, Juliet will go on to kill, not herself, but the name, thereby making herself an ethical subject, the kind of subject that Lacan locates in the analyst as 'a saint'.[38]

Derrida's reading of *Romeo and Juliet* can therefore be read as the second missed encounter between him and Lacan. This time around, Derrida's text is not a reply to Lacan's reading of *Romeo and Juliet* since such a reading doesn't exist; as we have seen, however, this doesn't prevent Derrida from furnishing his own reading of the play with an allusion to his reply to Lacan's reading of 'The Purloined Letter'. What follows is then an attempt to provide the missing link, the kind of interpretation of *Romeo and Juliet* to which Derrida's might serve as a reply along the lines of his reply to Lacan's 'Purloined Letter'; in short, the kind of reading of *Romeo and Juliet* that might retroactively render Derrida's reading a reply to it. This is of course a task both impossible and always already implicitly achieved by Derrida's allusion to Lacan's Poe; more importantly, it is the task of excavating an object that exists solely as an object of an allusion – which may actually be the only kind of excavation that Lacan, and Derrida, would subscribe to.

* * *

Dramatic action begins with Juliet receiving her father's demand to marry Paris. More precisely, her absent father's demand to marry Paris, coupled with her Nurse's obscene comments on Juliet's mother's delivery of the demand issued by Juliet's father. This coupling of the official but indirect interpellation and its unofficial but all too direct carnivalization is what triggers Juliet's desire. Her mother's semiotic expertise on Paris's noble face concludes with an incentive, 'So shall you share all that he doth possess, / By having him, making yourself no less' (1.3.93–4), which receives its obscene superego supplement in the Nurse's injunction to enjoy: 'No less, nay bigger. Women grow by men' (1.3.95). And despite Juliet's and her mother's attempts to make the Nurse stop talking, she has the final line as she supplements Juliet's mother's demand to join Paris with the following rhyme:

LADY CAPULET
    Juliet, the County stays.

NURSE
    Go, girl, seek happy nights to happy days.

(1.3.104–5)

The Nurse reminds Juliet twice that, as a two-year-old, she replied 'Ay' to the following piece of advice by the Nurse's husband: 'fall'st upon thy face? / Thou wilt fall backward when thou comest to age, / Wilt thou not, Jule?' (1.3.55–7).[39] So too, almost twelve years later, Juliet yields to the Nurse's injunction because she hears it without understanding it, more precisely, because she understands it by hearing it. Yet if hearing (or, in Lacan's French, *entendre*) was able to spark understanding (*compréhension*) without understanding (*entendre*) because of the infant's imaginary identification with the Nurse's husband, now that he is dead and his advice is turned by his widow into the injunction to enjoy (*Jouis!*),

Juliet can only reply along the lines of *I hear you* (*J'ouïs*). The *futur antérieur* of the suggestion becomes the haunting omnipresence of the injunction once its utterer is dead (as dead as Juliet's father is absent), and the utterance takes on a life of its own, forcing the Nurse to reiterate it, and Juliet to hear it, twice.[40]

Nurse's supplement to the law of Juliet's father makes Juliet acknowledge a certain lack in the law, forcing her to ask herself what the Nurse wants when she encourages her 'ladybird' (1.3.3) to search for enjoyment when it is already located in Paris, as her father ensures her. Deprived in this way of her trust in the signifier *Paris*, Juliet is faced with the object-cause of desire, the *objet petit a* that drives her action to the end. In her first attempt to cultivate the object's traumatic amorphism, she does what she is taught: she searches for another signifier of the object. And it is the binary logic of the signifier that brings her to *Romeo*, which in her mother's tongue (but not her mother tongue, that is, the Prince's tongue) signifies 'Montague, *ergo* the enemy of the Capulets, *ergo* Juliet's enemy, *ergo* not allowed, *ergo* non-Paris'. Thus, the first solution to the riddle of the two meanings of *plus-de-jouir* ('surplus of enjoyment', 'no more enjoyment') – the enigma of her surplus-enjoyment to which she should, according to the Nurse, remain faithful despite the father's demand – lies within the symbolic order, the Other, itself. Juliet fills her father's lack with his opposite: she totalizes his purely relational identity (*non-Montague*) by loving a *Montague*. She tries to suture the split (battle)field of the Other by identifying with *Romeo*, the signifier that was introduced to her precisely by the lacking Other. This symbolic identification with the name of the father as the Other is what overdetermines her imaginary identification with Romeo; her initial love of Romeo is an acting out for her father's gaze.

That is why the balcony scene makes most sense as a monologue. Since Juliet's addressee is, as Derrida stresses, but Romeo's name, Romeo's appearance in the orchard under the balcony makes no difference to the discourse of her speech. At one point, she does recognize Romeo as the empirical recipient of her utterances – utterances that, at the level of the enunciated, presume his absence (while lamenting it at the level of enunciation). But having recognized Romeo, she doesn't deny these utterances; on the contrary, she explicitly restrains from denying them (2.2.85–9). Romeo's dilemma 'Shall I hear more, or shall I speak at this?' (2.2.37) is then a false one, her monologue would go on in either case. It is the readers who have to ask themselves whether Romeo says 'She speaks. / O speak again, bright angel' (2.2.25–6) to himself or to Juliet.[41]

Due to her fantasy of the Other, Juliet can marry monologue to dialogue, imaginary identification to symbolic identification, Romeo to *Romeo*, Romeo to herself. She can instantly recognize Romeo's voice, for the voice is her own; she can trust that he will honour her[42] and his own love confession[43] since the honour is her own; and she can believe that, by giving, she is receiving,[44] as both the giving end and the receiving end are her own. The name of her father is then the object of her refutation, as Derrida maintains,[45] but also the condition of possibility of her very utterances. Finally, only if we read the scene as a monologue can we account for the strange circumstance that the Nurse is unable to hear Juliet's exchange with Romeo, hidden as he is in the orchard well under the balcony, while Juliet is able to hear the Nurse calling her from within the house.

For Juliet, Romeo embodies her choice in the form of a free, spontaneous solution to the riddle of the Other; conversely, in a symmetrical fantasy, Juliet embodies, for Romeo, the freedom that supposedly allows him, a 'young waverer' (2.3.85), to overcome his fixation with Rosaline and forget 'that name, and that name's woe' (2.3.42). Split between the father's demand and the Nurse's injunction, the desire of the Other poses a question to Juliet, a kind of 'Che vuoi?',[46] that she initially answers along these lines: *It is me, my enjoyment, that you, the Nurse, want; I in my enjoyment am what my father's demand lacks, so you chose to supplement it by turning Paris into Romeo.* By greeting the injunction, '*Jouis!*', with the apostrophe, '*J'ouïs!*', Juliet also apostrophizes (i.e. both addresses and bars) the absent father: she recognizes this Capulet's dependency on the signifier *Montague* and hence on the feud, which of course makes him dependent on his own absent father, the dead ancestor from whom he inherited the feud. Yet with this very gesture Juliet bars herself within the system of constraints that is language. For Romeo is but her ideal ego, while her ego-ideal is the name of the father; in other words, Romeo is the image in which she likes herself, while the name of the father provides the viewpoint from which she observes herself in that image; the presence that is the image in which she likes herself is overdetermined by the absence that is the viewpoint from which she likes herself.[47] Forbidding *Romeo*-as-enjoyment, the name of the father always already imposes *Romeo*-as-enjoyment on her, before eventually imposing on Romeo its own system of decoding Juliet's apparent death as a real death. The incommensurable, unconsummatable love is sadistically demanded by the obscene side of the law itself.

Like in the incest taboo, that which is already impossible is also forbidden. However, the surplus that the empty signifier *Romeo* rigidly designates is unobtainable, not because it is absent from Verona, but, on the contrary, this incestual love of *Montague* and *Capulet* is impossible because it is present in Verona (as well as in any other possible world), albeit in the form of an absence. In the families' discourses that govern Juliet, if not Verona, *Romeo* signifies either 'Montague, *ergo* friend' or 'Montague, *ergo* enemy'; in the Prince's impotent third way, as it were, it signifies 'citizen'; what remains a blind spot in this structure, and is as such retroactively instituted by it, is 'Romeo, *ergo* Juliet's lover', *objet* as absence of any positive object. For Juliet, *Romeo*'s signified is ultimately 'Juliet's lover'. The object-cause of Juliet's desire is herself as 'Romeo's lover', the impossibility that has the status of the real to Juliet.

Romeo's omnipresent absence confronts Juliet with a forced alternative. In Verona, *Romeo* as 'Juliet's lover' cannot be; in a different place, for example, Mantua, *Romeo* can be Juliet's lover, but not 'Juliet's lover'. For Juliet, hystericized by Verona's discourse, this simply is not it, outside Verona: only in Verona is Romeo also *Romeo*. Hence, Romeo's Socratic insight that 'there is no world without Verona walls' (3.3.17), which Friar Laurence immediately betrays with his plan of escape to Mantua, can be acknowledged only in Juliet's Socratic suicide. But first, when the Prince banishes Romeo from Verona, Juliet chooses Mantua, not knowing that the alternative is a forced one. This escape from the prison-house of her father's language therefore still relies on that language. Juliet makes her choice on the presumption that the name of the father is powerless outside Verona; but she enacts her choice on the presumption that her grammar of apparent death, her letter, her signifier to Romeo, will reach its addressee. Thus, the moment her father is for the first time present (feebly attached to the name of the father), and Romeo absent (detached from *Romeo*), namely in 3.5.126–95, Juliet substitutes, as the object of her symbolic identification, Romeo for father – in order, furthermore, to re-establish her imaginary identification with the banished Romeo. She answers her own question 'What's in a name?' as a naive nominalist who believes that Romeo cannot be reduced to *Romeo*, but also as a naive realist who believes that Romeo is in fact a hostage (though not a product) of *Romeo*. As soon as she nominalizes symbolic castration as so many empirically localizable discourses of Verona, she realizes Romeo as the addressee of the apparent death discourse that she designed to escape Verona – and nominalizes Romeo as her lover.[48]

The nominalism/realism contradiction turns the utterer of the question into a split subject. As the subject of the enunciated, Juliet dismisses the field of the symbolic ('That which we call a rose / By any other word would smell as sweet'), while addressing, as the subject of enunciation, her question ('What's in a name?') to none other than the Other, thus symptomatically acknowledging the symbolic (the symptom being, first and foremost, an address to the Other). At the first level, she limits herself to the opposition between word and object ('name' and 'rose'), and it is only at the second level that she tackles the crucial problem of the relation between name and word. Hence, she addresses the split between the empty signifier and the signifying chain (name and word) only by performing it, by being split; in this sense, Juliet in effect justifies the text-critical dilemma between 'any other name' and 'any other word' – before negating it in her suicide, that is, and thus becoming, in a way, her own editor.

This *mésalliance* of enunciation and the enunciated, realism and nominalism, the symbolic Romeo and the imaginary Romeo, Verona and Mantua – this unsuitable marriage is inherent in the answer itself, namely *a*. Juliet can hence resolve it only by negating the nominalism/realism frame and by embracing conceptualism, that is, by embodying *objet petit a* as a saint, instead of chasing it as a citizen of either Verona or Mantua. She will achieve this *passage à l'acte* by traversing the fantasy of being able to design one's own signifier. When her own letter to Romeo, the result of her shifting between the *mésalliance*'s axes *ad infinitum*, will amount to nothing, to *a*(bsence, -grammaticality, -morphism), she will finally identify with this result and perform 'the only act that can succeed without misfiring', to cite Lacan's definition of suicide once again.

Juliet's letter fails because, like any symptom, it goes directly to the Other, namely Romeo as 'the subject who is supposed to know',[49] beginning, in this case, with knowing the contents of Juliet's letter. The actually existing Romeo is, of course, deprived of this knowledge by 'the town' (and its 'searchers' (5.2.8), who quarantine Juliet's postman in Verona before he can head for Mantua), after he was already deprived of 'the town' itself (and its 'kind Prince' (3.3.25), who mercifully banished Romeo from Verona for killing Tybalt). Mantua remains a fantasy, and Romeo remains interpellated by Verona's discourse. Hence, he interprets Juliet lying in the tomb, not as a signifier of her living womb, but as a sign of her death: his reading is Verona's reading. Instead of Romeo reading

Juliet as a signifier that represents Juliet, as a subject, for another signifier, the letter, and Verona reading her as a sign that represents her death for the town, both Romeo and Verona read Juliet as a sign, 'as the manner of our country is' (4.1.109); the reading rests on the background belief of customs, the zero-degree of ruling ideology, where the belief is fulfilled as soon as it is employed, and so Juliet dies as soon as Romeo believes she is dead. The Other, be it Juliet's father or Romeo, is, of course, as clueless as the subject itself.

Here, Juliet is the hysterical director as well as the actress who symptomatically acts out, not for the present father, but for the new Other, the absent Romeo, who is supposed to know the letter. This pathological set of two elements (the director, the actress) one of which is the set itself (the director) is fantasy in its purest: the subject's illusion of being the director of its own relation to the object-cause of desire. Hence, Romeo can remain Juliet's object only as the presumed addressee of her letter, but also of her replies to her mother upon Tybalt's death, which are so many symptoms of her obscene enjoyment. Shedding tears for the banished Romeo and explaining them away to her mother as grief over Tybalt's death, Juliet displaces the meaning of practically every utterance from the meaning implied by, or intended for, her mother to the meaning intended for Romeo:

LADY CAPULET
>So shall you feel the loss but not the friend
>Which you weep for.

JULIET
>Feeling so the loss,
>I cannot choose but ever weep the friend.

LADY CAPULET
>Well, girl, thou weepst not so much for his death
>As that the villain lives which slaughter'd him.

JULIET
>What villain, madam?

LADY CAPULET
>That same villain Romeo.

JULIET
> Villain and he be many miles asunder.
> God pardon him. I do, with all my heart.
> And yet no man like he doth grieve my heart.

LADY CAPULET
> That is because the traitor murderer lives.

JULIET
> Ay madam, from the reach of these my hands.
> Would none but I might venge my cousin's death.

LADY CAPULET
> We will have vengeance for it, fear thou not.
> Then weep no more. I'll send to one in Mantua,
> Where that same banish'd runagate doth live,
> Shall give him such an unaccustom'd dram
> That he shall soon keep Tybalt company;
> And then I hope thou wilt be satisfied.
>
> (3.5.75–92)

In this exchange, Juliet shifts the meaning of 'friend' from the mother's 'friend Tybalt' to her own 'lover Romeo', and of 'satisfied' from 'revenged only by the Capulets' murder of Romeo' to 'sexually satisfied only by Romeo'. Similarly, she agrees with her mother's judgement of Romeo, 'and yet no man like he doth grieve my heart'. The 'wayward girl' (4.2.47) carries on with her obscene behaviour by replying to her mother:

JULIET
> Indeed I never shall be satisfied
> With Romeo, till I behold him – dead –
> Is my poor heart so for a kinsman vex'd.
> Madam, if you could find out but a man
> To bear a poison, I would temper it –
> That Romeo should upon receipt thereof
> Soon sleep in quiet. O, how my heart abhors

To hear him nam'd, and cannot come to him
To wreak the love I bore my cousin
Upon his body that hath slaughter'd him.

(3.5.93–102)

Here, the messages for Lady Capulet are 'My heart is with Tybalt', 'I want to poison Romeo' and 'If only I could crush, by my love for Tybalt, the one who killed him', while the messages for Romeo are 'My heart is with Romeo', 'I want to moderate Romeo poison' and 'If only I could hold, by my love for Tybalt, the one who killed him'.[50]

The truth of such obscene behaviour ('self-will'd harlotry', her father will call it (4.2.14)) is Juliet's utterance 'Indeed I never shall be satisfied / With Romeo, till I behold him – dead – / Is my poor heart'. Here, the first pause is for Romeo's ears, and the second is for the mother's. However, due to Romeo's absence, only the second one is heard: only Romeo's death will be able to 'satisfy' Juliet's desire, only then will she realize that, by obscenely carnivalizing her father's desire, she was reproducing it.

She manipulates her own split: the subject of the enunciated replies to the mother, while the subject of enunciation addresses Romeo; so too, staging her death in the tomb, she will be replying to her father's demand to marry Paris, while allowing Romeo to kidnap her. But since the subject of enunciation is the subject of the unconscious, immune to the intentions of the utterer, this manipulation is a fantasy. The price for overcoming the vicissitudes of the ideal ego, overdetermined as this imaginary instance is by the symbolic ego-ideal, is Juliet's ignorance of the illocutionary force of her utterances. She blinds herself to the fact that the uptake of her utterances depends on the Other, the symbolic order that refuses to give Romeo much leeway. Subject to 'the town', Romeo is unable to insert, as it were, the phallic signifier of Juliet's apparent death into the signifying chain of her letter. He is unable to read the staged death as an empty signifier that represents the subject, Juliet, for him as her newly appointed subject who is supposed to know, while representing nothing for her father, the original subject who is supposed to know. As a result, both Romeo and Capulet see in Juliet's fake death the thing itself, death sublimated in the unambiguous sign of the burial ritual. The second condition, namely that Juliet's staged death represent nothing for her father, is met: the Veronese receive Juliet's intended statement, *I am dead*, because they are blind to the message of her letter, *I am staging death*. But this message and with it the first condition, that Juliet's staged death represent living Juliet to Romeo, fails to meet Romeo, who receives its demand, *Acknowledge that I am alive!*, in an inverted, true form, namely *She is dead*. And since he is merely her ideal ego, not her ego-ideal, her demand returns to her in that form, *I am dead*. Her ignorance of the split between her present ideal ego and her absent ego-ideal proves fatal. In tragedy, one condition short equals nothing.

* * *

By failing to recognize the apparent death for what it is (to Juliet), Romeo turns it into real death. His rendition of Juliet's play is then ideological in the formal sense, a self-fulfilling prophecy, a translation of staged death into real death, a translation that retroactively, due to the effects of the very act of translation, becomes faithful. For the demand turns around the lack in Romeo's knowledge and returns to Juliet as *I acknowledged your death, and killed myself*; in other words, *I, Juliet, am not dead* returns as *I, Romeo, am dead* and, by extension, *I, Juliet, am dead*. From this point on – as the failure of Juliet's discourse of love is reiterated in, subjectivated as, the failure of her discourse of apparent death – she does not give ground relative to her desire to exit the Other as such rather than only its particular embodiments, such as Verona or Mantua. Between Verona and Mantua, between Capulet's and the Nurse's side of the Law, between *Romeo* and Romeo, she now chooses desire in its purest: the death drive. Seeing in the dead Romeo the result of her father's idio(syncra)tic not knowing, and in the latter the source of her initial presumption of Romeo's surplus – recognizing, that is, that the Other is split, and that the *objet* is an *abjet* – she subjectivates the situation, takes on its consequences, and identifies with the lack that always, after every secret wedding, staged death or escape, returns to its origin, namely herself. Faithful to her initial accidental encounter with love – faithful to fidelity as such – Juliet carries out the only act in which a subject can succeed.

And although her act is staged in Shakespeare's play as a singular act of suicide (and her death drive is staged as death), its subjective stance is depicted as a universally persistent action of a statue. After committing suicide, Romeo and Juliet will take the form of statues erected by their reconciled fathers:

CAPULET
>O brother Montague, give me thy hand.
>This is my daughter's jointure, for no more
>Can I demand.

MONTAGUE
>>But I can give thee more,
>For I will raise her statue in pure gold,
>That whiles Verona by that name is known,
>There shall no figure at such rate be set
>As that of true and faithful Juliet.

CAPULET
>As rich shall Romeo's by his lady's lie,
>Poor sacrifices of our enmity.
>>>>>>(5.3.295–303)

And although Capulet and Montague boast at length about the future form of these statues, it remains unknown to Shakespeare scholars whether 'statue' in 'For I will raise her statue in pure gold' means a statue or an image. This undecidable amorphism seems to echo the amorphism of the 'saints' of the lovers' first exchange. There, Romeo compares Juliet to a 'saint', and his own lips to pilgrims desiring a touch (1.5.92–5, 100, 102–3); Juliet rejects him playfully: 'For saints have hands that pilgrims' hands do touch, / And palm to palm is holy palmers' kiss' (1.5.99–9); and 'Saints do not move, though grant for prayer's sake' (1.5.104). The metaphor 'move' is, like any other metaphor, more than itself: 'Saints' in 'Saints do not move' can refer to statues of saints as well as to saints themselves. Juliet's subjective destitution in suicide therefore retroactively turns her original blindness, her initial refusal to recognize Romeo as a mere human, into an insight into his and her own non-human fate of a saint. This pulsation between 'saints' (1.5.100, 104) that may very well be statues of saints and 'statues' that may very well be mere images (5.3.298, 302), this drive pulsating around *objet* as absence, is what drives the action of *Romeo and Juliet*.

By refusing for the first time the desire of the Other, Juliet dispels not only the Nurse's final proposal to marry Paris after Romeo is banished (3.5.212–25) but also Friar Laurence's plea to seek refuge in a convent after Romeo commits suicide (5.3.151–9). Instead, she takes her life, redirecting the anxiety of '*Che vuoi?*' back to Verona. Now the Capulets, the Montagues and the Prince, all of whom have lost relatives (Juliet and Tybalt, Romeo and Lady Montague, and Mercutio and Paris, respectively), must themselves come to terms with the anxiety forced on them by the fact that the lovers' traumatic act cannot be explained away within the realm of the symbolic. By identifying with the *abjet* of the situation, Juliet becomes what she wanted to become in her feminine position on the stage: the phallus that the ruling discourse of Verona can socialize only through assigning it an empty signifier such as 'statue', a screen for projections of possible positive reasons for her suicide. The Veronese erect Juliet's name as their master-signifier. By inscribing the name, and the traumatic real of the suicide that it bears, into their contradictory language, they totalize the language, founding their community on the trauma of the suicide and evacuating the name into the void in their social structure, and under the 'statue'.

Far from remaining faithful to the event of the *passage à l'acte*, the Veronese try to domesticate the unbearable truth of the lovers' last will by reducing it to the sublimity of their first desire and to the Renaissance hubris of their fathers. However, against the backdrop of the pulsating drive of the statues' potential, undead activity, the final speeches of the two fathers seem anachronistic appropriations of the public funeral oration, a genre designed, according to Julia Reinhard Lupton, to appropriate traumatic deaths of members of a social body as deaths into citizenship.[51] The fathers' reconciliatory use of this community-building genre is haunted by a shadow of special interests and even boyish competitiveness, and so each lover is given a separate statue instead of a common one.

This positivization of the lovers' suicide betrays their act. The fantasy of being victimized by the givenness of fate, chance, Bloomian 'time's ironies' or blood feud spares the Veronese the anxiety of confronting the lack inherent in class society as such.[52] *Romeo and Juliet* gives ground neither to the melodrama to which Mantua would no doubt lead nor to the tragedy of Verona. Both compromises, along with escaping to Paris or to the convent, would prolong Juliet's naming of the unnameable in Romeo, the naming, 'Juliet's lover', that has been betraying the real itself, the unsymbolizable of their love. In her final act, Juliet replaces this naming with the silence of the suicide. In this way, she compels Verona itself to name and betray the real of this silence by erecting the 'statue'. Whereas hegemony needs culture for its totalization, *Romeo and Juliet*, as a work of art rather than a piece of culture, refuses to stand in for the fulfilment of the cultural programme of the mourning fathers, as their reconciliation is no longer fully contained by the play's mimetic frame.[53]

Read as an element of a text, that is, of a syntagmatic elaboration of the paradigmatic logic of the signifier, Juliet, having subjectivated the monologue of the balcony scene, does become a tragic 'character as destiny', despite acting in a 'bad tragedy'. She ignores the Shakespeare studies commonplace of *Romeo and Juliet* as a 'bad tragedy', and she does it by ignoring yet another such topos, the text-critical dilemma between 'any other name' and 'any other word'. As such, she becomes the quintessential editor of her own utterance regarding any other name/word.

3

# Necessary possibility as necessary actuality: Butler finds poetry in every parasite

In Chapter 1, we looked into J. L. Austin's speech act theory as the first phase in a three-phase process that has led from his bracketing off of literature as a parasitic speech act, to Jacques Derrida's valorization of the parasite as a necessary possibility of speech acts, to Judith Butler's reappropriation of this necessary possibility as a necessary actuality. We have so far seen in some detail how this developed in the first two phases, so let us now focus on the final phase. As we know from Chapter 1, Austin constitutively excluded literary and other etiolated performatives from the scope of his theory of the performative; we will see below, however, that Butler decided no less than to ground her theory of performativity in just such etiolations. In other words, that which Austin's analytic philosophy took great pains to expel from the notion of the performative, Butler's continental philosophy made sure to elevate to the level of the very notion of the performative. This was the price that the nomothetic theory of the performative ultimately had to pay to become the basis of an idiographic theory of performativity. On this conceptual travel across the epistemological sea, something that started, with Austin, as a theoretical intervention in the 'critical' ideology of logical positivism ended up, with Butler, as the 'topical' ideology of cultural performativity. This chapter will be our last chance to see if we can take something from this development in a time when Butler's cultural translation seems more canonical than Austin's language philosophy ever was.

Recently, translation was said to have become 'a more prolific, more visible and more respectable activity than perhaps ever before', even 'a model of time-space, of geopolitical relations, of postnational identities, and ultimately … a metaphor of culture itself'. Both these claims, by prominent postcolonial scholar Harish Trivedi and leading video artist and cultural commentator Hito Steyerl respectively, were followed by a critique of the conception of cultural translation, as Steyerl questioned the 'optimistic predictions about a new globalised cosmopolitism based on cultural translation', while Trivedi even claimed that, quite often, 'cultural translation is not so much the need of the migrant, as Bhabha makes it out to be, but rather more a requirement of the society and culture to which the migrant has travelled; it is a hegemonic Western demand and necessity'.[1]

In a prefiguration of Steyerl's critique of cultural translation, her colleague Boris Buden talks about the public space and the third space as the two possible social scenes of translation; writing for what an authoritative account of translation studies calls a 'superb multilingual website',[2] Buden distinguishes between therapeutic and cultural translation.[3] In the first case, Jürgen Habermas speaks of returning excluded individuals into the community by translating their pathological private discourses into the discourse of the public space.[4] In the second case, Homi Bhabha but also Judith Butler (who, as Buden notes, explicitly connects Bhabha's notion of cultural translation with the problem of universality)[5] speak of universalizing the public space itself by making it recognize its own excluded other; this other is excluded constitutively, it defines the public space as its other, and will hence never be fully translatable into it; the public space, no matter how universalized, remains separated from the private space, and this separation itself introduces a third space, the space of the very negotiation between the two: the space of cultural translation.[6]

According to Buden, the difference between these two models of emancipatory translation amounts to the difference between negation and negotiation or between dialectics and transgression; in Habermas's therapeutic translation, the integration of the private into the public leads to its dialectical negation as the other of the public, while in Butler's or Bhabha's cultural translation it leads to a transgressive renegotiation of the public itself. But building on Buden, we could perhaps even speak of two kinds of dialectics here, a positive one in Habermas and a negative one in Butler and Bhabha, as well as of two kinds of transgression, transgression demanding therapy and transgression limiting therapy; in Habermas, dialectical negation of private transgressions of the public sphere is just a step in the positive process of affirming that sphere, while in Butler or Bhabha it truly is a negative movement, one where no therapeutic translation can fully negate the private as the negation of the public.

In this sense, we can only agree with Butler's and Bhabha's own critiques of Habermas,[7] insofar as his universal pragmatics subsumes otherness under equivalence, and only Butler's and Bhabha's proposals of cultural translation grant otherness the status of difference, where equivalence among discourses is a matter of endless negotiation and transgression rather than something that simply precedes the discourses. As such, and in the words of yet another authoritative source on translation studies, 'cultural translation … offers a dissolution of some key categories of translation studies: the notion of separate "source" and "target" language-cultures and indeed binary or dualistic models in general'.[8]

However, as we have seen following Buden, both therapeutic and cultural translation ultimately regard translation as a kind of social bond, with one located in the public space and the other in the third space. From this perspective, we could argue that, if Habermas's therapeutic translation makes social action redundant, Butler's and Bhabha's cultural translation makes it atomized, asocial and as such, again, redundant. As Buden himself notes, by the time Bhabha's cultural universality was picked up by Butler, 'universality has become the problem of cross-cultural translation', which Butler explains 'in a way similar to the Habermasian "excommunication model"';[9] for Buden, cultural translation, like therapeutic translation, ultimately seeks the post-political 'balance of impossibilities' instead of facing the 'impossibility of balance'.[10]

As Bhabha is less crucial for the development of speech act theory in contemporary continental thought, let us focus on Butler's version of cultural translation. In her approach, cultural translation is an endless process in which identities excluded from the legal notion of universality are translated back into it, and in turn retroactively universalize this universality itself. According to Butler, in contemporary multicultural societies it is no longer possible either to universalize a particular culture or to define a universal trait of cultures. Hence, the universalization of recognition depends not on the universalist law and the state but on cultural translation as a process in which excluded identities resignify the speech acts through which they have been excluded.[11]

As we will see below, this belief in the power of the addressee of exclusionary speech to subvert this speech rests on a misreading of Austin's speech act theory, a misreading mediated by an older misreading of Austin, the one introduced by Derrida. Butler's voluntarist belief that exclusionary speech is sooner or later resignified by its addressee, and that hence state censorship denies both the speech and its resignification, seems alien to Austin and Derrida as her two main sources. A more attentive reading of these sources can therefore help us appreciate the institutional overdetermination of both speech acts and their potential resignifications.

But first let us look at an example. Martin Luther King, Jr provided us with a sublime case of cultural translation when he proclaimed that he was indeed black – and beautiful:

> Somebody told a lie one day. They couched it in language. They made everything Black ugly and evil. Look in your dictionaries and see the synonyms of the word Black. It's always something degrading and low and sinister. Look at the word White, it's always something pure, high and clean. Well I want to get the language right tonight. I want to get the language so right that everyone here will cry out: 'Yes, I'm Black, I'm proud of it. I'm Black and I'm beautiful!'[12]

Indeed, this is what Butler's cultural translation is all about: countering exclusionary speech, not with a Habermasian therapeutic neutralization on behalf of some universal target language – racist speech already is part of what is perceived as universality in 1960s America – but with a reappropriation in the language of the addressees themselves, a re-enactment capable of showing that universality itself is not universal until it recognizes the excluded and admits that, for example, black is beautiful. However, it is safe to say that King would never give up in advance any institutional resource in his fight, despite the strength of his own speech.[13] And not everyone's speech matches that of King, so even if King was too modest in his assessment that the strength of his speech acts is not enough to resignify the hate speech addressed to him, this would still only constitute a solution for him and for those few who can match the strength of his speech acts. Everybody else would have to seek refuge outside the realm of speech acts and their resignification.

But the point is that even King, while providing paradigmatic examples of what we can today call cultural translation, never stopped fighting for a broader institutional transformation. By the 1990s, when Bhabha and Butler championed the idea of cultural translation, this insufficiency of aesthetic re-enactment of hate speech was already the butt of a joke. The joke comes from African American stand-up comedian Dave Chappelle as part of a set that helped launch his unprecedented comedic career. Chappelle takes a white friend who loves hip hop to a hip hop party where all his black friends greet each other with the N-word and enjoy themselves until his overexcited white friend tries the greeting and in turn gets beaten by Chappelle himself.[14]

Here, Butler's aesthetic re-enactment of hate speech is just the premise of the joke, the punchline being its failure, the inability, even self-imposed inability, of re-enactment to cross the boundaries of its original producers, the addresses of hate speech, and to become available to a person who happens to be of the same colour as the original producers of hate speech. The channel that used to deliver the slur from the utterers to the addressees has been refracted – the slur has become a term of endearment – and yet the two ends of the channel remain as distant as ever, if not more. Let us see if we can find something in the theory itself that may be the cause of this frustration.

* * *

As mentioned in the incipit of this chapter, Butler's cultural translation will be approached in this book as just the latest stage in a three-stage process in which the parasite of non-seriousness is treated first as a mere possibility, then as a necessary possibility, and finally as a necessary actuality of so-called serious speech acts. Let us then briefly revisit the basic contours of the first two stages in this process, represented respectively by Austin's ordinary language philosophy and Derrida's deconstruction of Austin, as we know them from Chapters 1 and 2.

In *How to Do Things with Words*, Austin challenges the metaphysical presuppositions of logical positivism by discovering a class of utterances that, far from reproducing the metaphysical gap between subject and object, produce intersubjective relations. This distinction between constatives and performatives allows Austin to achieve an epistemological break with the tradition of logical positivism. But as soon as he adds performatives to constatives he discovers that constatives, too, can in the right circumstances say something and thereby perform something other than just saying something. Hence, he reframes the distinction between constatives and performatives as belonging to a special theory of the performative within the general theory of speech acts. In this new theory, each utterance has the locutionary force of uttering a sentence, the illocutionary force of producing intersubjective relations by this utterance, and the perlocutionary force of influencing subsequent utterances.

In 'Signature Event Context', Derrida recognizes in Austin's theory of illocutionary acts a forerunner of his own theory of writing. A written sign is written in order to be able to function outside its original context and even after the death of both the writer and the addressee. The possibility of this kind of functioning of a written sign is therefore a necessary possibility. Consequently, the possibility of additional citation of a written sign outside that original context is a necessary possibility, too. A written sign can hence be repeated beyond the addressee's or even the writer's original intentions, and to this degree a written sign can also be altered; both repeatable and alterable, a written sign is, in a word, iterable, according to Derrida. The possibility that a citation is going to be unfaithful to the original intentions or the original context in general is thus immanent, rather than external, to a written sign; it is a necessary possibility. And if the possibility of iteration is not external to a written sign, neither is a written sign itself merely external to a spoken sign, for a spoken sign is equally vulnerable to citations outside its original context. Every sign is therefore necessarily iterable and as such unable to express any original, idiosyncratic intention, which in turn means that communication cannot be a means of exchange of such intentions.

As we also know from Chapter 2, in 'Signature Event Context', Derrida praises Austin for reducing intention and reference to so many effects of illocutionary formulas themselves. But this similarity between speech act theory and deconstruction is, for Derrida, just a backdrop for a certain fundamental difference, his own *différance*. Unaware that language is marked by a difference that, as writing illustrates best, is always already deferral or, in a word, *différance*, Austin's deconstruction of communication remains steeped in logocentrism and its favouring of speech over writing, according to Derrida. More precisely, Austin is said to regard locution as a mere contingent expression of the illocutionary formula, rather than as its necessary and potentially altering incarnation. In order to escape the precariousness of locution, Austin clings to monosemy, according to Derrida, guaranteed by the serious intention and the conventional context in general. Hence, finally,

Austin's infamous dismissal of jokes, citations and literature as non-serious, etiolated, parasitic speech acts. In Austin, etiolations are merely a possibility that remains external to serious illocutions, and the citation is not a necessary possibility in the fate of any sign. For Derrida, on the other hand, the possibility of etiolation is a necessary possibility that makes every speech act precarious and as such non-redundant, meaningful.

In her 1997 book *Excitable Speech*, Butler misreads Derrida's necessary possibility of etiolation as a necessary actuality. According to Derrida, the performative's 'possibility ... to be "quoted"' is 'the very force and law of its emergence'; Butler's report, however, reads: 'Derrida claims that the failure of the performative is the condition of its possibility, "the very force and law of its emergence."' Here is the relevant passage from Derrida:

> The possibility for every performative utterance (and a priori every other utterance) to be 'quoted' ... Austin ... excludes, along with what he calls a 'sea-change,' the 'non-serious,' 'parasitism,' 'etiolation,' 'the non-ordinary' ..., all of which he nevertheless recognizes as the possibility available to every act of utterance. It is as just such a 'parasite' that writing has always been treated by the philosophical tradition, and the connection in this case is by no means coincidental.
>
> I would therefore pose the following question: is this general possibility necessarily one of a failure or trap into which language may *fall* or lose itself as in an abyss situated outside of or in front of itself? What is the status of this *parasitism*? In other words, does the quality of risk admitted by Austin *surround* language like a kind of *ditch* or external place of perdition which speech [*la locution*] could never hope to leave, but which it can escape by remaining 'at home,' by and in itself, in the shelter of its essence or *telos*? Or, on the contrary, is this risk rather its internal and positive condition of possibility? Is that outside its inside, the very force and law of its emergence? In this last case, what would be meant by an 'ordinary' language defined by the exclusion of the very law of language? In excluding the general theory of this structural parasitism, does not Austin, who nevertheless claims to describe the facts and events of ordinary language, pass off as ordinary an ethical and teleological determination ...?[15]

And this is what Butler makes of the passage:

> When Austin wrote that all conventional acts are subject to infelicity and 'all conventional acts are exposed to failure,' he sought to isolate the conditions of failure, in part, as circumstantial. Derrida, however, argues that there is a

conventionality and a risk of failure proper to the speech act itself (15) – a failure that is the equivalent of the arbitrariness of the sign. The sense of convention in Austin, augmented by the terms 'ritual' and 'ceremonial', is fully transmuted into linguistic iterability in Derrida. ...

... Performatives fail either because, for Derrida, they must fail as a condition of their iterability or, for Bourdieu, they are not backed by the appropriate expressions of social power. Derrida claims that the failure of the performative is the condition of its possibility, 'the very force and law of its emergence.' (17) That performative utterances can go wrong, be misapplied or misinvoked, is essential to their 'proper' functioning: such instances exemplify a more general citationality that can always go awry, and which is exploited by the 'imposture' performed by the mimetic arts.[16]

In this way, 'the very force and law of its emergence' no longer resides in the performative's 'possibility ... to be "quoted"', but instead in 'the failure of the performative', as if to be quoted is always already to fail, when it comes to speech acts. And as we can see, this slippage occurs not only between Derrida's text and Butler's report but is repeated also in the course of Butler's report itself, when 'a risk of failure' becomes simply 'a failure', which then reappears as the performative's 'condition of ... possibility' before it is subordinated again to 'a risk' in the notion that 'performative utterances can go wrong' (rather than simply 'go wrong'). But this reunion of 'failure' and its 'risk' is brief, as Butler effectively goes on to take Derrida's necessary possibility of performative failure and use it in Pierre Bourdieu's problematic of social power to come up with the necessary actuality, rather than possibility, of performative failure: beyond Derrida's 'linguistic iterability', in 'expressions of social power', performatives not only can, but also do go wrong, for Butler, just as they always go wrong in 'the "imposture" performed by the mimetic arts'.[17]

The performative's possibility to be cited thus becomes the failure of the performative; a possibility in Austin becomes a necessary possibility in Derrida – only to become a necessary actuality in Butler. So, for her, every speech act is sooner or later 'aesthetically reenacted',[18] resignified, reappropriated by the addressee. The literary and other etiolations that Austin excluded from his attempt to grasp speech acts are used by Butler as the very object of her own attempt.

Butler is interested in providing a theoretical argument for introducing universality beyond its legal institutionalization. In her analysis, the law necessarily particularizes universality because it censors, in the name of universal rights and liberties, any utterance that prevents its addressee from uttering. Hate speech, as a silencing of its addressee, is particularist and hence censored in the name of universality. If the law were to protect such particularist speech on behalf of universality, it would conduct a performative contradiction, 'an act of speech that in its very acting produces a meaning that undercuts the one it purports to make'.[19] So, if the universalist law is to avoid such a contradiction, it must refrain from ratifying non-universalist utterances. But according to Butler, it is precisely by trying to escape the performative contradiction that the law misses the contradiction that simply is universality, namely universality as precisely the process of ratifying, universalizing, non-universalist utterances:

> Consider, for example, that situation in which subjects who have been excluded from enfranchisement by existing conventions governing the exclusionary definition of the universal seize the language of enfranchisement and set into motion a 'performative contradiction,' claiming to be covered by that universal, thereby exposing the contradictory character of previous conventional formulations of the universal. This kind of speech appears at first to be impossible or contradictory, but it constitutes one way to expose the limits of current notions of universality, and to constitute a challenge to those existing standards to become more expansive and inclusive. In this sense, being able to utter the performative contradiction is hardly a self-defeating enterprise; on the contrary, performative contradiction is crucial to the continuing revision and elaboration of historical standards of universality proper to the futural movement of democracy itself.[20]

This demands a substitution of nonconventional idealization, conceived by Habermas as 'always already there', with Bhabha's cultural translation, as Habermas's notion of consensus

> short-circuits the necessarily difficult task of forging a universal consensus from various locations of culture, to borrow Homi Bhabha's title and phrase, and the difficult practice of translation among the various languages in which universality makes its varied and contending appearances. The task of cultural translation is one that is necessitated precisely by that performative contradiction that takes place when one with no authorization to speak within and as the universal nevertheless lays claim to the term.[21]

Finally, if Habermas is out, hate speech is in:

> Indeed, it seems important to consider that standards of universality are historically articulated and that exposing the parochial and exclusionary character of a given historical articulation of universality is part of the project of extending and rendering substantive the notion of universality itself. Racist speech, to be sure, contests current standards governing the universal reach of political enfranchisement. But there are other sorts of speech that constitute valuable contestations crucial to the continuing elaboration of the universal itself, and it would be a mistake to foreclose them.[22]

On her way to positing universality beyond its institutional, legal notion, Butler refers to Hegel's critique of Kant's formalist distinction between subjective categories and the objective world. According to Hegel, the individual participates in universality insofar as he or she subjectivates the objective sphere of customs, *Sittlichkeit*, which consists of the family, civil society and the state. For, alienated into this sphere, the individual can be recognized within the community of other subjects of *Sittlichkeit*. Participation in universality is guaranteed by participation in *Sittlichkeit*. But since Butler views contemporary societies as multicultural communities, she claims that, today, universal recognition demands the work of cultural translation.

> In fact, if Hegel's notion of universality is to prove good under conditions of hybrid cultures and vacillating national boundaries, it will have to become a universality forged through the work of cultural translation. And it will not be possible to set the boundaries of the cultures in question, as if one culture's notion of universality could be translated into another's. Cultures are not bounded entities; the mode of their exchange is, in fact, constitutive of their identity.[23]

Multiculturalism is said to require a practice of translating between the particular and the universal, a politics of translation that is able to recognize all particular identities as participating in universality and hence to universalize the institutionalized notion of universality. In short, the politics of cultural translation is a politics of recognition.

This means that Butler equates *Sittlichkeit* with the sphere of culture. This equation, where the family, civil society and the state are reduced to culture, seemingly allows her to derive universality, whose material existence is for Hegel *Sittlichkeit*, from the purely cultural overcoming of the purely cultural differences that supposedly characterize contemporary societies. This culturalization of *Sittlichkeit*, however, is a regression in relation to Hegel. In Hegel, *Sittlichkeit* universalizes not only abstract law but also morality as the universalization of this law; and within the sphere of *Sittlichkeit* itself, the state universalizes not only the family but also civil society as the universalization of the family. So when Butler returns to the sphere of culture, accusing the state of rigidity, her reliance on *The Phenomenology of Spirit* and *The Philosophy of Right* is illegitimate. Granted, *The Philosophy of Right* does envisage such a return from the state to civil society, insofar as it views the universalization that propels the triad of family, civil society and the state as more than just a linear negation of the first two elements of the triad by the third one. But this return is by no means without consequences for universality: it proves regressive as soon as *The Philosophy of Right* is read with *The Phenomenology*, in which the state, far from negating civil society, overdetermines it, rendering any return to civil society without any regard for the overdetermining state regressive, just as it would be a regression to view the family as a haven unmarked by civil society. After all, 'if we fail in our attempt to climb the social ladder we cannot simply return back to our family: there is nothing more painful and uncanny than to face your family members once they know that you *had to* return'.[24]

So, in order to grant culture more universality than the state, Butler has to reduce the negation of the family and civil society by the state to a mutual dependence of all three institutions of *Sittlichkeit*. Only then is she able to talk about the dependence of the state's legal apparatus on the norms of the family and civil society (e.g. the dependence of the legal definition of universality on patriarchal homophobic politics), and then deploy this hinging of the state upon culture in her struggle against the hegemony of the existing state. But in her reading of Hegel she seems to neglect the fact that the negation of both the family and civil society by the state does not lead to the mutual dependence of these three institutions since the two negated institutions – not only the family but also civil society, the institution that she defends against the state – are overdetermined by the negating one, the state.

This neglect of the overdetermining role of the state is not without consequences for her own demand that universality be a Derridean process to come, rather than a Habermasian sphere that is already institutionalized in the modern nation-state. This demand, instead of taking the state into consideration, is itself overdetermined by the viewpoint of the contemporary state, insofar as that type of state is the result of precisely the institutionalized, state-led regression of the nation-state to the post-national identity community. This kind of regression of the state to culture that characterizes the contemporary state itself seems to be at work also in Butler's reading of *Sittlichkeit*. In this sense, her anti-statism is the anti-statism of the contemporary state itself; her culturalist reduction of *Sittlichkeit* is the reduction that simply is the contemporary state. Defending civil society against the state amounts here to exposing it to the logic of the state.[25]

* * *

In her analysis of the general performative contradiction of the law, Butler shows that the contemporary legal apparatus of the United States cannot escape reproducing the contradiction between the First Amendment to the Constitution, which guarantees freedom of speech, and the Fourteenth Amendment, which guarantees equality in exercising rights and liberties. The legal system is faced with its own contradiction whenever it processes hate speech and other utterances that do not yield to the legal notion of universality, according to Butler. The system is forced to draw the line beyond which hate speech is no longer protected by the First Amendment and instead becomes subject to the Equal Protection Clause of the Fourteenth Amendment, as hate speech prevents its addressees from exercising their freedom of speech.[26]

From this account one could conclude that the normal functioning of the legal system produces, when faced with hate speech, a contradiction between the utterers' and the addressees' freedom of speech. But the law is, of course, nothing if not the apparatus installed to resolve dilemmas engendered by the normal functioning of state institutions. There is indeed a contradiction here between the First and the Fourteenth Amendments, but there is also the law as precisely the supplementary institution that does the work of resolving such inherent institutional contradictions. Butler seems to underestimate this reproductive function of the law, placing all her hopes on the contradiction alone in her desire to reject the law in the name of utterances that contradict the legal ideal of the universalist utterance.[27]

Butler notices that the legal apparatus tends to resolve this dilemma by resorting to conservative ideologies. In most cases, it protects hate speech by referring to the First Amendment because the addressees – who, as addressees of hate speech, are denied the rights guaranteed by the Fourteenth Amendment

– are usually members of sexual, religious, racial and other kinds of minorities. Or, at best, the law censors hate speech so as to protect its utterers from becoming addressees of public protests that might arise if the hate speech in question were not censored.

So, Butler in effect shows us how the antinomy between censoring and protecting hate speech is resolved by censorship of both hate speech and the anticipated public outrage over hate speech. One might even say that the contradiction between censorship and protection is resolved simply by more censorship: by the direct censorship of hate speech, and by the indirect censorship of the protesters who otherwise might take the job of censoring hate speech in their own hands. While the law censors hate speech, it interprets this censorship as an unavoidable step, a preventive measure against the spontaneous, public, non-legal censorship of the hate speech in question: the law places the responsibility for its act of censorship on the public, whose protests it both presupposes and suspends. The legal apparatus presents its act of censoring hate speech as a means of preventing public outrage over the legal protection of hate speech – and at the same time it censors this public, leaving it without a reason to protest; in one and the same gesture, the law anticipates and prevents public protests. The law, it seems, suspends not only hate speech but also any public suspension of it.

Once again it seems that Butler's deconstruction of the law misses the point: contradictory as the law may be in its actions, it only fulfils its role of an ideological state apparatus as it makes this kind of *bricolage* of its own possibilities, its own Amendments, in order to strike a compromise between censoring hate speech and censoring public, extra-legal censorship of such speech. The law simply sets in motion a typical institutional mechanism whenever it disavows the First Amendment in anticipation of spontaneous public exercise of law. For Butler, however, such disavowal is proof that the law fails even when it delivers and decides to protect the victims of hate speech; that is, the law fails even when it does not fail, according to Butler. Stressing the contradictory practices of the law and failing to see that such supplementation of the contradictions of other institutions is the very goal of the institution of law, she denounces the legal manner of addressing hate speech.[28] Reading censorship as the law's conservative bias, she looks for an alternative to censoring hate speech and finds it in the subversion of hate speech by its addressees themselves.[29] Failing to see that contradiction is the institution's aim, not mistake, she looks for the solution outside the institutional field, and she finds it in cultural translation and, in the last analysis, in the individual addressee's potential to rearticulate hate speech.

Indeed, Butler believes that hate speech can be resignified by its addressees via aesthetic re-enactment and other transgressive acts that need not resort to state institutions. Moreover, not only can such resignifications of hate speech do without the state – the state even disables them as it censors hate speech, the very object of resignification. It seems that Butler can believe this because she interprets hate speech as the illocutionary act of threat, the act that triggers a temporality that can be brought to a close only by the threatened act itself, which is the perlocutionary effect of the threat. In this interval between the threat and its realization lies the opportunity to subvert hate speech,[30] that is, the possibility of the threat's misfiring, according to Butler.[31]

Building on what we know already from Austin, we can say that Butler neglects the fact that the perlocutionary effects of a threat are much less institutionally mediated, and as such much more in the hands of the utterer, than those of, say, a marriage or a verdict. And the reason for this is that the same holds true for the felicity conditions of these illocutions, as classified by Austin: the conditions of felicitous execution of such illocutionary acts as a threat are much less institutionally mediated, much more manageable by their utterer, than those of a marriage or a verdict.[32] The only institution necessary is language itself: hate speech can be viewed as the result of the delocutive derivation of a verdictive; it consists of words derived from illocutionary acts of verdict. To return to the Benveniste example that we already know from Chapter 1, the verb *to okay* is derived not from *okay* the noun, but from 'Okay!' the locution;[33] hence, the verb *to okay* simply means 'to say: "Okay!"'. So too, in the case of hate speech, the word *Idiot!*, far from being a diagnosis, means 'I call you "Idiot!"'. If called an idiot, a person is designated, not as someone who fits the description made by the word *idiot* (whatever that description may be), but as someone who is called an idiot (and who as such fits the only pertinent description). From a word that metaphorically designates its addressee as having a certain property (say, idiocy, whatever that may mean) is derived, via continuous use, a homonym that designates its addressee as precisely the addressee of that word. Far from describing its addressee, hate speech makes him or her hateable, addressable by hate speech.

Consequently, Austin's first of the three pairs of felicity conditions is satisfied by definition, in the case of a threat: there is a conventional procedure with a conventional effect (A. 1), and the involved persons and circumstances are appropriate (A. 2), as they are retroactively constituted by the very invocation of the procedure. Due to this invocation, this utterance, the threat is also executed correctly (B. 1) and completely (B. 2), which satisfies the second pair of Austin's felicity conditions. The four conventionalist conditions are therefore easily met, in the case of a threat. So, there remain two felicity conditions, the intentionalist conditions, namely the sincerity of the speech act (Γ. 1) and subsequent adherence to it (Γ. 2).[34] These two conditions, however, do not have to be met at all, because even without them the act is, not a misfire, but rather a mere abuse; for, when a speech act is abused, 'the act *is* achieved', writes Austin, 'although to achieve it in such circumstances, as when we are, say, insincere, is an abuse of the procedure', so that, 'when I say "I promise" and have no intention of keeping it, I have promised but …'.[35] Butler seems to forget here that a threat, as an utterance that embodies the rift between illocution and perlocution, can only be abused, not misfired.

Thus, the felicity conditions of a threat are met as soon as the threat is uttered. Which means that in the absence of state censorship anyone can make a threat. And anyone with sufficient authority can also execute a threat, thereby satisfying the final of the six felicity conditions (Γ. 2). By warning against the power of censorship, Butler in effect exposes the addressees of hate speech to those in power.

Butler is right to say that hate speech can be stopped only in the gap between what it does as an utterance and what it does as the cause of later events, that is, in the rift between its illocutionary force and its perlocutionary effects.[36] As we have seen, Derrida claims that the possibility of this gap is a necessary possibility, one that makes any speech act precarious and hence meaningful, non-redundant, and Butler effectively misreads this necessary possibility as a necessary actuality. As she herself argues, Derrida, with his interpretation of Austin in the direction of pure 'linguistic iterability', stops short of analysing the institutional conditions for the actualization of this necessary possibility.[37] She, on the other hand, does look for such institutional conditions, but she seems to find them precisely in the disintegration of an institution, namely the state institution of censorship. The law, she claims, cancels the gap between illocution and perlocution as it defines hate speech (illocution) as conduct (perlocution) in order to be able to censor it.[38] By doing so, the law deprives threatened identity groups of the opportunity to resignify a given speech act of threat before the gap between this act and the threatened act is closed.[39] And she believes in this resignification because she thinks that all hate speech is sooner or later resignified in the very process of its uncensored dissemination since it is iterable, that is, repeatable and as such prone to resignification.

But as Butler may very well know, suspension of both the act of threat and the threatened act is made increasingly difficult, not by the legal apparatus but, on the contrary, by its neoliberal commodification. Addressees of hate speech are forced to rely on the option of resignifying a threat only after a greater threat has been realized, namely the threat of dismantling public institutions. Only after institutional sanctions against illocutionary acts of threat are no longer an option does a suspension of the perlocutionary effects of such acts become a real option, if not the only one (which, as the only option, is, of course, no option at all). But at that point, the institutional measures necessary to control these perlocutionary effects of acts of threat become unavailable as well (and the only option literally becomes a non-option). As soon as individuals have to suspend the perlocutionary effects of threats, it is too late. For without the help of censorship, addressees can resignify hate speech only if each case of hate speech is always already misfired – which, as we have seen, is untenable, as hate speech is abused at best, rather than misfired, and can as such hardly be resignified by its addressees alone. In fact, we can prevent the realization of a threat only if we treat the threat as always already realized, and then silence it.

Hence, Butler's politics is a politics of allowing the dissemination of hate speech in order that it be aesthetically resignified in its iterability. This politics, however, disavows the fact that institutions alone are able to intervene in hate speech, insofar as hate speech, as Butler herself knows, pertains to rigid designations, empty signifiers (*Idiot!* means nothing but 'I call you "Idiot!"', and it means this rigidly, in all possible worlds). As the result of delocutive derivation, hate speech is inherently institutional, inscribed in the national language, which is why it can only be resignified institutionally. For a rigid designator cannot be resignified without a transformation of the very institutions that support the belief in the object of such a designator. There is hence no resignification without the institution, so any attack on the institution in the name of resignification is an attack on resignification itself.[40]

3: *Necessary Possibility as Necessary Actuality* 107

In short, in a situation where the addressee of hate speech is deprived of any legal and social support, we should not believe that only if hate speech is not censored can the addressee resignify it; on the contrary, we should assume that if hate speech is not censored the addressee can only resignify it, that is, only re-enact it in a new context without, however, thereby effecting its misfire. And Butler's critique of censorship indirectly contributes to such a situation. Moreover, her attack does not seem to lose its force despite the ongoing economic crisis in which multinational capital is by now externalizing its costs to entire nation-states, that is, to the very institutions that claim to protect individuals from the anti-social excesses of capital, including hate speech addressed to racial and ethnic minorities, migrants, women and other traditional low-income groups. For example, in her 2009 book *Frames of War* she writes:

> Precarity ... characterizes that politically induced condition of maximized precariousness for populations exposed to arbitrary state violence who often have no other option than to appeal to the very state from which they need protection. ... To be protected from violence by the nation-state is to be exposed to the violence wielded by the nation-state, so to rely on the nation-state for protection *from* violence is precisely to exchange one potential violence for another.[41]

It seems that, if Derrida develops the philosophical consequences of Austin's theoretical practice, then Judith Butler inadvertently develops the ideological consequences of Derrida's project. If Derrida produces a philosophical category, Butler produces ideological legitimation for the commodification of the state.

\* \* \*

As mentioned above, Butler herself feels that Derrida fails to fully reflect on the social dimension of speech acts. As we have seen in the previous two chapters, this has consequences for his theory first and foremost, which neglects the conventionalism developed already by Austin. Butler, however, supplements Derrida's linguistic iterability with her notion of the social iterability of the speech act in order to grasp the iterability of hate speech without having to grant such speech the status of delocutively derived rigid designation whose meaning can be changed solely with the help of those institutions that she wants to deconstruct. In effect, she finds Derrida's linguistic iterability unsatisfactory insofar as Derrida insists that a sign, due precisely to its iterability, can maintain its conventional meaning even in new contexts, functioning as a rigid designator immune to its addressee's conscious attempts at subversion. Derrida may not consider the institutional conditions of a sign's rigid designation, but from his position it at least follows that it takes more for hate speech to be subverted than its recontextualization performed by its own addressee.

This is why Butler has to disavow Derrida: in her reading, iterability guarantees for the changeability of the meaning of a sign,[42] not for the persistence of the sign's conventional meaning beyond the sign's original context. According to Derrida, iterability guarantees for the unchangeability of a sign's meaning despite the changeability of the sign's original context; according to Butler, however, Derrida's iterability guarantees for the changeability of the very meaning of a sign, the possibility of its 'resignification', 'restaging', 'revaluation'.[43]

Returning to 'I know well, but all the same …', Mannoni's succinct formula of fetishistic disavowal that closed Chapter 2 on Derrida, we could sum up her belief as follows: *I know well that hate speech is a rigid designator effective in every possible world, but all the same I believe that it can be rearticulated without, and only without, institutional intervention.* From this perspective, we shouldn't overhear her expressions of faith when she writes, for example, that 'attacks by one's enemies can paradoxically boost one's position (one hopes)'.[44] Butler believes, or 'hopes'; and the same register persists in the rest of the sentence – 'especially when the broader public has no desire to identify with the manifest aggression represented by their tactics' – where a difference between one's enemies and the broader public is simply presupposed without any analysis of the conditions of its possibility. Instead of an argument, we are offered faith in a kind of iterability, a sort of surplus of the utterance's effects over the intention of the utterer.[45]

This replacement of the necessary possibility of etiolation with a necessary actuality allows Butler to maintain her belief in the rearticulation of hate speech by its addressees. By forsaking possibility for actuality, she can upgrade Derrida's linguistic iterability to social iterability, where hate speech is bound to be subverted by its addressees. Because only if, as she seems to think,[46] the condition of possibility of hate speech lies, not in the possibility of its misfiring, but in its actual misfiring, only then is every actual case of hate speech always already misfired – and as such vulnerable to extra-institutional resignification. In this sense, Butler's idiographic expert knowledge on the ways in which the social effects of hate speech can be managed by the addressees themselves is based on a pre-theoretical reading of Derrida's deconstruction of Austin's nomothetic theory.

She is right to say that Derrida, while managing to derive from Austin's problematic the general conditions of meaning and to produce the category of iterability, does not use this new category to analyse the social effects of speech acts. But she is wrong to think that she herself can develop this social problematic without relinquishing the category of iterability fetishized as the solid basis for the subversion of the social effects of speech acts. The only way in which she can take the category of iterability with her on her path to the social problematic is by demoting this philosophical category to the level of an ideological notion: Derrida substantialized the structuralist concept of the empty signifier to produce the category of iterability as the general condition of the unchangeability of the utterance's meaning despite the changeability of the utterance's context; Butler took this philosophical categorial use of a theoretical concept and transformed it into the ideological notion of the social iterability as the changeability of the utterance's meaning, a notion that is ideological insofar as it reflects neither on Derrida's philosophical appropriation of a theoretical concept nor on its own appropriation of the unchangeability of meaning postulated in this category.

Unlike Derrida, Butler raises the question of the social conditions of subverting a speech act, but she finds the answer in iterability as the law of performativity,[47] that is, in the very category that Derrida insists on in his attempt to answer, as it were, the question that he never raises. Her answer regarding the material conditions of a performative is performativity: she equates the conditions of a phenomenon with its essence,[48] instead of studying these conditions precisely in order to avoid contemplating the mystery of the essence. As such, her answer to the question of conditions is tautological. However, as she herself shows, the speech act itself is a tautological act of symbolization.[49] Her account of the speech act is thus as tautological as the speech act itself. In this sense, her account reproduces its object – which makes it a pre-theoretical account.

Her argument reproduces its own object insofar as the absence of institution in her analysis of hate speech uncannily fits the absence of institution from the list of felicity conditions of a threat. Butler's argument neglects the fact that the very action that it proposes, the disintegration of institutions such as censorship, helps bridge the gap between the act of threat and the threatened act. Because she rejects the nation-state as the institutionalized social bond that censors hate speech, she unwittingly helps promote hate speech itself to the status of the social bond.

So, instead of following, for example, Eve Kosofsky Sedgwick or Shoshana Felman in their adherence to Butler's Austin, or even J. Hillis Miller and Erika Fischer-Lichte in their revisions of Butler's Austin,[50] we should reach beyond her horizon of the atomized addressee. And who better to lead us beyond the atomized individual if not Austin himself, whose original speech act theory places so much importance on the institutional conditions of speech acts.

# *Ad* 3: Butler's poetry of parasites in *We Are All Jews and Germans*

Martin Luther King wanting 'to get the language so right' that everyone cries out 'I'm Black and I'm beautiful!' is, of course, not the only passage one could take from King to exemplify Judith Butler's, if not Homi Bhabha's, ideal of cultural translation. As noted by our source of the King passage,[1] King used language in this way in other speeches from 1967 as well, including his famous address 'Where Do We Go From Here?', where he said the following:

> The Negro must boldly throw off the manacles of self-abnegation and say to himself and to the world, 'I am somebody. (*Oh yeah*) I am a person. I am a man with dignity and honor. (*Go ahead*) I have a rich and noble history, however painful and exploited that history has been. Yes, I was a slave through my foreparents, and now I'm not ashamed of that. I'm ashamed of the people who were so sinful to make me a slave.' (*Yes sir*) Yes [*Applause*], yes, we must stand up and say, 'I'm black, but I'm black and beautiful.'[2]

Nor is the Dave Chappelle bit used in the previous chapter to illustrate a limit to cultural translation the only mainstream joke about a white man making the mistake of joining in when his black friends use an anti-black slur to greet each other. Recent examples include a white man hiring a black man to say the slur for him whenever he wants to use it in a conversation with a black friend, and a white man swapping bodies with a black man and realizing that he can now use the slur to greet black people.[3] In both cases, hate speech is reappropriated by its addressees and then made available even to members of the group that is most likely to utter such hate speech; culturally translated, hate speech enters the realm of universalist speech and thereby exposes this realm itself to the kind of universalization that Butler expects from cultural translation. However, the price for this universality in the first example, from 2013, is that the white man has to bribe one of the black men to sell out the other black man, while in the second, 2018 example, the price is no less than body swapping.

But as we also know from the previous chapter, King would never limit his politics to cultural translation to begin with, as brilliant as he was in it. His politics was much more radical; so radical, in fact, that it ended with his assassination just a month before it was in many ways revived on a global plain by the events of May 1968.

\* \* \*

In the official memory of May 1968, no one epitomizes the spirit of May better than one man. For fifty years now, this man has embodied the revolt of 1968. Born just before the end of the Second World War, and raised by a Germanic family in a Romance culture, this man was still in his early twenties when he made his name with a feat that shook France and the rest of Europe. Passionately active throughout the 1970s and 1980s, he always found time to reflect on his achievements in numerous books, articles and interviews. His image graced posters the world over. In the 1990s, he was elected to the European Parliament as a member of the Greens. His views spark controversy in all camps to this day. This man is, of course, Daniel Cohn-Bendit. But it could easily also be Reinhold Messner.

Born in 1944 to a German family in South Tyrol, Italy, Messner soon became one of the best climbers of his generation, a status he secured as early as 1969 when he made the first solo ascent of the Droites north face in the French Alps. During the 1970s and 1980s, Messner climbed all fourteen eight-thousanders as well as the highest peaks of all seven continents, spending the time between the climbs writing books and giving interviews. In 1999, he became a member of the European Parliament for the Greens, just like Cohn-Bendit had five years earlier. To be sure, just like Cohn-Bendit, Messner rejected the national flag during May 1968; he may not have gone on the record that 'the French flag was made to be torn apart and turned into a red flag',[4] a statement that earned Cohn-Bendit immediate interdiction of the stay in France, but Messner's and Messner's generation's decision to give up the ritual of displaying the national flag on mountain tops had no less impact in the world of climbing.[5]

Indeed, the events metonymically termed *May '68* resonated both on the roof of the Sorbonne Chapel, where students displayed one of their red flags, and on the summits of the Himalaya, where the foremost climber of the era ceased to display the national flag; protesters included both anonymous industrial workers in Southern France and already (in)famous student leaders in Paris;

the movement engulfed both students in Mexico or Jamaica and workers in Italy or Japan, and students both of Columbia University and of South Carolina State University. But the events were also met with disapproval both by liberal and by socialist regimes; they were criticized both by incorrigible humanists like Theodor Adorno and by provocative anti-humanists like Jacques Lacan; finally, and perhaps crucially, silence was the ultimate message both of students and of workers as they tried in vain to lead the revolt together.

In terms of cultural translation, King's pleas to his fellow African Americans to assert 'I'm black, but I'm black and beautiful' are continued in May '68 by slogans like 'Nous sommes tous des Juifs et des Allemands' ('We are all Jews and Germans'). The utterance was launched by a poster, and celebrated as a slogan, following the interdiction of the stay in France issued on 21 May 1968 against Cohn-Bendit. Leader of the Movement of 22 March (Mouvement du 22 mars) at the University of Paris at Nanterre, Cohn-Bendit featured as early as 2 May on the front page of the far-right newspaper *Minute* as 'the German Cohn-Bendit, the chief commando of the vandals'.[6] The very next day, the French Communist Party echoed this label on the front page of its own newspaper, *l'Humanité*, by calling him a 'German anarchist' inclined to 'fascist provocations'.[7] By 21 May, when he was supposed to return to France after a brief tour of German student occupations, Cohn-Bendit was referred to as a German Jew across the political spectrum in France, including the outlets of Charles de Gaulle's government. A representative product of the Atelier Populaire ('Popular Studio'), as students dubbed the lithography studios of the École des beaux-arts art school when they occupied them during May, the poster was created by Bernard Rancillac on the basis of Jacques Haillot's photograph of Cohn-Bendit singing the *Marseillaise* in the face of a helmeted riot police officer after a meeting with administrators at the Sorbonne on 6 May. Along with Gilles Caron's photograph of a somewhat less confident Cohn-Bendit facing what appears to be the same officer,[8] Haillot's image soon circled the globe on its own, but its true fame comes from what Rancillac and then the protesting masses did with it.

And what the masses did with the poster was not unimportant. For, on the morning of 22 May, the poster didn't leave the Atelier Populaire with the original sign 'Nous sommes tous des Juifs et des Allemands'; instead, it read 'Nous sommes tous "indésirables"' ('We are all "undesirables"'), 'in an apparent effort', as an interviewer of Rancillac reports, 'by those in the workshop aligned with the French Communist Party to avoid further tensions with ... the party leadership'.⁹ The original sign, however, nonetheless reached the protesters and became their chant, 'which Rancillac took as a sign of the power of the street over those at the Atelier'.¹⁰ Instead of being streamlined, the slogan was only abbreviated to 'Nous sommes tous des Juifs allemands' ('We are all German Jews'), and it was made famous in this form by the demonstrations of 31 May.

'In his physical absence', the interviewer of Rancellin goes on, 'Cohn-Bendit was evoked in reference to the subjective annihilation of the Holocaust and, according to philosopher Jacques Rancière, given "a form of visibility conferred upon something that is supposedly non-visible or that has been removed from visibility."'¹¹ Granted, Rancière uses these words to define a political subject, not Cohn-Bendit, but his example is indeed the slogan 'Nous sommes tous des Juifs allemands'. In fact, 'Nous sommes tous des Juifs allemands' is not only an utterance that Rancière likes to cite as an example of political subjectivation but also the utterance that opened up for him, as he claims, 'an entire field of understanding speech acts as political gestures'.¹²

In the light of our previous chapters, we could say that the slogan condenses the difference between the Derridean notion of performativity and Rancière's own conception, while also pointing, as we will see in the next, concluding chapter, to the dimension where this difference shrinks and allows us to approach both Rancière's thought and the Anglo-American Derridean misreadings of it as a totality where Rancière's thought is the source of the misreadings, rather than their victim. So, what might Derrida and Butler have to say about 'Nous sommes tous des Juifs allemands'?

Derrida would perhaps choose to approach the slogan as a speech act of identification that, as an example of identification with a predicate of the other, is non-serious, parasitic and, as such, an embodiment of the necessary possibility of any act of identification, a supplement without which serious identifications would be redundant. Butler, for her part, could perhaps focus on the way in which the slogan parasitizes – and thus exposes the truth of – the neo-fascist, communist and Gaullist utterances about Cohn-Bendit: resignifying these utterances, the slogan embodies the necessary actuality of their etiolation and thus secures an identity to its own utterers, who, as a group claiming 'Nous sommes tous des Juifs allemands' can now participate in and thereby universalize the universal. Rancière, however, interprets the slogan, neither as an etiolated identification nor as a resignified identification, but as a disidentification: an identification with an identity that, as an excluded, empty identity, is available to anyone, not just to the utterers, and as such a source of the verification of equality. In the article referenced earlier, Rancière approaches the slogan as an example of an 'impossible identification', a 'nameless subjectivation of a gap between two citizenships' that

> inverted a name that was meant to stigmatize by turning it into the principle behind an open subjectivation of the uncounted, but it did not politically confuse them with any representation of an identifiable social group. What is it that gives the political sequence punctuated by May 68 … its specificity? … It is the rediscovery of what a political subject (proletarian or otherwise) is: the manifestation of a wrong, a counting of the uncounted, a form of visibility conferred upon something that is supposedly non-visible or that has been removed from visibility.[13]

In other words, in Derrida's horizon, the slogan could be read as an etiolated identification and hence a testament to the potential etiolation that is universal to identity utterances; in Butler's horizon, it could be viewed as a reappropriated identification and hence a universalization of the field of identities that have received recognition so far; Rancière, however, approaches the slogan as a disidentification and hence a verification of a universal competence, the constant possibility of rejecting a given part in the distribution of the sensible. In Derrida's horizon, 'Nous sommes tous des Juifs allemands' could become political only with something like the addition of negation: 'Nous sommes (et ne sommes pas) tous des Juifs allemands'; in Butler's, it would probably be most political if Cohn-Bendit himself were to confirm his German Jewishness and say something like: 'Oui, je suis un Juif allemande' (which is more or less what he actually said in 2005 when the national secretary of the French Communist Party, Marie-George Buffet, suggested that he should not campaign for the French European Constitution referendum);[14] Rancière, on the other hand, is able to grant politics to the utterance as it is, the actually existing slogan, insofar as, for him, the possibility of politics is presupposed, rather than deferred to Butler's Derridean 'futural movement of democracy itself' (to reiterate one of her phrases cited in the previous chapter).

\* \* \*

But if we add the perspective of the theory of the signifier, we can notice that what 'Nous sommes tous des Juifs allemands' also does to the neo-fascist, communist and Gaullist utterances about Cohn-Bendit is to reproduce them as its own pretext, that is, as both its textual material and its excuse. The utterance 'Nous sommes tous des Juifs allemands' includes a signifier, 'Juifs allemands', that has no linguistic signified (or else the slogan would simply be contradictory), but instead has two loci of inscription: the utterance to which it belongs, and the neo-fascist, communist and Gaullist utterances to which it refers. The signifier 'Juifs allemands' begins to make sense and thereby to totalize the whole utterance only after it is inscribed in a chain of signifiers that, unlike 'Juifs allemands' itself, are absent from the utterance 'Nous sommes tous des Juifs allemands', but can nonetheless be reconstructed as the utterance's pretext, namely all the hateful utterances about Cohn-Bendit.

As such, the signifier 'Juifs allemands' represents for these hateful utterances the subject that is the metaphor 'Nous sommes tous des Juifs allemands', the subject that is split between the position of enunciation ('Nous') and the position of the enunciated ('Juifs allemands'), the zero-degree difference whose meaning – a parodic rejection of the hateful utterances that make up the pretext – is discernible only to those who always already know these hateful utterances. 'The subject is only a moment in the putting-together of the utterance, a function of its construction',[15] writes Rastko Močnik in a recent formalization of 'Nous sommes tous des Juifs allemands'. And since Močnik acknowledges an unpublished version of the interpretation presented in this chapter,[16] let us look at his argument more closely.

With a signature gesture of the by now world-renowned school of Lacanian theory that he co-founded in Ljubljana around the time when Rancière established himself in Paris, Močnik approaches Rancière's problematic from the perspective of the very theory that Rancière thought was necessary to leave behind to develop this problematic. In his approach to Derrida's theory of writing, Močnik, as we have seen in Chapter 2, adds to Derrida's seminal critique of Husserl a key insight of Husserl's own semiology to concretize writing as a signifying practice.[17] So too, in his reading of 'Nous sommes tous des Juifs allemands', he builds on the theorist who supervised and published with Rancière before the student came into his own with a book-length critique of the supervisor (and of the very notion of supervision) in the name of none other than the students and workers who use slogans like 'Nous sommes tous des Juifs allemands'; this theorist and supervisor is, of course, Louis Althusser.[18]

Althusser's Leninist insistence on 'the authority of Science and the Party', as Rancière puts it, is the most far-reaching political consequence of his philosophical thesis that ideology exists materially in the practice of institutions to interpellate individuals as subjects by representing their imaginary relation to their real conditions of existence.[19] If ideology is as omnipresent as institutions and if, as such, its reach extends to the level of individuals, then the only way in which the individuals can counter ideological interpellation is indeed if they theorize their situation and organize accordingly behind the vanguard of a party and its own alternative ideology. Rancière's response to such an uncompromising view of ideological struggle is to leave Althusser and his reading of Marx with Lacan altogether, and to focus instead on a much more Foucauldian archaeology of those political strategies that have been invented by the masses themselves. Močnik's solution is to follow Althusser farther than Althusser himself was willing to go, as it were, and to show how his theses about ideology can be subtilized by an even more resolute entry into the Lacanian problematic.

Within this problematic, Močnik notices a certain contradiction in Althusser:

> Either ideology operates within the imaginary ... register, as Althusser explicitly claims – but then it does not affect the symbolic instance of the subject; or else ideology interpellates individuals as subjects, ... as Althusser also claims – but then his text only offers an incomplete presentation of the ideological process, and omits its essential dimension where ideology operates as symbolic mechanism.[20]

Opting for the first possibility, Althusser describes, according to Močnik, 'reproductive practices where the interpellated individual routinely and unknowingly submits to ideology', but fails to conceptualize 'practices of resistance, moments of radical rupture', while also leaving unanswered 'the question of the instance of identification: what instance does the interpellated individual identify with?'[21] As a result, we could add, Althusser presents us, somewhat like Lacan's armed robber yelling out 'Your money or your life!', with a forced choice between a missing concept of symbolic interpellation and an imaginary interpellation that is conceptualized, but not fully, because it is missing precisely the concept of symbolic interpellation. Močnik, without formulating the alternative in this way, in effect approaches it as such: he refuses, not one of the options, but the choice itself, and allows for ideological interpellation both as an effect of identification and as a mode of subjectivation.

To present these two types of interpellation, Močnik looks at two student movements (both of which he, incidentally, participated in as a student and an invited speaker respectively): the student movement in France during May '68, and the Croatian chapter of the Occupy movement in 2009.

The student occupation of the Faculty of Humanities and Social Sciences at the University of Zagreb was an early example of what a few years later spread globally under the name of the Occupy movement. Known for its 'manual',[22] *The Occupation Cookbook*, the Croatian movement started with the demand for the abolition of tuition fees, but soon developed into a struggle for the universal access to free education. This 'ideological development from a position defending a particular interest to a general slogan that really effectively mobilises people' is read by Močnik 'in terms of referring to one's own past discourse as another's discourse'.[23] Here is his Ducrotian analysis: 'The first discourse D displays two enunciators: enunciator E1 presents fees as unjust, and enunciator E2 says: *as* they are unjust, we will not pay them. And the way in which the fees are presented articulates the two enunciations together.' This is followed by the second position, the discourse D', where 'enunciator E1' ... presents education as a public good, and *as* a public good it should be free for all, which is the conclusion drawn by enunciator E2".[24] According to Močnik, 'the two discourses D and D' are running in the same direction ..., as D' only generalises what was already present ... in the discourse D'. Hence, 'in order to submit to interpellation, it is enough for the interpreter to identify herself or himself at the point offered as the one at which one should identify oneself: that is, at the level of the binding "evidence"'.[25] Ideological interpellation in this case 'proceeds by identification' and, ultimately, 'by self-objectivation, by objectification of one's own discourse'.[26]

Interpellation by identification is reproductive, according to Močnik: 'It reproduces the same ideological horizon across subsequent discourses'; it 'occurs whenever it appears that a locutor has used an expression in its "normal", "evident", "lexical" sense'; it is 'the ideology that Althusser speaks of when he says that ideology reproduces relations of production'.[27] On the other hand, there is interpellation as subjectivation, and Močnik's example is none other than 'Nous sommes tous des Juifs allemands': 'Discourses implicated in this utterance run in opposite directions: the ideological process operates an inversion of the other's discourse. The elegance of the manoeuvre consists in that the two discourses meet only at the point where they disagree.'[28] Here is Močnik's formalization:

> The discourse D consists of two enunciations by E1 and E2. Enunciator E1 presents these acts as objectionable; E2 ties to this the idea that, being objectionable, they were instigated by a German Jew. ... And then there is the second discourse D', opposing the first one, where E1' presents the locutors, 'us', as the agents of those acts, and E2' draws the conclusion: if we are the agents who conceived and performed these acts, we are all German Jews, according to your definition.

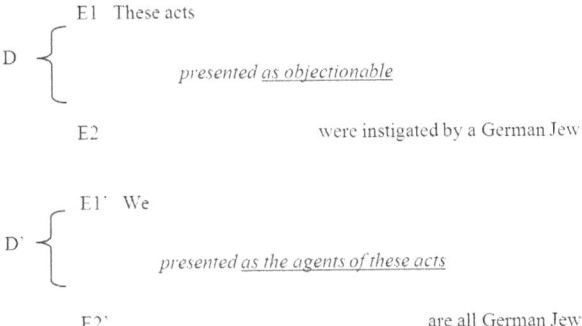

> Here, interpellation does not proceed by identification: it *is* subjectivation. ... 'German Jews' as S1 ... defines the situation, while receiving its meaning only when supplemented by S2, the concatenation of evidences D' and D 'as the agents of these acts ... presented as objectionable'. There is no 'inherent meaning' to the expression 'German Jews' in this sequence: despite its being stabilised by the supplementation provided by S2, it only possesses 'contextual meaning'.[29]

As for the subject, it emerges

> within the distance between S1 as meaningless and S1 as meaningful: however, this distance only signifies the cleavage between the subject of *énonciation* ('we') and the subject of *énoncé* ('German Jews'): the cleavage between the two is irreducible, and the momentarily emerging subject is irremediably split. The cleavage is inscribed within the utterance as the incongruity of predication: there is no chance of identifying the subject with the predicate. In this case, the subject cannot be supposed: it is not an instance guaranteeing the sense of the utterance from its inaccessible

hidden centre obfuscated by the mechanism of identification. The subject is only a moment in the putting together of the utterance, a function of its construction. Subjectivation remains open – hence the mobilising effect of the slogan.[30]

This is indeed much more radical than the Croatian case. There, for the hailing to succeed, the addressees only needed to identify with the ideological supposition that fees are unjust because education is a public good. There are many egalitarian ideologies, both in the recent Croatian past and in present neighbouring societies, where the latter is indeed just a positive formulation of the former and the status of a public good can serve as an argument for the unjustness of its commodification. Hence, the addressees of the Croatian slogan are able to identify with it without having to undergo the unconscious process of subjectivation demanded by 'Nous sommes tous des Juifs allemands'. Indeed, one of the slogans of the Zagreb student occupation simply takes the famous May '68 slogan 'Soyons réalistes, demandons l'impossible' ('Let's be realistic, let's demand the impossible'), adds ''68' to it, and rewrites it as 'Budimo realni, tražimo moguće '09' ('Let's be realistic, let's demand the possible '09').[31]

There is no such ideology available in the Parisian case. When *l'Humanité* as well as *Minute* and the government present Cohn-Bendit's acts as objectionable, there is no supposition at hand that can identify Cohn-Bendit with the addressees of *l'Humanité*, *Minute* and the government; these have to subjectivate Cohn-Bendit's acts themselves by uttering precisely 'Nous sommes tous des Juifs allemands'. Which indeed opens an entirely new level of mobilization; the only problem is that the mobilizing effect of this particular interpellation did not last. As Močnik himself warns us, the difference between the two types of ideological interpellation 'does not judge in advance their practical effects':[32] 'Interpellation by identification has established Croatian students as representatives of the general interest. Interpellation by subjectivation has, for a short moment, established French students as a political group apart. Croatian students may have triggered a political process that will last in the future. French students have sunk into historical myth.'[33]

* * *

Thanks to *Minute* and *l'Humanité*, Cohn-Bendit became the student leader whom the entire French political class identified, in the course of May, as a

German Jewish troublemaker. Thanks to the poster *Nous sommes tous des Juifs et des Allemands*, however, the movement identified with the German Jewish troublemaker. The protesters chose to confront the enemy with cultural translation, instead of realizing that the enemy that is split between positions as divergent as those of *Minute* and *l'Humanité* is a barred Other that should be replaced in an institutional struggle rather than sustained as the subject of the hate speech that the poster is supposed to performatively reappropriate. By using 'Juifs allemands', an empty signifier that only makes sense against the backdrop of the hate speech of *Minute*, *l'Humanité* and the government, the poster and the subsequent slogan are closer to an acting out than to a genuine Lacanian passage to the act; closer to reproducing hate speech than to suspending it. From the fact that Cohn-Bendit's nationality is referred to both by *Minute* and by *l'Humanité* the protesters somehow derive, not that the Other is barred, but, on the contrary, that it is ubiquitous. Even before neoliberalism becomes hegemonic, the neo-fascists and the French Communist Party are perceived, by the poster and the slogan, as two sides of the same evil coin.

Just as, for example, 'la pègre' ('riff-raff'), a signifier used, less than a week earlier, both by Minister of the Interior Christian Fouchet and the Party's *l'Humanité*, was immediately reappropriated by Marguerite Duras, Maurice Blanchot and other members of the Action Committee,[34] so too, the hate speech about Cohn-Bendit launched by both *Minute* and *l'Humanité*, and most likely also by the new Minister of the Interior, is resignified by demonstrators without delay, instead of being read as a final bar over the Other (A̶), the final proof that power is ready to be seized. Éric Hazan writes in 2002:[35]

> The two rival organizations of Gaullism and the 'Communist' party, in solidarity with one another in the police order of the time, only appeared to triumph with the demonstration of the Champs-Élysées and the Pompidou-Séguy agreements at Grenelle. They did not realize that they were already running on empty, like those characters in comic books who continue their chase beyond the edge of the cliff. It took a bit of time to look at the ground and begin the famous nosedive.

The problem is that the majority of the protesters, too, acted (or, acted out) as if they did not realize that the two rival organizations had already been running on empty. That is at least what Kristin Ross seems to suggest in her Rancièrian account of May '68, written in the same year as Hazan's:

> To look back at a moment after it has passed – a moment when ministers, the prime minister, and the president of the republic had all vacillated and lost consistency, when the government had become a shadow and had all but evaporated into smoke or dust like the witch in the *Wizard of Oz* – is to raise the question in all its poignancy of a missed opportunity, despite the fact that the notion of 'seizing state power' was for the most part not central to the workings of May.[36]

Hence the abstract and institutionally naive character of the slogan that, in Sarah Hammerschlag's words, has 'allowed for the easy (although obviously unfair) analogy between the de Gaulle government, Petain, and, by proxy, National Socialism'.[37] And although the unfairness of the analogy might not be as obvious as it seems to Hammerschlag, its easiness is, at least in the sense in which Mladen Dolar – building on Frantz Fanon's critique of both victimization and culpabilization to comment on the current global refugee crisis – warns us that, in political struggles, the term *fascism* tends to function 'as the name of the absence of the concept', since 'the implication of the term is: don't think, condemn'.[38]

It is in this sense that Lacan warns student radicals, in December 1969, that their revolution is a plea for a master and that it will succeed;[39] aligning himself neither with the conservative nor with the liberal faculty, Lacan simply accuses the students 'of not being radical enough', as Joan Copjec puts it[40] – an accusation not unlike the one voiced by militant Pierre Goldman in 1975, during his imprisonment and four years before his assassination, for whom 'the students spreading out onto the streets, in the Sorbonne, represented the unhealthy tide of an hysterical symptom'.[41] In this sense, it is perhaps unproductive to search for the political potential of May '68 in the transgressive slogans that capital had no problem quilting onto a new signifying chain, the one that quickly gave the student slogans against the family, the factory and the school a neoliberal meaning as the students were indeed freed from the family, the factory and the school. The signifier 'Juifs allemands' has become the object of Derridean etiolated identification and Butlerian resignification as well as Rancièrian universalization; what it has not become is the object of a revolutionary institutional sanction capable of subverting that signifier and quilting it onto a new signifying chain.

## Ad 3: Butler's Poetry of Parasites in We Are All Jews and Germans

Finally, as mentioned above, Rancière's reading of 'Nous sommes tous des Juifs allemands' can help us escape the lure of treating his thought as a mere victim of Anglo-American Derridean misreadings, and instead delineate a certain totality where Rancière's thought is the very source of the misreadings. It is therefore not at all misguided when, for example, Mark Robson interprets Rancière's aesthetic exposure of art to life in terms of Derrida's aesthetic potential of the speech act,[42] referring in the process to Andrew Parker, who in turn reads Rancière's cases of political subjectivation as so many proto-literary speech acts.[43] The performativity thesis, the misreading according to which Rancière equates the aesthetic regime with political subversivity, can indeed be justified, although not because the aesthetic regime is nonetheless somehow politically subversive, but because Rancièrian politics itself may not be fully subversive. As argued by such readers of Lacan as Jelica Šumič-Riha or Slavoj Žižek,[44] Rancière's own examples of political subjectivation imply and thereby reproduce a non-barred Other, the Other as an autonomous instance of granting words to bodies. In this sense, Rancière's own horizon ought to be broadened in the direction that can be traced, with some charity of interpretation, all the way back to Austin, especially to those propositions in which Austin effectively presents speech act theory as a theory of the Other embodied in convention and institution.

\* \* \*

The critique of Rancière outlined in this chapter is, surprisingly or not, already presupposed in his own theory. There, it is called 'metapolitics', which is the kind of politics that, starting with Marx, is said to be invested in looking hysterically behind the appearance of actually existing politics in an attempt to uncover, via symptomatic reading, the anti-political truth of actually existing politics.[45] Needless to say, 'metapolitics', with its opposition between truth and appearance, is rejected by Rancière (who, however, strangely gives the alternative, the politics of aesthetic regime, the same name, as he incessantly ascribes to this regime of art 'a politics or, more exactly, … a metapolitics').[46]

Yet our critique uncovers the truth (the insufficient subversivity of the May '68 slogan, of the aesthetic regime, and of political subjectivation itself) not behind the appearance, but in it (i.e. in the materiality of the slogan's empty signifier, in a characteristic Anglo-American misreading of the aesthetic regime and in the aesthetics of political subjectivation). As a result, both the appearance and the truth behind the appearance have become parts of the same surface (and even this reflection on our critique, far from offering a metanarrative, sees the truth of the critique in its appearance, its manifest unfolding). As such, our critique has analysed hysteria, rather than practicing it, insofar as it has granted appearance the dignity of a staging, a hystericization, of truth. This critique of both the aesthetic regime and its performativist reception participated in symptomatic reading merely in the strict psychoanalytical sense in which, as Lacan shows,[47] the notion of the symptom was introduced precisely by Marx and in which Rancière's theory itself was reproached for clinging to a certain hysterical presupposition of the existence of the Other – the Other whose only actual existence, namely the non-all realm of institutions (starting with the institution of language), is the focus precisely of symptomatic reading.

It is this focus that ought not to be lost today, when, a century after the Left seized power, and half a century after it seized speech rather than power, the United States shows the global Right how to seize power-as-hate-speech. In the United States, a year before student protesters shouted 'Nous sommes tous des Juifs allemands' in front of the National Assembly in Paris, King had wanted 'to get the language right', as we have seen in the previous chapter: 'I want to get the language so right that everyone here will cry out: "Yes, I'm Black, I'm proud of it. I'm Black and I'm beautiful!"' Today, in the same country, it is political correctness that wants to get the language right. In this framework, 'cultural and identity struggles inspire so much more passion and engagement than the political and the economic issues' that, as Dolar notes, we now have a full-fledged academic culture of safe spaces and trigger warnings that, however, cannot 'shield anyone from stepping outside the university and being exposed to the crudest kind of politically incorrect speech by none other than the American president'.[48]

It is not difficult to agree with the way in which Kristin Ross builds on Rancière's reading of 'Nous sommes tous des Juifs allemands' to praise the grassroot tendencies of May '68,[49] where change came from below rather than from a Leninist vanguard party.[50] It is more difficult to come to terms with the fact that this entailed the kind of change where what was meant to be seized was, not power per se, but speech. Perhaps the time has come to disentangle these two pairs — vanguard versus grassroot, power versus speech – as the second year of the current American president's first term is coming to an end without being bothered by the hegemony of political correctness. Perhaps change fifty years after May '68 demands a seizure of power, not just of speech; grassroot, if not party-led, but nonetheless a seizure of power.

This at least is suggested by the current development of a certain movement that started in French social media exactly fifty years after the May of 1968 and spread onto the streets of France and beyond by the end of the year. The participants in the 'Yellow vests movement' ('le mouvement des Gilets jaunes' in French) put on the high-visibility vests that the French law had required all motorists to obtain in 2008 as a safety measure, and took to the streets to demand real safety measures from the government, including the reintroduction of the solidarity tax on wealth. Causing the most violent protests in France since May '68, the demonstrators nonetheless managed to secure solidarity even from sections of the police, judging, for example, by the statement of retired policeman Ronald Guillaumont titled 'Nous sommes tous Gilets Jaunes !!!' ('We Are All Yellow Vests!!!').[51] Only time will tell if this echo of May '68 and its most iconic slogan will bring about more than just its singular form, 'Je suis Gilet Jaune', which is already available as, for example, a sticker that anyone can use instead of protesting – just as, for example, 'Nous sommes tous des Charlie', the response of the majority of associations of French journalists to the 2015 *Charlie Hebdo* terror attack,[52] was embraced outside journalistic collectives around the world as the much more comfortable 'Je suis Charlie', while 'Nous sommes Paris', the sign displayed by fans of Olympique de Marseille in solidarity with their Parisian football rivals after the 2015 Paris terror attacks,[53] spread outside France simply as 'Je suis Paris'.

# Conclusion: Literature and political disagreement from Austin to Rancière to Ducrot

The final chapter of this book will be our final opportunity to return to J. L. Austin's ordinary language philosophy and its fate in the hands of Jacques Derrida and Judith Butler. It will be a chance to delineate the limits of Derrida's and Butler's mining of Austin for notions of aesthetics and politics; these limitations are suggested by Oswald Ducrot's intervention in Austin's speech act theory, at one end of the Austin–Derrida–Butler sequence, and by Butlerian appropriations of Rancière's aesthetics, at the other end. In what follows, Ducrot's alternative to Austin's inauguration of this sequence will be critically concretized, and the Butlerian continuation of the sequence will be questioned.

Let us begin with the circumstance that an important part of the current reception of Rancière in the United States and the United Kingdom is able to align Rancière with Butler only at the cost of reducing Rancière's theory of the aesthetic regime to the level of a pre-Austinian notion of art as an unproblematic, non-heteronomous practice. But far from pursuing a Manichean view of a French philosopher victimized by English-speaking literary types, let us instead consider the option, already sketched in the previous chapter, that such appropriations of Rancière are more than just evil abuse, insofar as Rancière's theory itself downplays the institutional field of the symbolic as the condition of possibility for any political subjectivation.

As a way out of this dead end, the Lacanian theory of the signifier will be used, by way of conclusion, to valorize Ducrot's polyphonic theory of enunciation. For Ducrot's basic idea is that the difference between the utterance and its enunciation is the source, not of the Austinian etiolation of sense, but of sense itself. Ducrot's key example, ironic negation, will prove contradictory itself, though. This contradiction can be solved, as we will see, if we recognize in ironic negation the structure of the Lacanian expletive *ne*, and in Ducrot's example of ironic negation a case of the Lacanian discourse of the university, which, according to Althusser's famous definition, is the central ideological apparatus of the capitalist state.

\* \* \*

In his lecture of 28 March 2000, published in 2005 as the penultimate chapter of his book on the twentieth century, Alain Badiou spoke about the intimate link between art and politics that had characterized the century but seemed so remote as the century drew to a close. This link had been based, according to Badiou, on the thesis that art has an intrinsic political value and impact: 'The avant-gardes even went to the extreme of saying that there is more politics to be found in the formal mutations of art than in politics "strictly speaking". This conviction was still held by the *Tel Quel* group in the sixties. Today, some of Jacques Rancière's writings provide a sophisticated echo of it.'[1]

Today, this kind of link between art and politics seems even more remote than in 2005, let alone in 2000, and Rancière even more dedicated to it. Badiou's twentieth century is itself, among other things, the sequence in which this link was invented, practised and thought; as such, the century starts with the surrealists and ends with *Tel Quel*.[2] Or, in terms that are both less Gallocentric and more Badiousian, the century begins sometime around October 1917 and ends sometime around May 1968. October 1917 is a more or less obvious metonymy for most of Badiou's entries into the century, from an Osip Mandelshtam poem written 'during the first years of Bolshevik power', or a Saint-John Perse poem published, like Mandelshtam's, forty years before a Paul Celan poem of the same title (*Anabasis*), to such events of the 'prologue' to the century as a 1902 pamphlet by Vladimir Ilich Lenin, the leader of the October Revolution, and a Sigmund Freud case history dating, 'like the first Russian revolution', from 1905.[3] May 1968, conversely, is arguably the best approximation of the end of the respective sequences inaugurated by these events, be it the 'chronic preoccupation with purging' from Freud to Lacan, the above-cited thesis linking art and politics from the surrealists to *Tel Quel*, or the *Anabasis* topos from Perse to Celan;[4] indeed, 'for Badiou, anabasis becomes the name for a "small century" interrupted on the eve of May '68', even 'a mini-century in need of subtraction from the global period of Restoration that began in the 1980s'.[5]

In any case, October 1917 and May '68 delineate the twentieth century, or *le Siècle*, as Badiou sees it in 2005, with Rancière constituting, according to Badiou, a rare echo of that century in the next one. A thinker whose interventions dedicated to the specific twentieth-century link between art and politics have only intensified since 2005, Rancière is also, as we know from the previous chapter, a contributor to the famous Leninist reading of Marx's *Capital* that Althusser and his students published in 1965, a student activist by May '68 and an early critic of Althusser's Leninism by 1974. In this sense, Rancière's work on art and politics, and the way in which this work has been read in terms of speech and the act, seem to provide a relevant backdrop against which we can approach our own conjuncture, when, a hundred years after the Left seized power, and fifty years after it seized speech instead of power, the United States shows the global Right how to seize, if not power, then at least power-as-speech. Power-as-hate-speech, to be precise.

Indeed, in the United States, the home of speech act theory long before the current president's speech act practice, Rancière's studies on aesthetics, building on his archaeological phase to refashion the conceptual apparatus of continental aesthetics and political philosophy, are, as we have also seen in the previous chapter, often received against the backdrop of Anglo-American speech act theory – as it is read, granted, by Jacques Derrida's continental thought.

Rather than speak about art as a homogenous practice, Rancière chooses to distinguish between the ethical, the representative and the aesthetic regimes of art. Whereas the ethical regime strives for Platonic ideologically guided projections of images onto ideas, and the representative regime aspires to Aristotelian poetologically guided projections of forms onto materials, the aesthetic regime introduces Schillerian unguided projection of words onto things. In contrast to Platonic external criteria of the social bond and truth as well as to Aristotelian internal criteria of poetics, the aesthetic regime ascribes words to things without any criteria, according to Rancière. Its distribution of the sensible is hence not reproductive and policing, but transformative and political – more precisely, metapolitical, since, by transforming the relations between words and things, the aesthetic regime not only practises but also enacts the political struggle for the recognition of voices as speech (rather than as mere signals). As such, the aesthetic regime is 'autonomous/heteronomous':[6]

free of criteria and hence penetrable by anything, as any thing is now worth mentioning.

It is not difficult to find a textual basis for the thesis that Rancière attributes a performative force to the aesthetic practice even though he does not talk about this force in terms of the theory of the performative. In 'The Politics of Literature' (both the article and the otherwise heavily rewritten chapter for the book of the same title),[7] Rancière draws the line between the representative and the aesthetic regime of art precisely along the rift between the conventional speech act and the mute letter of the speech act that has no conventional utterer, reference or addressee and is as such available to anyone. But he uses the same kind of distinction already in his 1998 book on 'mute speech', where the representative and the aesthetic regime are still called 'representative' and 'expressive poetics' respectively.[8] Incidentally, in the same year, writing for the second edition of the book whose first edition was translated as *On the Shores of Politics*, Rancière also reproaches John Searle – for whom a literary text is a speech act that is even more conventionalized than non-literary speech acts – for simply turning upside down Plato's opposition between mute writing and living speech.[9] Which is a reproach unusually reminiscent of Derrida's reply to Searle's rejection of his deconstruction of John Austin. And as we have seen in previous chapters, Rancière's kind of emancipation of the speech act from conventional context is a necessary possibility for any speech act, according to Derrida, or even a necessary actuality, according to Judith Butler; moreover, both Derrida and Butler treat this de-conventionalization, this etiolation of the speech act, as a condition of possibility for the act's aesthetic functioning.

However, despite all this textual basis, the thesis about the performativity of the aesthetic regime implies a pre-theoretic notion of performativity. In other words, we should begin by noting the internal insufficiency of the thesis, namely its spontaneous notion of performativity, before we even attempt to corroborate the external equivalence between the aesthetic regime and performativity, as if these are fully produced and unquestionable concepts. For Austin's theory of the performative constitutively presupposes a certain separation between performative and aesthetic utterances: as we already know from Chapter 1, performatives (orders, promises, christenings …) reproduce the social bond within ordinary language, while aesthetic utterances etiolate and parasitize performatives. But once we manage to avoid the pre-theoretic identification of aesthetic and performative utterances, there emerges an even greater misconception of the thesis about the performativity of the aesthetic regime, namely the misconception of the subversive character of the aesthetic regime. For the thesis ascribes to Rancière's aesthetic regime not only performativity but also subversivity.[10] As such, the performativity thesis ignores not only Austin's distinction between aesthetic and performative utterances but also Rancière's differentiation between the heteronomous autonomy of the aesthetic regime and the impossible pure autonomy of art: Austin treats aesthetic utterances as etiolations of performatives (which he in turn treats as hierarchically codified utterances that, as Rancière might say, reproduce the given distribution of the sensible), while Rancière treats them as gestures of suspending, not subverting, ideological practices (which he in turn sees as hierarchically codified practices that, as Austin might say, include performatives). In short, Austin separates aesthetic practices from performativity, and Rancière separates them from subversivity.

According to Rancière, art in the aesthetic regime subverts ideology only insofar as it is irreducibly involved in ideology. It emancipates itself from ideology merely by performing discursive operations on ideologemes; in other words, since art possesses no ideology of its own, it has to constantly rely on existing ideologies for its material. Art becomes autonomous when it relinquishes its Platonic and Aristotelian criteria, and with them its distinctiveness in relation to non-art, life: art becomes autonomous when it becomes heteronomous.[11] This insight enables Rancière to 'locate the break with representation precisely in novelistic realism, the supposed crown achievement of the literature of representation'.[12] In *The Politics of Literature*, Rancière even separates political disagreement, as the relation between conventional, policing speech and new, subjectivated speech, from literary misunderstanding between conventional, canonical speech and its estrangement, the estrangement that, unlike political disagreement, produces no new speech.[13] Art in the aesthetic regime is a practice, not imitation of a practice; it is a practice of uttering, not the kind of utterance that becomes a practice only if it meets the felicity conditions of performative utterances. This concept of relative, heteronomous autonomy of art is therefore the positive concept that enables us to supplement Austin's purely negative differentiation between ordinary and aesthetic language.

Moreover, aesthetic regime's heteronomous autonomy is a positive concept that we can refer back to Austin's problematic of the ordinary as the ideological if we read it, for example, with Pierre Macherey's conceptualization of theory and aesthetic practice as the two discourses that interrupt, in the sphere of ideological practices, the imaginary dialogue of spontaneous language:[14] according to Macherey, a co-author, like Rancière, of the above-mentioned canonical reading of *Capital*, literature is autonomous only insofar as it can refract any discourse, or, as Rancière would later argue, only insofar as it can cite and displace any discourse. So, if influential representatives of the Anglo-American reception of Rancière want to grant the aesthetic regime performativity so as to be able to grant it subversivity, they should argue that, quite the contrary, the aesthetic regime is not a performative practice, but something beyond the performative, beyond interpellation, beyond that which positions individuals on positions from which they can utter felicitous and hence ideological performative utterances.

This equation of aesthetic practice, performativity and subversivity seems to reflect the influence of Butler's intervention in Derrida's deconstruction of speech act theory. But if we actually compare this intervention with Rancière's, it becomes obvious that his aesthetic regime cannot be reduced to performativity-as-subversivity. Between Austin and Butler, aesthetic utterances transition from the constitutive other of speech act theory to the very object of the conception of performativity. When Austin discovers performatives – utterances that perform an act in naming it – he relegates their etiolation by way of citation (as in a joke, a recitation or a poem) to a mere possibility that says nothing about non-etiolated performatives. According to Derrida, this possibility is in fact a necessary possibility that makes any speech act precarious and hence non-redundant, meaningful: the performative's 'possibility ... to be "quoted"' is 'the very force and law of its emergence,'[15] as we have seen in Chapter 2. Butler, as we know from Chapter 3, takes this point, but her actual report reads as follows: 'Derrida claims that the failure of the performative is the condition of its possibility, "the very force and law of its emergence."'[16] Thus, in Butler, 'the very force and law of its emergence' no longer resides in the performative's 'possibility ... to be "quoted"', as Derrida claimed, but in 'the failure of the performative'. The performative's possibility to be quoted becomes the failure of the performative; a possibility in Austin becomes a necessary possibility in Derrida – only to become a necessary actuality in Butler. For her, every speech act, even hate speech, is sooner or later 'aesthetically reenacted' by the addressee.[17]

So, whereas Butler translates Derrida's necessary possibility of etiolation as necessary actuality, Rancière in effect reaffirms Derrida's necessary possibility. And, unlike both Butler and Derrida, he reaffirms Derrida's necessary possibility of etiolation not in order to ontologically limit politics to a necessary possibility that is only to come (as in Butler's Derridean 'futural movement of democracy itself'),[18] but, on the contrary, in order to recognize politics in etiolation itself, in the emancipation from the master-signifier, from the ideology in accordance with which the sensible is distributed. Rancière is interested less in Derrida's testamentary character of writing, the irreducible possibility of etiolation-as-disidentification, than in the emancipatory character of writing, the irreducible possibility of etiolation-as-subjectivation. For Rancière, the possibility of etiolation, where the master-signifier can be appropriated by anyone, is less the condition of a certain impossibility, the impossibility of an original imaginary intention and an original context of the signifier, than the condition of a certain possibility, the possibility of a symbolic, discursive functioning of the signifier. It is less the necessary possibility of the utterer's loss of origin than the necessary possibility of the addressee's emancipation from his or her original part in the given distribution of the sensible. In Rancière, writing is not, first and foremost, the testament of the writer, but the birth certificate of the reader – any reader.

Because Butler grants the status of universality only to the Derridean universality to come, only to universalization-as-etiolation, only to universalization-as-resignification-of-master-signifiers,[19] she must misread 'the failure of the performative' as 'the condition of its possibility' and treat etiolation as a necessary actuality, if she wants to present universalization itself as a necessary actuality. And vice versa, because Rancière sees in universality equality presupposed, and in etiolation the subjectivation of this equality (rather than the unavoidable outcome of uttering performatives, which is how Butler understands etiolation), he treats etiolation – emancipation from the signifier that distributes the sensible – as a necessary potentiality. In other words, because equality of everyone in their relation (or, subordination) to writing is already here, already a given, while 'the failure of the performative' is, for Rancière, not quite 'the condition of its possibility', etiolation as the emancipation from hegemonic speech is a necessary potentiality. Rancière therefore replaces not only Butler's necessary actuality with a necessary potentiality but also

Derrida's necessary impossibility of originality with the necessary possibility of verifying equality. Rancière himself, incidentally, differentiates between Derrida's deferral of equality and his own presupposition of equality in terms of the difference between *à venir* (the 'to come') as Derrida's supplement-to-democracy and *à venir* as his own supplement-as-democracy.[20]

Today, the Butlerian conception of performativity is therefore used to simplify not only Austin's speech act theory but also Rancière's aesthetic theory. But as we have seen in the previous chapter, Rancière's theory is itself unable to provide a way out of the dead end of the continental pressing of Austinian ordinary language philosophy for a concept of aesthetics or politics. This was at least the conclusion to be drawn from Rancière's reading of the May '68 poster *Nous sommes tous des Juifs allemands*, compared to the reading that Rastko Močnik provided on the basis of his Lacanian valorization of Ducrot's polyphonic theory of enunciation. Let us then shift our attention from the current, Butlerian stage of speech act theory to its earliest, Austinian stage and take a look at a very different kind of alternative to Austin, namely the one effectively offered by Ducrot.

\* \* \*

'It seems to me that research on language, over at least the past two centuries, has taken for granted the fact that every utterance has one and only one author – an idea that has seemed so obvious that it has not been overtly formulated.' This is a citation from 'Esquisse d'une théorie polyphonique de l'énonciation' ('Outline of a Polyphonic Theory of Enunciation'), the final chapter of Ducrot's book *Le dire et le dit* (The Saying and the Said).[21] Far from merely formulating this idea, the aim of Ducrot's chapter (regarded in Bakhtinian discourse studies as somewhat 'famous')[22] is to refute it. Moreover, both projects of Ducrot's descriptive semantics, the polyphonic theory of enunciation and the theory of argumentation, are designed to prove that, ultimately, words do not mean anything.[23] In the remainder of this book, we can limit our attention to the first theory, as this theory is, at least for Ducrot himself, the basis of all his work.[24] As we will see, Ducrot's polyphonic theory of enunciation misses its aim precisely where it should prove most productive, arguably due to its failure to conceptualize subjectivation as ideological interpellation in a situation of a forced choice.[25]

According to Ducrot, every act of enunciation requires a splitting of the speaking subject between the subject of the enunciated and the subject of enunciation, or, in Ducrot's own terms, between the locutor and the enunciator. Polyphonic utterances, where the author's voice is ventriloquized by the voices of others, are merely a case in point, for Ducrot. The speaking subject is able to claim responsibility for the utterance merely as a locutor that identifies with the enunciator. And the enunciator is but a viewpoint from which a part of the utterance is enunciated, a partial perspective opposed to other perspectives that are also enacted in the utterance. Therefore, Ducrot distinguishes not only between the speaking subject and the producer of the utterance but also, within the speaking subject, between the locutor and a number of partial enunciators. Formalizing Bakhtin's *dispositif* of author/narrator/hero as producer/locutor/enunciator, Ducrot wants to make Bakhtin's approach capable of grasping polyphony in singular utterances as well as in texts comprised of utterances. Returning to the belief held by linguists that every utterance has only one author, Ducrot writes:

> A similar belief has reigned in literary theory for a long time and has only been explicitly questioned during the last fifty years, especially since Bakhtin developed the concept of polyphony. For Bakhtin, there is a whole category of texts, and in particular literary texts, for which we must recognise that many voices are speaking at once, without any of them being dominant or judging the others. … But the theory of Bakhtin, to my knowledge, has only been applied to texts, that is to say, to sequences of utterances, and never to utterances in which these texts are constituted. So it has not led to questioning the postulate that an isolated utterance allows the audibility of only one single voice.[26]

In this way, Ducrot can show that there is merely a seeming contradiction in utterances such as the following: 'John won't come, and I regret it, because it would have been nice.'[27] The utterance is contradictory only if we disavow the split between the locutor and the enunciator. For the locutor, inscribed in the utterance by the pronoun 'I', can characterize 'it' as both unfortunate and nice because the two occurrences of *it* are not enunciated by the same enunciator: the first enunciator claims that John won't come, and the second one asserts that he will come. And, to interpret Ducrot from the viewpoint of the theory of the signifier, while the first enunciator represents the locutor in the utterance, the second one, the Other, preconditions this representation in two inversely symmetrical ways: as the object of the locutor's actual refutation (the locutor refutes the second enunciator) and as the object of the locutor's potential identification (the locutor believes that the second enunciator's decoding of the two instances of *it* is identical to his or her own encoding). The utterance avoids redundancy as well as unintelligibility insofar as it is addressed to the subject who is supposed to not know about John as well as to know how to switch between the two instances of *it*. The supposed Other is actually ignorant and potentially all-knowing, thus filling in the split between the *its* and with it the split between the locutor and the enunciator.

With its dependence on disavowal, the contradiction of 'John won't come, and I regret it, because it would have been nice' is homologous to the contradiction of the liar paradox, which, as Lacan demonstrates, persists only insofar as we disavow the split between the subject that enunciates 'I am lying' and the subject of the enunciation 'I am lying'.[28] A classical pre-theoretic take on this disavowal is given in the *Postscript to* The Name of the Rose, where Umberto Eco depicts the postmodern lover who can declare his love only by citing a declaration of love that is well known to his addressee: the lovers know that the declaration is a cliché, but they accept it nonetheless; it is the act of citation, the ironic distancing from the cliché, that allows them to subjectivate it and answer its interpellation.[29] Lacan's solution to the liar paradox, his conceptualization of the split between the subject of the enunciated and the subject of enunciation,[30] can hence be read as a critique of postmodernism *avant la lettre*.

Ducrot's interest is primarily limited to ordinary language. To illustrate that the irreducibility of enunciators is constitutive of all discourse, let us look at an example that in no way resembles ordinary language: 'He has no money; he has no name; he has no importance. I value such things and I have the courage to say it; I think they're very precious. Many other people think the same, and they show it. But they give some other reason.'[31] One need not read *The Portrait of a Lady* to understand that 'such things' are 'money', 'name', 'importance', not the absence of 'money', 'name', 'importance'; any misunderstanding is pre-emptively averted by the spontaneous background belief provided by commodity fetishism, which makes 'money' the universal equivalent of 'value' while making the interpellated individuals anxious about this 'value'.[32] One then only needs to be a subject, such as, say, a mouse – but not a duck:

'[Mouse:] I proceed.
 "Edwin and Morcar, the earls of Mercia and Northumbria, declared for him: and even Stigand, the patriotic archbishop of Canterbury, found it advisable –"'

> 'Found *what*?' said the Duck.
>
> 'Found *it*,' the Mouse replied rather crossly: 'of course you know what "it" means.'
>
> 'I know what "it" means well enough, when I find a thing,' said the Duck: 'it's generally a frog or a worm. The question is, what did the archbishop find?'
>
> The Mouse did not notice this question, but hurriedly went on, '"– found it advisable to go with Edgar Atheling to meet William and offer him the crown. ..."'[33]

This interpretation of Ducrot's analysis of 'John won't come ...' already enables us to introduce interpellation without having to stray from Ducrot's path. But it seems productive to proceed with an example that forces us to formulate this introduction more radically. For the absence of the concept of interpellation is even more problematic in Ducrot's analysis of an example that condenses a certain tension inherent to his approach, namely the contradiction between ocularcentrism and *différance*.

\* \* \*

Ducrot's example 'John won't come, and I regret it, because it would have been nice' is able to illustrate polyphony, as he notes himself, because it is an example of explicit negation of a presupposed utterance. So when he goes on to analyse utterances that employ irony as well as negation, the results should be even more impressive. Yet this seems to be the point where, quite the contrary, Ducrot's theory turns back on itself, as it were. It finds itself pulsating between introducing examples of designations of extradiscursive reality, on the one hand, and multiplying enunciators in order to estrange this reality, on the other. Unable to suspend this bad infinity with the concept of ideological interpellation, Ducrot's project itself seems to begin to participate in that which it set out to conceptualize, namely ideology.

Here is his example of ironic negation: 'Z claimed that he would finish his article on time, and N maintained that it couldn't be done. After finishing the article on time, Z showed it to N with the ironic remark: "As you can see, I didn't finish the article on time."'[34] Ducrot finds that his usual analysis of irony, where irony is viewed as the impossibility of assimilating any enunciator with the locutor, fails here. He offers an alternative analysis, but he also admits that, ultimately, he cannot decide between the two.[35] As this alternative seems a telling detail that may turn the whole theory on its head, let us look at it in its entirety:

> Rather than placing all the enunciators on the same plane, let us place them on two levels. On the first level, there is enunciator E0, the ridiculed enunciator assimilated with N in the second conversation. Now, N's reply is no longer absurd merely because he refuses Z's claim that he will finish the article; rather, it is absurd because he places, on another level, two enunciators, E1 and E2, the protagonists of the complete negative exchange. There, E1, assimilated with Z at the moment of producing the article, would observe that the article has been finished on time, while E2, assimilated with E0 (and hence indirectly with N), would deny the assertion. In this approach, the assimilation of E1 with L [the locutor] is avoided, as E1 is itself a construction by E0. We can now see how this alternative solution differs from the previous one. N is no longer ridiculous because he denies an obvious fact, but because he imagines, upon completion of the article, the complete exchange during which E2 denies something that is obvious and as such asserted by the reasonable enunciator, E1, which has been put on stage by E0 (assimilated with N) as well. Thus, N is blamed not for directly (as E2) adopting denial as one of the two positions implied by the negative utterance, but for staging, as E0, two attitudes, assertion and denial, in order to take on, still as E0, the one that is unacceptable in this case.
>
> The theoretical problem of this second solution is that it implies the possibility of subordinating enunciators to other enunciators. ... This may, at least to some extent, jeopardise my locutor/enunciator opposition: the enunciator becomes dangerously similar to the locutor once it is itself, as in this case, able to put enunciators on stage. On the other hand, by taking the liberty of limitlessly subordinating enunciators to each other, we spare ourselves the need to ground sense in 'contents', objects of the attitudes that are taken by the enunciators and which seem to represent reality directly. We can always see 'contents' as perspectives of enunciators of lower degrees. This seems an important achievement if we are to regard the very 'things' that discourse allegedly conveys as so many crystallisations of a discourse on other things, which can themselves be resolved into other discourses.[36]

To remain a man of his word, N has to at least imagine, as E0, concurring with E2. It is this stubbornness of the signifier faced with reality, this rigidity of the designator of reality, that is comical and not merely 'absurd', not simply available to 'ridicule' or 'irony'. This negation is the empty signifier that organizes the entire exchange; and it can do that because it is not only imagined by N, but, as we will see below, uttered, and by none other than N's adversary, Z.

As already mentioned, Ducrot's key examples of irony rely on designations of extradiscursive reality. Irony for him is basically the result of the discrepancy between the asserted and the seen. His three central examples of irony, including both examples of ironic negation, are introduced by the prefix 'As you can see';[37] the first one is as follows: 'Yesterday I told you that Peter would come to visit me today, and you refused to believe me. Today, having convinced you of Peter's presence, I can say to you ironically: "As you can see, Peter didn't come to visit."' Even the example 'My dachshund used to be a St Bernard,'[38] which Ducrot finds 'less artificial,'[39] presupposes that nature is given. And when Ducrot finally tries to get rid of these 'things', these 'contents', he can only think of a 'limitless' supplementation of enunciators with their own kind.

Ducrot is right to refuse to decide between the ocularcentrism of 'As you can see' and the *différance* of 'limitlessly subordinating enunciators to each other'; he is right to reject this forced choice between want and excess of signification. His error is rather in focusing on N's, the underdog's, supposed failure, instead of analysing the greater failure of Z. If he focused on Z, Ducrot would be able to identify the real loser and, more importantly, break the horizon of the dialogue itself and grasp its material conditions. He could suspend the pulsation of his project if he identified the empty signifier in his example, which in this case functions, as we will see, like a case of *ne explétif*. Moreover, if he recognized the function of an empty, meaningless and even senseless signifier around which words are structured into utterances, he could achieve his ultimate goal, namely, as mentioned at the onset, to prove that words have no given meaning.

Z's utterance 'As you can see, I didn't finish the article' is saturated neither by the givenness of its referent nor by the endless supplementation of enunciators with enunciators of lower degrees: the enunciator is inscribed in the utterance, as the utterance is reflected by the signifier 'didn't', or, more precisely, 'not'. For this 'n't' functions like a pleonastic negative, *ne explétif*, such as the 'ne' in, for example, 'Je crains qu'il ne vienne' (literally: 'I'm afraid he may not come'). On the level of the enunciated, the expletive *ne* is just a filler here, a pleonasm, that is, an expletive; on the level of enunciation, however, this *ne explétif* figures as the signifier of the subject, or, in short, as a non-expletive.[40]

Since our interpretation of Ducrot's example of ironic negation should not hesitate to touch on the theme of modern science as such, let us look at one of Descartes's examples of *ne explétif*: 'Puis, outre cela, i'auois des idées de pluſieurs choſes ſenſibles & corporelles : car, quoyque ie ſuppoſaſſe que ie refuois, & que tout ce que ie voyois ou imaginois eſtoit faux, ie ne pouuois nier toutefois que les idées n'en fuſſent véritablement en ma penſée … .'[41]

But instead of analysing Descartes's desire,[42] let us return to 'As you can see, I didn't finish the article.' The signifier 'n't' represents Z insofar as it belongs to an entity other than either Z or N. Z attributes 'didn't', not to N, but to an enunciator that is supposed to claim its view regardless of reality: Z attributes 'didn't' to an entity that is allegedly immune to reality – and can as such be shared by, referred to, Z and N despite their different ideas of reality. It is this Other that Z is bragging to, and reassuring, with his article.

As opposed to the word *did*, which would refer to the already produced article and make the utterance redundant, the word 'didn't' designates nothing but the utterance itself. The article in Z's hand is thus transformed from a given to an accomplishment of subjective action. For the utterance no longer represents for N that which he 'can see', but the subject of enunciation for the discourse of the addressee, which is merely indirectly assimilated with N.

The word 'n't' shakes the indisputability, the objectivity of the statement *As you can see, I did finish the article*. It makes this statement counterfactual and as such inhabitable for the subject, the subject of enunciation, that takes on, subjectivates, the nonsense of 'I didn't finish the article', turning the above statement into this utterance. The word 'n't' functions like the Husserlian difference between pure psychic experience and transcendental consciousness, the difference that, to reiterate once again Derrida's classic formulation, 'without altering anything, changes all the signs';[43] in a word, 'n't' functions like a master-signifier.

But how did the subject come about here? For Lacan, the subject is an effect of the signifier in general and of modern science in particular. Modern science is constituted by the divorce of thinking and being. Cartesian thinking is materialized in the signifying chain, which is a system of relations that gives material existence to modern, mathematicized science; and after the break with Greek wisdom (*episteme*), being unaffected by thinking can only be an idiosyncrasy, non-being. Hence, the choice between thinking and being is a forced choice, as thinking is the only option. Thinking can materially exist as a signifying chain if that chain of signifiers is able to rely on no authority other than itself. And the chain can indeed authorize itself if it is able to suspend the endless metonymical displacement of its purely relational elements. Without any reliance on external authority, this can be achieved only if one of these elements is made to relate only back to itself. This kind of element, a signifier that refers to no signifier outside itself, is a signifier without a signified; by default, as it were, this kind of signifier signifies signification, or the chain, itself. This senseless, empty signifier represents for other signifiers their limit, non-sense, the being that enunciates the empty signifier; in short, this signifier represents the subject. The pathology, mathematically speaking, of the relation between the member representing the entire set and all the other members of that set is taken on by, and supplemented with, the subject of enunciation, which is no less than the disembodiment of the speaking subject.

However, evacuated in an empty signifier supplemented with the subject of its enunciation, the metonymical nature, the non-sense, of signifiers is merely sublated, reiterated on a higher level, which is the second level of Lacan's graph of desire;[44] the subject's answer to the enunciated interpellation poses the question of the enunciation of the interpellation. Represented for the order of sense by the non-sensical signifier, the subject itself faces the metonymy, the non-sense, of the chain, which makes the lack between the signifiers the subject's own lack. And this lack in the chain is, in the final dialectical turn, compensated for precisely by that which the forced choice, the Lacanian *vel* of alienation, defined as the impossible choice, the subject as being. The choice repressed through the interpellee's alienation into the order of signifiers returns via the interpellee's separation from the lack in that order. Being, rendered unconscious for the subject whose being is reduced to the enunciation of a signifier with its signified repressed, returns as the subject's projection onto the lack in the chain. The answer to the uncanny question of the want of the interpellating sense is the subject as non-sensical being; in other words, the answer to the question of what the Other wants is the subject as that which the subject was alienated from by interpellation itself. The question, then, is its own answer: Why does the Other address me, if not because I am that which is not the Other, that which the Other lacks. The subject thus saturates the chain by giving it what was already given, repressed; the subject's unconscious – the subject as being, or, the subject as this which is always already lost – strictly coincides with the lack in the signifying chain.[45]

So, the structure of modern science is the structure of the signifying chain; as such, it is authorized by its own criteria rather than by referring to some external being that is supposedly untarnished by the signifying practice of formalization. Far from describing so-called real objects from a seemingly spontaneous, non-reflexive viewpoint, science constructs objects of knowledge, models of real objects, from the perspective established by science itself precisely via its critique of such spontaneous descriptions. Science does not describe facts; it replaces ideological descriptions of so-called facts with propositions that are falsifiable by subsequent scientific propositions, which, in turn, intervene, not into facts, but into the ideological remnants of the existing scientific propositions on these so-called facts. In short, science describes facts as being always already described in unfalsifiable, pre-scientific ways.

Science therefore exists as a signifying chain that is totalized by one of its own links, namely the one that signifies nothing and hence signification, the chain, itself, representing the utterer for this chain. The utterer is thus not a being external to the chain, but a being reduced to the uttering of the signifier without the signified – the signifier, that is, that signifies the chain as a whole. The utterer is neither the Philosopher who authorizes pre-modern scholasticism, nor the ironic simulation of the Philosopher that authorizes postmodern metaphysics; instead, the utterer is a Cartesian subject authorized by the uttering of the signifier that renders the chain of signifiers sensible and is itself made sensible as the chain's signifier. This utterer is neither the source of the pre-modern argument with authority nor the object of postmodern anti-argumentative ironization; it is simply that which remains of the utterer's being once any reference to it has been forbidden by modern science as the argument ad hominem.[46]

Lacan's location of the subject in the modern break with *episteme* allows us to historicize his structural analysis in the context of the discourse to which Ducrot's example pertains, namely the discourse of the university. This is how Phillip E. Wegner unpacks Lacan's schema of the university discourse:

$$\frac{S_2}{S_1} \quad \frac{a}{\$} :$$

In what we would take as its most 'normal' situation, that of a classroom unfolding within the discourse of the university, the professor occupies the 'agential' role of the conduit of an apparently objective knowledge (S2), while the student is the 'other' filled with the desire to learn (a). The 'product' of this exchange will be a disciplining of the student's desire in the formation of the proper subject ($) we call the graduate. ... What must remain hidden in this relationship is the 'truth' that the professor is in fact always already a master (S1) – that is, any apparently objective knowledge is also subjective, fabricated, and interested.[47]

In the case of 'As you can see, I didn't finish the article', what alienates the speaking subject into the signifying chain, what constitutes it as the subject of knowledge, is the forced alternative that nothing sums up quite as elegantly as the motto *Publish or perish!* Echoed, for example, in Jean-François Lyotard's 'be operational ... or disappear',[48] this motto is used by postmodernists to subjectivate and legitimize their position within late capitalism in general and in the contemporary academia in particular.

In this context, we could turn to one example in particular of what we already know from Chapter 1 as Lacan's negative protreptic, a device that Lacan liked to use in his seminars to defamiliarize the spontaneous ideologies of his audiences. His word of caution to the academic audience in his 1969–70 seminar that a worker is merely a 'unité de valeur',[49] which is French for a university course as well as for a unit of labour, could retroactively be understood as an anticipation of the neoliberal appropriation of the May '68 revolt against the rigid university system. Indeed, not unlike Althusser, who sees the school system as the modern equivalent of the pre-modern church and of its role as the dominant ideological state apparatus,[50] Lacan sees in the university discourse the contemporary realization of the master's discourse. As Juliet Flower MacCannell argued in a recent essay, in this seminar, 'Lacan is ... determined to think about how the dovetailing of ... [the university] discourse with the new stages of capitalism points to a rather bizarre future – a then-future that is now our present ... with our students now openly called "consumers" or "clients"'.[51] And Močnik, a member, like MacCannell, of Lacan's audience in 1969–70, recently described neoliberalism as a return of the demands from May '68 in their inverted, true form: the freedom from the bourgeois welfare-state has returned as the freedom to sell one's labour in the subsidiary state with privatized education, healthcare and pension funds.[52]

If Ducrot's example is to be pertinent for a materialist analysis, it should be placed in no less complex a situation; only then can we explain Z's overinvested reaction to N and account for the amount of affect triggered by a remark as passing as N's. To this end, let us introduce the assumption that Z interprets N's remark against the backdrop of a forced choice such as *Publish or perish!*, which, as precisely a forced *vel*, is effectively an injunction to publish. This is what forces Z to supplement N's remark that he won't finish the article on time with the notion that he won't finish it on time like this. Z cannot omit writing the article; all he can, and must, omit is the way in which he is writing it, the non-thinking that is the other of knowledge within the university discourse. But as an academic whose initial announcement that he would meet the deadline triggered N's remark in the first place, he has already omitted non-thinking. Z is already alienated into the institution of knowledge, he has already subjectivated *Publish!*, the signifier that forms the opposition only with its absence, perishment, signifying the signifier as such, the act of publishing as such. With his publications, Z already reproduces the institution that has forced this empty signifier upon him. For him, non-thinking is merely the impossible, repressed alternative; to N's remark on his non-thinking he can respond only with the empty affect of anxiety, so he has to dismiss the remark with irony – and even this he can do only after he has already met the actual deadline.

The signifier of the denial of the publication, 'n't', thus signifies the injunction to publish. As part of N's remark, it activates the *Publish or perish!* topos as the remark's background belief; and as reiterated in Z's ironic rejoinder, it represents Z, alienated as he is from the choice of not publishing, for all the other signifiers that give the institution its material existence. Just like a *ne explétif*, the signifier 'n't' does the work of Freudian negation; it negates Z's choice of being, of not publishing, and thus signifies Z's unconscious desire, the status of which this choice has obtained following Z's alienation. But as it is ironically ascribed, returned, to N, 'n't' is also the agent of the separation of the already alienated Z from the uncanny lack in N's remark: 'n't' resolves Z's question of what it is that N wants by turning N's remark into a sign that N and with him the institution want their other, Z's being, Z as someone who is impossible ever since the alienation took place.

The irony allows Z to give to the Other his very being, the being that he obtains merely as someone who is lost ever since the Other interpellated him, through N, with the forced choice. The irony manages to distance Z from N, who, as E0 identified with E2, clings on, like in a Freudian joke, to the signifier 'n't', rigidly designating with it the absence of the article in every possible world. Yet this absence of knowledge is merely the object-cause of Z's own repressed desire to desire: Z transfers his own unconscious desire to E0 as the silent N of the second dialogue, that is, of the monologue that is the truth of Ducrot's polyphony. In a loving gesture, he corrects N with that which he himself does not have:[53] Z supplements N with the always already repressed being, the being that N's remark discomfortingly reminded him of as it returned to him, in its inverted, true form, his initial, unprovoked claim that he would meet the deadline, his initial choice of thinking over being.[54] In a final mythologizing act of making a narration out of Lacan's schema of the university discourse,[55] we might say that the *vel* ($S_1$) of the university ($S_2$) changes Z from a student or a theorist (*a*) to an academic ($).

\* \* \*

Ducrot's neglect of the institutional context of his example of ironic negation makes his analysis of the university discourse resemble its own object; as such, it is pre-theoretical both as a case of university discourse and as a discourse that is indistinguishable from its object of inquiry. His dilemma between designation (ocularcentrism) and dissemination (*différance*) remains 'undecidable' merely if we fail to break with the horizon shared by Z and N. We can suspend this dilemma as soon as we institutionalize, so to speak, Z and N by locating their dialogue within the university as the material existence of the dialogue's ultimate addressee. Ducrot could do this himself if – instead on focusing on the fact that the Bakhtinian conception of polyphony is restricted 'to texts, that is to say, to sequences of utterances', as he puts it – he read Bakhtin's concept of 'varidirectional double-voiced discourse' against the backdrop of Valentin N. Vološinov's 'intersecting of differently oriented social interests within one and the same sign community, i.e., ... *class struggle*'.[56] According to Vološinov and the rest of the Bakhtin Circle, such varidirectional double-voiced speech is polyphony in its purest, the practical existence of differently oriented class interests; hence, our articulation of polyphonic speech into a theory of social institution is conceivable already within the Bakhtinian horizon that Ducrot himself tries to reactivate.

From this perspective, Z and N are simply two sides of the same message; they are the same subject. The subject of enunciation and the subject of the uptake of the utterance are interpellated by the same Other and are hence the same subject: the one that receives, from the Other, its own messages in their inverted, true form. Z and N differ only as far as N naively believes that the word 'article' means more than what is institutionally referred to as 'article', while Z shamelessly accepts this delocutive derivation of the word's meaning; this is the difference between a fool and a knave, to use the parlance of Geoffrey Chaucer.[57] In a word, both Z and N are a product of the institutionalized practice of publications as Lacanian 'poubellications',[58] or, as we could perhaps also say, *oublications*.

# Notes

## Chapter 1

1. J. L. Austin, *How to Do Things with Words* (Oxford: Oxford University Press, 1962), 13.
2. Ibid., 89.
3. See Stanley Cavell, *Philosophical Passages: Wittgenstein, Emerson, Austin, Derrida* (Oxford: Blackwell, 1995), 71–2, 51–2, 48, 61; and David Gorman, 'The Use and Abuse of Speech-Act Theory in Criticism', *Poetics Today* 20, no. 1 (1999): 109. Cavell also shows here that Derrida neglects Austin's epistemological break with logical positivism, a point crucial to Chapter 2. (That Paul de Man, a key colleague of Derrida, might have even mistakenly aligned Austin with logical positivism, is conjectured in Toril Moi, *Revolution of the Ordinary: Literary Studies after Wittgenstein, Austin, and Cavell* (Chicago: The University of Chicago Press, 2017), 139–40.)
4. Austin, *How to Do Things with Words*, 46.
5. Ibid., 147.
6. Ibid., 150–1.
7. Ibid., 147.
8. J. Hillis Miller, *Speech Acts in Literature* (Stanford: Stanford University Press, 2001), 13.
9. Austin, *How to Do Things with Words*, 142.
10. Cavell, *Philosophical Passages*, 52, 57–8.
11. '*Your money or your life!* If I choose the money, I lose both. If I choose life, I have life without the money, namely, a life deprived of something.' (Jacques Lacan, *The Four Fundamental Concepts of Psychoanalysis: The Seminar of Jacques Lacan, Book XI*, ed. Jacques-Alain Miller, trans. Alan Sheridan (London: Hogarth Press and the Institute of Psycho-Analysis, 1977), 212.)

    See 'Conclusion' for more on Lacan's *vel*, or forced choice, of alienation, the subjectivating alternative between being and thought that forces being (I) to choose thought (the subject), as institutional laws prohibit being from choosing itself as being and thus make being possible only as thought without being.

12 Incidentally, Austin's turn from categories to the words that philosophers use to talk about categories arguably shines through the most at the point where philosophy seems to be the farthest away from the materiality of language, namely the point of Truth. In his eponymous essay from 1950, Austin starts by offering a classification of ordinary philosophical questions pertaining to the ontological status of Truth, and then goes on to say the following: 'But philosophers should take something more nearly their own size to strain at. What needs discussing rather is the use, or certain uses, of the word "true."' (J. L. Austin, 'Truth', *Proceedings of the Aristotelian Society*, Supplementary Volumes 24, no. 1 (1950): 111.)

13 See Rastko Močnik, 'Toward a Materialist Concept of Literature', *Cultural Critique* 4 (1986): 180, n. 13.

14 Ibid.

15 Austin, *How to Do Things with Words*, 89–90, 134. Here and elsewhere, the emphasis is in the original.

16 Lewis Carroll, 'Alice's Adventures in Wonderland', in Carroll, *The Complete Works of Lewis Carroll*, ed. Leonard S. Marcus (London: Bracken Books, 1994), 75–6.

17 Ibid., 86.

18 Ibid., 23, 80, 108, 117.

19 Nakul Krishna, 'How Not to Be a Chucklehead', *Aeon*, 23 November 2016. Available online: aeon.co/essays/how-the-thought-acts-of-the-oxford-don-j-l-austin-live-on (accessed 1 April 2019).

20 Robin Tolmach Lakoff, 'Lewis Carroll: Subversive Pragmaticist', *Pragmatics* 3, no. 4 (1993): 377.

21 Ibid., 381.

22 Jean-Claude Milner, 'Considerations of a Work', trans. James Penney, *Journal for Lacanian Studies* 4, no. 1 (2006): 149.

23 Ibid., 156, n. 17.

24 Austin, *How to Do Things with Words*, 21–2, 104.

25 Or, in the words of Stanley Fish: 'Here the argument turns on the word "seriously" which seems to mean straightforwardly or non-metaphorically and *therefore* productive of action in the world. The claim, in short, is that only when the words of an utterance refer to empirically specifiable conditions can it be called serious. But such a rigorous definition of serious would exclude many of the perlocutionary acts we perform daily. Surely, for example, the politician who incites the eagle of liberty to soar would be doing so seriously, in part because he would be attempting to make his hearers *do* something by making them think of themselves as extensions of the eagle of liberty.' (Stanley Fish, 'With the Compliments of the Author: Reflections on Austin and Derrida', *Critical Inquiry* 8, no. 4 (1982): 706.)

26 Oswald Ducrot, *Slovenian Lectures: Introduction into Argumentative Semantics*, trans. Sebastian McEvoy (Ljubljana: Pedagoški inštitut, 2009), 12–13. Available online: https://www.pei.si/ISBN/978-961-270-014-0/index.html (accessed 1 April 2019).

27 Not least because there may be no Whitman text with that kind of motif; but there definitely is one and only one utterer of 'Then you shouldn't talk' identified in Carroll's text, and Austin ignores that utterer as well ('the Caterpillar or whoever it was').

28 See John R. Searle, 'The Logical Status of Fictional Discourse', *New Literary History* 6, no. 2 (1975): 324–32.

29 For Searle, see Ducrot, *Slovenian Lectures*, 19–23.

30 Austin, *How to Do Things with Words*, 90.

31 Claude Lévi-Strauss, *Introduction to the Work of Marcel Mauss*, trans. Felicity Baker (London: Routledge & Kegan Paul, 1987), 28.

32 Jef Verschueren, *Understanding Pragmatics* (London: Edward Arnold; New York: Oxford University Press, 1999), 196; see ibid., 131–2, for a critique of speech act theory from the perspective of pragmatics.

33 Needless to say, Alice thinks very highly of her own opinions: '"I must be getting somewhere near the centre of the earth. Let me see: that would be four thousand miles down, I think –" (for, you see, Alice had learnt several things of this sort in her lessons in the school-room, and though this was not a *very* good opportunity for showing off her knowledge, as there was no one to listen to her, still it was good practice to say it over) "– yes, that's about the right distance – but then I wonder what Latitude or Longitude I've got to?" (Alice had not the slightest idea what Latitude was, or Longitude either, but she thought they were nice grand words to say.)

… Alice … felt very glad to get an opportunity of showing off a little of her knowledge.' (Carroll, 'Alice's Adventures in Wonderland', 17, 61.)

But 'the representatives of nonsense', as Milner calls the Hatter & Co., do manage to wrench Alice from *doxa* by scolding her; in the process, they even make her literalize her own 'I don't think …': '"You see the earth takes twenty-four hours to turn round on its axis –"

"Talking of axes," said the Duchess, "chop off her head!"

Alice glanced rather anxiously at the cook, to see if she meant to take the hint; but the cook was busily stirring the soup, and seemed not to be listening, so she went on again: "Twenty-four hours, I *think*; or is it twelve? I –"' (Ibid., 61.)

In time, negative protreptic makes Alice question even her name and the pronoun 'I' (ibid., 25–6, 48–9, 100).

34  For a classic reading of the empty signifier as a rigid designator, see Slavoj Žižek, *The Sublime Object of Ideology* (London: Verso, 1989), 89–92.
35  Harold Bloom, *The Anxiety of Influence: A Theory of Poetry*, 2nd edn (Oxford: Oxford University Press, 1997), 116, 123.
36  Ibid., 123.
37  Ibid., 133–4.
38  Ibid., 93.
39  Franco Moretti, *Modern Epic: The World-System from Goethe to García Márquez*, trans. Quintin Hoare (London: Verso, 1996), 67.
40  Ibid., 65.
41  Ibid., 66.
42  Ibid.
43  Ibid., 67.
44  See Harold Bloom, *The Western Canon: The Books and School of the Ages* (New York: Harcourt Brace, 1994), 265–6.
45  Karl Marx, *Capital*, vol. 1, trans. Ben Fowkes (Harmondsworth: Penguin; London: New Left Review, 1976), 280.
46  Austin, *How to Do Things with Words*, 48–50, 95–6, 135–7, 145.
47  Ibid., 149.
48  For the phatic act and the rhetic act, see ibid., 92–3.
49  '[The poetic] function, by promoting the palpability of signs, deepens the fundamental dichotomy of signs and objects' (Roman Jakobson, 'Closing Statement: Linguistics and Poetics', in *Style in Language*, ed. Thomas A. Sebeok (New York: Wiley, 1960), 356). See also Jakobson's observation that the poetic function renders the reference, the utterer and the addressee 'ambiguous' (ibid., 370–1, 366).
50  Let us take a look at a pair of idioms that, as signs, can respectively mark the beginning and the end of an exchange, while designating, as signifiers, the utterer's relation to this exchange. If an idiom like *How do you do?* can mark the start of a conversation, and if an idiom like *We must have lunch someday* can end the exchange, then, taken together, they signify how the utterer has subjectivated him/herself in relation to the other – reducing at the outset the absolute otherness of the other to an image of an acquaintance, before cutting the final anxiety about the future of the relationship by treating this relationship as precisely one without lunch appointments.

   Moreover, if the opening greeting may still be able to support the illusion that the signifier is reducible to a sign, then in the case of the closing invitation any breaking down of the idiom to its lexical components would inevitably lead to an awkward misunderstanding. In other words, if a literal answer to the rhetorical question *How do you do?* might still be excused as a slight case of rudeness, any attempt on the side of the addressee of *We must have lunch someday.* to fill this empty phrase with a positive meaning by, say, pulling out his or her pocket planner would retroactively tarnish the already formal relationship, as it would force the utterer to explain that the implication was, quite the opposite, to leave things to the drift of time.

51 'A signifier is that which represents a subject. For whom? – not for another subject, but for another signifier. In order to illustrate this axiom, suppose that in the desert you find a stone covered with hieroglyphics. You do not doubt for a moment that, behind them, there was a subject who wrote them. But it is an error to believe that each signifier is addressed to you – this is proved by the fact that you cannot understand any of it. On the other hand you define them as signifiers, by the fact that you are sure that each of these signifiers is related to each of the others. And it is this that is at issue with the relation between the subject and the field of the Other' (Lacan, *The Four Fundamental Concepts of Psychoanalysis*, 198–9).

52 Emile Benveniste, 'Delocutive Verbs', in Benveniste, *Problems in General Linguistics*, trans. Mary Elizabeth Meek (Coral Gables, FL: University of Miami Press, 1971), 242.

53 Oswald Ducrot, *Le dire et le dit* (Paris: Minuit, 1984), 123–4 (my translation).

54 M. M. Bakhtin and P. N. Medvedev, *The Formal Method in Literary Scholarship*, trans. Albert J. Wehrle (Baltimore: Johns Hopkins University Press, 1978), 16; and Pierre Macherey, *A Theory of Literary Production*, trans. Geoffrey Wall (London: Routledge & Kegan Paul, 1978), 63.

55 Austin, *How to Do Things with Words*, 4.

56 Ibid., 23.

57 Igor Ž. Žagar, 'How to Do Things with Words: The Polyphonic Way', in *Speech Acts: Fiction or Reality?*, ed. Igor Ž. Žagar (Ljubljana: Inštitut za družbene vede, 1991), 80.

58 Ibid., 79.

59 Lacan, *The Four Fundamental Concepts of Psychoanalysis*, 112.

60 Ducrot, *Le dire et le dit*, 130 (my translation).

61 Ibid., 117.

62 Ibid., 123.

63 For Ducrot's articulation of the delocutive analysis of the performative, see ibid., 127–43.

64 Jacques Lacan, 'Science and Truth', in Lacan, *Écrits: The First Complete Edition in English*, trans. Bruce Fink in collaboration with Héloïse Fink and Russell Grigg (New York: Norton, 2006), 734.

65  Shoshana Felman, *The Scandal of the Speaking Body: Don Juan with J. L. Austin, or Seduction in Two Languages*, trans. Catherine Porter (Stanford: Stanford University Press, 2003), 20–1, 46.

## *Ad* 1: Austin's poetry in *Dead Poets Society*

1  See Ducrot, *Slovenian Lectures*, 20, 24.
2  Rastko Močnik, 'Laokoon, oder über Grenzen der Filmkunst und Poesie', in Močnik, *Extravagantia* (Ljubljana: ŠKUC and ZIFF, 1993), 125 (my translation).
3  See *Dead Poets Society*, dir. Peter Weir (Touchstone Pictures, 1989); and N. H. Kleinbaum, Dead Poets Society *(New York: Hyperion, 1989)*.
4  Ibid., 3; the boys' private translation of tradition, honour, discipline and excellence as travesty, horror, decadence and excrement is neatly absent from this novelization.
5  Ibid., 14.
6  Ibid., 26. Later on, when this strategy will help Keating make the students compose poems of their own, his plea that they make their lives extraordinary will soon be followed by his injunction to not let their poems be ordinary.
7  Ibid., 25.
8  Ibid., 26–7. If we locate the source of Keating's citation, we can also spot Freud's original objects of desire, the breasts and the faeces: 'Gather ye rosebuds while ye may' is the first verse of *To the Virgins, to Make Much of Time*, a poem Keating that finds particularly suitable for his students – but also a poem alluded to in the following piece of cultural history: 'Men desire access to the vagina, but also fear it and are disgusted by it. They see it as a gaping maw, at times toothed, frighteningly insatiable. At other times a literature of seduction blames the woman for being too reticent or scrupulous about making her vagina available. The argument is the well-known gather ye rosebuds while ye may, which alternates flattery with the threat of horror and disgust that ultimately attends such scrupulosity' (William Ian Miller, *The Anatomy of Disgust* (Cambridge, MA: Harvard University Press, 1997), 102).
9  Močnik, 'Laokoon, oder über Grenzen der Filmkunst und Poesie', 114 (my translation).
10  'That which is light looks at me, and by means of that light in the depths of my eye, something is painted – something that is not simply a constructed relation, the object on which the philosopher lingers – but something that is an impression, the shimmering of a surface that is not, in advance, situated for

me in its distance. This is something that introduces what was elided in the geometral relation – the depth of field, with all its ambiguity and variability, which is in no way mastered by me. It is rather it that grasps me, solicits me at every moment, and makes of the landscape something other than a landscape, something other than what I have called the picture' (Lacan, *The Four Fundamental Concepts of Psychoanalysis*, 96). Here, 'a landscape' is chosen to translate 'une perspective' (Lacan, *Le Séminaire. Livre XI : Les quatre concepts fondamentaux de la psychanalyse: 1964*, ed. Jacques-Alain Miller (Paris: Seuil, 1973), 89).

11  'Were the Law to give the order, "*Jouis!*" ["Enjoy!" or "Come!"], the subject could only reply "*J'ouïs*" ["I hear"], in which the jouissance would no longer be anything but understood [*sous-entendue*]' (Jacques Lacan, 'The Subversion of the Subject and the Dialectic of Desire in the Freudian Unconscious', in Lacan, *Écrits*, 696).

12  'Far from the dialectic of what occurs in the subject's unconscious being able to be limited to the reference to the field of *Lust*, to the images of beneficent, favourable objects, we have found a certain type of objects which, in the final resort, can serve no function. These are the *objets a* – the breasts, the faeces, the gaze, the voice' (Lacan, *The Four Fundamental Concepts of Psychoanalysis*, 242).

13  Judging by the excerpt Keating makes one of the students read out loud, the Pritchard textbook is modelled on Laurence Perrine's *Sound and Sense: An Introduction to Poetry* (New York: Harcourt, Brace & World, 1956).

14  *Kleinbaum*, Dead Poets Society, 39. In the film itself, the word is the same as the boys' private word for the pillar called 'Excellence'.

15  Ibid., 41–2.

16  Ibid., 38.

17  Ibid., 24.

18  Ibid., 38. As we have seen in Chapter 1, we need this kind of fluency to fully understand, not just poetry, but simple prosaic statements like 'The cat is on the mat'. But this, as we will see in this chapter, is precisely the point: 'The cat is on the mat' can function as a ready-made poem.

19  Mladen Dolar, 'Freud and the Political', *Unbound: Harvard Journal of the Legal Left* 4 (2008): 27.

20  Juliet Flower MacCannell, *The Regime of the Brother: After the Patriarchy* (London: Routledge, 1991). Dolar himself uses MacCannell's concept in the original, Slovenian-language version of the essay cited above: Mladen Dolar, 'Freud in politično', *Problemi* 44, nos. 7–8 (2006): 303–4.

21  Kleinbaum, *Dead Poets Society*, 46.

22  Ibid., 38.
23  Lacan, *The Four Fundamental Concepts of Psychoanalysis*, 96.
24  Ibid., 225.
25  Henry A. Giroux, *Breaking in to the Movies: Film and the Culture of Politics* (Malden, MA: Blackwell, 2002), 84, 85, 89.
26  Ibid., 84.
27  'What we see here, then, is that the gaze operates in a certain descent, a descent of desire, no doubt. … Modifying the formula I have of desire as unconscious – *man's desire is the desire of the Other* – I would say that it is a question of a sort of desire *on the part of* the Other, at the end of which is the *showing* (*le donner-à-voir*).

How could this *showing* satisfy something, if there is not some appetite of the eye on the part of the person looking? This appetite of the eye that must be fed produces the hypnotic value of painting. For me, this value is to be sought on a much less elevated plane than might be supposed, namely, in that which is the true function of the organ of the eye, the eye filled with voracity, the evil eye' (Lacan, *The Four Fundamental Concepts of Psychoanalysis*, 115).

For Whitman's 'tyrannical eye' and 'gaze', see, respectively, Bloom, *The Anxiety of Influence*, 133; and Moretti, *Modern Epic*, 66.
28  Kleinbaum, *Dead Poets Society*, 75.
29  Ibid., 76.
30  Močnik, 'Laokoon, oder über Grenzen der Filmkunst und Poesie', 114 (my translation).
31  Kleinbaum, *Dead Poets Society*, 76.
32  Ibid., 74.
33  Lacan, *The Four Fundamental Concepts of Psychoanalysis*, 263.
34  For this point about the *Ode*, see Slavoj Žižek, '"Ode to Joy," Followed by Chaos and Despair', *The New York Times*, 24 December 2007, A17. Available online: www.nytimes.com/2007/12/24/opinion/24zizek.html?_r=0 (accessed 1 April 2019).
35  See Vincent Canby, 'Review/Film; Shaking Up a Boys' School With Poetry', *The New York Times*, 2 June 1989, C00008. Available online: www.nytimes.com/1989/06/02/movies/review-film-shaking-up-a-boys-school-with-poetry.html (accessed 1 April 2019).
36  See Giroux, *Breaking in to the Movies*, 99, n. 16.
37  Kleinbaum, *Dead Poets Society*, 70.
38  Soon after the incident, Keating is shown to share a casual laugh with a colleague whom he had accused of cynicism not long before the incident and who, after

the incident, chose to side with his colleagues, that is, the entire teaching staff save for Keating. This detail may look like a narrative inconsistency, but is in fact fully consistent with the superego duplicity that we see in all these examples of Keating's hystericization of the students.

39  Another detail that our approach is able to appreciate as indeed a detail, rather than just a coincidence, is the moment when Neil's father takes off his slippers to take his well-deserved nightly rest and pats them twice before leaving them at his side of the bed. In that bedroom, this neurotic twitch is too quick and slight to be discernible by anyone else than the Other, the presupposed guarantor of Neil's father's place in society; his gesture makes sense only as a 'good night' to the instance that watches over his slowly yet steadily accumulated capital and saves it from any antagonism that might prevent his investment in his son from yielding extra profit.

40  On hearing Keating's advice to talk to his father, Neil quickly ends the conversation, realizing that Keating cannot even imagine how strict his father really is. On this basis, it is possible to assume that the boy never even tried to talk to his father.

41  'Suicide is the only act that can succeed without misfiring', quips Lacan in a famous case of negative protreptic (Jacques Lacan, 'Television', trans. Denis Hollier, Rosalind Krauss and Annette Michelson, in Lacan, *Television; A Challenge to the Psychoanalytic Establishment*, ed. Joan Copjec, trans. Denis Hollier, Rosalind Krauss, Jeffrey Mehlman and Annette Michelson (New York: Norton, 1990), 43). Jacques-Alain Miller, the interviewer on this occasion, formalized Lacan's idea in his article 'Jacques Lacan: remarques sur son concept de passage à l'acte', *Actualités Psychiatriques* 18, no. 1 (1988): 50–6.

Shortly after the film's release, Zupančič provided a reading that misses (in its original version) or at least downplays (in the English-language edition) the fact that Neil's reply to Keating is a lie and that Keating chooses to ignore that (see, respectively, her essays 'Dejanje, Svoboda in Zlo', in *Beseda, dejanje, svoboda*, ed. Miran Božovič (Ljubljana: Društvo za teoretsko psihoanalizo, 1990), 228, and 'A Perfect Place to Die: Theatre in Hitchcock's Films', in *Everything You Always Wanted to Know about Lacan (But Were Afraid to Ask Hitchcock)*, ed. Slavoj Žižek (London: Verso, 1992), 99). As a result, her Keating is a Lacanian who teaches Neil to act according to the one desire he has that is irreducible to the desire of the Other. This enables Zupančič to counter the public moralistic outrage over the transgressive character of Keating. But if we acknowledge Keating's resigned acceptance of Neil's lie, we don't have to choose between the immoral seducer and the ethical analyst. There is a third position we can attribute to Keating, a stance Zupančič herself theorized so influentially just a few years after her take on *Dead Poets Society*, when she drew a distinction between the superego injunction and the categorical imperative in a way that corrects Lacan's own identification of Marquis de Sade and Immanuel Kant without falling back on pre-Lacanian critiques of the former on behalf of the latter (for the bestselling English-language edition of this 1993 reading of Kant with Lacan, see her book *Ethics of the Real: Kant and Lacan* (London: Verso, 2000)). With this distinction in mind, Keating appears as neither the immoral nor the truly ethical alternative to official morality, but as the latter's obverse and truth – in a word, the superego.

42  See Kleinbaum, *Dead Poets Society*, 123–4.
43  Ibid., 63–4.
44  Sigmund Freud, 'Totem and Taboo', trans. James Strachey, in *The Standard Edition of the Complete Psychological Works of Sigmund Freud. Vol. 13 (1913–1914): Totem and Taboo and Other Works*, ed. James Strachey in collaboration with Anna Freud, trans. James Strachey et al. (London: Hogarth Press and the Institute of Psycho-Analysis, 1955), 143.
45  'The only thing one can be guilty of is giving ground relative to one's desire', reads Lacan's ethical imperative (Jacques Lacan, *The Ethics of Psychoanalysis, 1959–1960: The Seminar of Jacques Lacan, Book VII*, ed. Jacques-Alain Miller, trans. Dennis Porter (New York: Norton, 1992), 321).
46  Kleinbaum, *Dead Poets Society*, 165.
47  Walt Whitman, *The Works of Walt Whitman*, vol. 1 (New York: Minerva Press, 1969), 306.
48  A losange, that is, like the one Lacan used to formalize the fantasy as a screen that separates the subject from the object, '$ ◊ a [*barred S, punch, petit a*]' (Lacan, *The Four Fundamental Concepts of Psychoanalysis*, 209).
49  'The priest is a "functionary of the Holy"; there is no Holy without its officials, without the bureaucratic machinery supporting it, organizing its ritual, from the Aztec's official of human sacrifice to the modern sacred state or army rituals. The saint, on the contrary, occupies the place of *objet petit a*, of pure object, of somebody undergoing radical subjective destitution. He enacts no ritual, he conjures nothing, he just persists in his inert presence.

    We can now understand why Lacan saw in Antigone a forerunner of Christ's sacrifice: in her persistence, Antigone is a saint, definitely not priestess' (Žižek, *The Sublime Object of Ideology*, 116–17). See also Chapter *Ad* 2.
50  Kleinbaum, *Dead Poets Society*, 41. The first student to betray Keating to the headmaster also reports that, under Keating, he and his classmates covered the Romantics and some post-Civil-War writers, and confirms the headmaster's

suspicion that they skipped most of realism. As a 'realist' identifies also the above-mentioned teacher when Keating accuses him of 'cynical' disbelief in the individualism of each student (ibid., 44). And the society Keating sums up to the students by telling them that the members were Romantics. Keating is therefore a Romantic regardless of whether the label names a concept in literary theory, a philosophical category or an everyday ideological notion.

51  Tom Schulman, *Dead Poets Society (1989): Shooting Script* (Alexandria, VA: Alexander Street Press, 2003), 42. Just like the students' profanation of the four pillars of the school, the scene is missing from Kleinbaum's novelization.

52  Hopkins's word 'cat', though not a part of *to be on the mat*, the idiom inscribed in the very system of language, is automatically received by Hopkins's audience as an integral part of the idiom, and not only due to the rigid, meter-like rhythm of 'The cat sat on the mat', but also because the frequency of the word *cat* in idiomatic phrases and other kinds of paradigmatic, iconic syntagms. Austin himself uses, in his 1955 lectures, the word 'cat' in a proverb: 'There are more ways of killing a cat than drowning it in butter' (Austin, *How to do Things with Words*, 48). Besides, given the film's chronotope, it is possible to imagine that our heroes have resolved their Oedipus complex with the help of, among other things, *The Cat in the Hat*, Dr. Seuss's bestselling children's book from 1957 whose considerable influence on ordinary language owes in no small measure to its title.

53  For Whitman's debt to the Enlightenment, see Harold Bloom's musings cited in Chapter 1 (Bloom, *The Anxiety of Influence*, 123); as for Keating's debt to the Enlightenment, here is Giroux one last time: 'He appears to represent the classic modernist teacher whose pedagogical sensibilities have been spawned by Enlightenment thinking, with its narratives of unending progress, faith in a unified social world, and the power of an unencumbered individualism' (Giroux, *Breaking in to the Movies*, 85).

54  Kleinbaum, *Dead Poets Society*, 40.

55  Ibid., 40.

# Chapter 2

1  See Richard Ohmann, 'Speech Acts and the Definition of Literature', *Philosophy and Rhetoric* 4, no. 1 (1971): 1–19.

2  See, respectively, Pratt's studies *Toward a Speech Act Theory of Literary Discourse* (Bloomington: Indiana University Press, 1977), 89–99; and 'Ideology and Speech-Act Theory', *Poetics Today* 7, no. 1 (1986): 62.

3   *Différance* is Derrida's translation of G. W. F. Hegel's use of the Latin verb *differre* to define the present as both a differing and a deferring relation, the two senses only the former of which, as Derrida notes, pertains to the Greek verb, *diapherein*, that *differre* is supposed to merely translate (see Jacques Derrida, 'Différance', in Derrida, *Margins of Philosophy*, trans. Alan Bass (Chicago: The University of Chicago Press, 1982), 7–8, 13–14).

4   Jacques Derrida, 'Signature Event Context', in Derrida, *Limited Inc*, trans. Samuel Weber and Jeffrey Mehlman (Evanston, IL: Northwestern University Press, 1988), 15.

5   Ibid., 7.

6   Jacques Derrida, 'Signature événement contexte', in Derrida, *Marges: de la philosophie* (Paris: Minuit, 1972), 380.

7   Edmund Husserl, *Husserliana, Band XIX/1: Logische Untersuchungen, Zweiter Band, Erster Teil*, ed. Ursula Panzer (The Hague: M. Nijhoff, 1984), 59.

8   Edmund Husserl, *Logical Investigations: Volume 1*, trans. J. N. Findlay (London: Routledge & Kegan Paul; New York: The Humanities Press, 1970), 292–3.

9   Derrida, 'Signature Event Context', 12. Unlike Searle in his reading of Derrida, this translation fails to provide the original formulation of Derrida's example 'Where has the green gone (of the lawn: the green is where)', namely 'Où est passé le vert (du gazon: le vert est où?)' (Derrida, 'Signature événement contexte', 381).

10  John R. Searle, 'Reiterating the Differences: A Reply to Derrida', *Glyph* 1 (1977): 203.

11  Derrida, 'Signature Event Context', 12. As Constantine V. Nakassis notes in a recent essay, 'Derrida is right to emphasize that the citation underwrites the performative – but perhaps for the wrong reasons', reasons that ultimately lead him away from the fact that, 'while all acts are iterable or citable, not all are reflexive about that fact' (Constantine V. Nakassis, 'Citation and Citationality', *Signs and Society* 1, no. 1 (2013): 68, 69).

12  Derrida, 'Signature Event Context', 11.

13  For the grave accent on the French proposition *à* as an empty signifier neglected by Derrida in his deconstruction of Lacan's interpretation of Poe's *Purloined Letter*, see Barbara Johnson, 'The Frame of Reference: Poe, Lacan, Derrida', *Yale French Studies* 55–6 (1977): 495.

14  As Marko Kržan demonstrates, no grammar can do without a supplement external to the field of signifiers if it is to function as an apparatus for furnishing formal elements with meaning. For example, transformational grammar needs a logicistic supplement that inscribes it into the tradition of the ancient Greek

and the Port-Royal grammar, the logism of which is stressed by Ferdinand de Saussure; Kržan, on the other hand, calls for a 'discursivist' supplement that could be derived from Ducrot's argumentative semantics (Marko Kržan, '"Tuji govor" ter razmerje med lingvistiko in pragmatiko', *Slavistična revija* 56, no. 1 (2008): 76).

15  This kind of Husserlian critique of Derrida has been developed in Kevin Mulligan, 'Searle, Derrida, and the Ends of Phenomenology', in *John Searle*, ed. Barry Smith (Cambridge: Cambridge University Press, 2003), 271–6; see also Nam-In Lee, 'Phenomenology of Language beyond the Deconstructive Philosophy of Language', *Continental Philosophy Review* 42, no. 4 (2010): 465–81. Within historical materialism, the shortcomings of Derrida's reluctance to analyse what I discuss here as the institutional conditions of the iterability of the sign were outlined, for example, in Jack E. Marsh Jr, 'Of Violence: The Force and Significance of Violence in the Early Derrida', *Philosophy & Social Criticism* 35, no. 3 (2009): 280–4.

16  Jacques Derrida, 'Limited Inc a b c …', in Derrida, *Limited Inc*, 81.

17  Jacques Derrida, *Voice and Phenomenon*, trans. Leonard Lawlor (Evanston, IL: Northwestern University Press, 2011), 10.

18  Jean-Claude Milner, *For the Love of Language*, trans. Ann Banfield (Basingstoke: Palgrave Macmillan, 1990), 76.

19  Ibid., 106.

20  Ibid., 108, n. 7.

21  Derrida, 'Limited Inc a b c …', 84.

22  Derrida, 'Signature Event Context', 10.

23  Ibid., 9.

24  Ibid., 14.

25  For a critical account of the intentionalism that is unwittingly shared by Derrida and Searle, see Raoul Moati, *Derrida/Searle: Deconstruction and Ordinary Language*, trans. Timothy Attanucci and Maureen Chun (New York: Columbia University Press, 2014), 88; Moati also shows that both Derrida and Searle tend to reduce Austin to a theorist of communication (see ibid., 13–14). In matters of intention, Austin is much closer to Lacan and his overdetermination of intention by intersubjectivity, according to Moati, who, however, is careful not to reduce Lacan to Austin's anti-intentionalist conventionalism: see Raoul Moati, '*The Performative from Ordinary Conventions to the Real*', The Symptom 9 (2008). Available online: www.lacan.com/symptom/the-performative.html (accessed 1 April 2019). For a Lacanian valorization of Austin, see also Geoff Boucher, 'The Lacanian Performative: Austin after Žižek', in *Žižek and Performance*, eds.

Broderick Chow and Alex Mangold (Basingstoke: Palgrave Macmillan, 2014), 13–32.
26  Derrida, *Voice and Phenomenon*, 75.
27  See Searle, 'Reiterating the Differences', 207–8.
28  Ibid., 202.
29  See Derrida, 'Signature Event Context', 21.
30  Rastko Močnik, 'Glas in fenomen – danes', in Jacques Derrida, *Glas in fenomen*, trans. Rastko Močnik and Zoja Skušek-Močnik (Ljubljana: ŠKUC and ZIFF, 1988), 124 (my translation).
31  Ibid., 127–8.
32  Ibid., 131. Among Heideggerians, Paul Ricoeur dismisses Martin Heidegger's label 'Western metaphysics' as a case of 'laziness in thinking' (Paul Ricoeur, *The Rule of Metaphor*, trans. Robert Czerny with Kathleen McLoughlin and John Costello, SJ (London: Routledge & Kegan Paul, 1978), 311). Responding to similar critiques of his own use of the label, Derrida says, unconvincingly, that he has been using it purely 'for pedagogical reasons' (Jacques Derrida, 'Marx and Sons', trans. G. M. Goshgarian, in *Ghostly Demarcations: A Symposium on Jacques Derrida's Specters of Marx*, ed. Michael Sprinker, trans. Kelly Barry et al. (London: Verso, 1999), 229).
33  Octave Mannoni, 'I Know Well, but All the Same …', trans. G. M. Goshgarian, in *Perversion and the Social Relation*, ed. Molly Anne Rothenberg, Dennis A. Foster and Slavoj Žižek (Durham, NC: Duke University Press, 2003), 70, 71, 79, 80.
34  Derrida, *Voice and Phenomenon*, 85.
35  As Moati demonstrates, Derrida neglects the conventionalism developed already by Austin (see Moati, *Derrida/Searle*, 42–3, 19, 21, 61) and even reduces Austin to a representative of intentionalism (see ibid., 65–7). As a consequence, the only alternative to logocentrism Derrida can provide is Nietzschean voluntarism, which, however, Austin's conventionalism would by itself be able to reject as easily as it rejects logocentrism (see ibid., 60, 64).

## *Ad 2*: Derrida's parasite in *Romeo and Juliet*

1  Jacques Derrida, 'Aphorism Countertime', trans. Nicholas Royle, in Derrida, *Acts of Literature*, ed. Derek Attridge, trans. Geoffrey Bennington et al. (New York: Routledge, 1992), 419–20.
2  Ibid., 419, n. 6.
3  Jacques Lacan, 'Seminar on "The Purloined Letter"', in Lacan, *Écrits*, 30.

4  See Jean-Claude Milner, *Détections fictives* (Paris: Seuil, 1985), 9–44.
5  See Johnson, 'The Frame of Reference', 502.
6  See Slavoj Žižek, *Enjoy Your Symptom! Jacques Lacan in Hollywood and Out* (London: Routledge, 1992), 20–3.
7  Jacques Derrida, 'The Purveyor of Truth', trans. Alan Bass, in *The Purloined Poe: Lacan, Derrida & Psychoanalytic Reading*, eds. John P. Muller and William J. Richardson (Baltimore: The Johns Hopkins University Press, 1988), 187.
8  Jacques Derrida, *Resistances of Psychoanalysis*, trans. Peggy Kamuf, Pascale-Anne Brault and Michael Naas (Stanford: Stanford University Press, 1998), 32.
9  Derrida, 'Aphorism Countertime', 419, n. 6.
10  Nicholas Royle, *Jacques Derrida* (London: Routledge, 2003), 23.
11  Jacques Derrida and Derek Attridge, '"This Strange Institution Called Literature": An Interview with Jacques Derrida', trans. Geoffrey Bennington and Rachel Bowlby, in Derrida, *Acts of Literature*, 67.
12  See, respectively, Harold Bloom, *Shakespeare: The Invention of the Human* (New York: Riverhead Books, 1998), 4–5, 745; and Derrida and Attridge, '"This Strange Institution Called Literature"', 65, 67.
13  See, respectively, Bloom, *Shakespeare*, 87; and Derrida, 'Aphorism Countertime', 432.
14  See, respectively, Bloom, *The Western Canon*, 50; and Derrida and Attridge, '"This Strange Institution Called Literature"', 67.
15  Harold Bloom and Imre Salusinszky, 'An Interview with Harold Bloom', *Scripsi* 4, no. 1 (1986): 84.
16  See Derrida and Attridge, '"This Strange Institution Called Literature"', 67–70.
17  Bloom, *The Western Canon*, 59, 53.
18  Ibid., 53.
19  Bloom, *Shakespeare*, 10.
20  See, for example, David Schalkwyk, *Speech and Performance in Shakespeare's Sonnets and Plays* (Cambridge: Cambridge University Press, 2007), 151–77; Catherine Belsey, 'The Name of the Rose in *Romeo and Juliet*', *Yearbook of English Studies* 23 (1993): 126–42; Kiernan Ryan, *Shakespeare*, 3rd edn (Basingstoke: Palgrave Macmillan, 2002), 72–83; and Laurie Maguire, *Shakespeare's Names* (Oxford: Oxford University Press, 2007), 50–73.
21  See, for example, Julia Kristeva, 'Romeo and Juliet: Love-Hatred in the Couple', in Kristeva, *Tales of Love*, trans. Leon S. Roudiez (New York: Columbia University Press, 1987), 209–33; Alexander Leggatt, *Shakespeare's Tragedies: Violation and Identity* (Cambridge: Cambridge University Press, 2005), 29–58; and Lloyd Davis, '"Death-marked love": Desire and Presence in *Romeo and Juliet*', *Shakespeare Survey* 49 (1996): 57–67.

22  See Leggatt, *Shakespeare's Tragedies*, 29–58; and Davis, '"Death-marked love"'. This identity between the extrinsic and the intrinsic is clear already in Kristeva's unmotivated move from Shakespeare's text (as informed by love-hatred) to biography (in which the love of Romeo and Juliet – suddenly detached from hatred – is the hapless Bard's fantasy). By adding to Kristeva's reading the idea that the play is 'a *fantasy representation* of desire overdetermined by the trauma of mutability', Jonathan Dollimore in effect avoids this need to move from the text to the author – but goes on to reiterate, at the textual level, Kristeva's victimization of the lovers by their ambivalent desire (see Jonathan Dollimore, *Death, Desire and Loss in Western Culture* (New York: Routledge, 1998), 109, 112–3).

23  Bloom, *Shakespeare*, 87; René Girard, 'The Passionate Oxymoron in *Romeo and Juliet*', in *Shakespeare et l'excès*, eds. Pierre Kapitaniak and Jean-Michel Déprats (Paris: Société Française Shakespeare, 2007), 48–9; and 'Lévi-Strauss, Frye, Derrida and Shakespearean Criticism', *Diacritics* 3, no. 3 (1973): 37; Northrop Frye, *Northrop Frye On Shakespeare* (New Haven: Yale University Press, 1986), 33.

24  According to R. S. White, something similar was the case throughout the twentieth century, when predominant appropriations of *Romeo and Juliet*, revisions of either Freud or Marx, unknowingly shared the presupposition that human freedom is impossible (see R. S. White, 'Introduction: What is This Thing Called Love?', in *Romeo and Juliet: Contemporary Critical Essays*, ed. R. S. White (Basingstoke: Palgrave Macmillan, 2001), 4). And tracing the opposition between 'creative' and 'scientific' Shakespeare criticism back to the Victorian critique of Romanticism, Michael Taylor writes: 'Whatever its origins, the struggle between the two approaches surfaces in a variety of forms throughout twentieth-century criticism of Shakespeare' (Michael Taylor, *Shakespeare Criticism in the Twentieth Century* (Oxford: Oxford University Press, 2001), 4).

25  On these two clichés, see, respectively, Avraham Oz, '"What's in a Good Name?" The Case of *Romeo and Juliet* as a Bad Tragedy', in *'Bad' Shakespeare*, ed. Maurice Charney (Rutherford, NJ: Farleigh Dickinson University Press; London: Associated University Presses, 1988), 133–42; and David Farley-Hills, 'The "Bad" Quarto of *Romeo and Juliet*', *Shakespeare Survey* 49 (1996): 27–44.

26  White, 'Introduction', 1.

27  2.2.43–4. All further references to the play appear parenthetically in text and follow the Arden edition, second series: William Shakespeare, *Romeo and Juliet*, ed. Brian Gibbons (London: Methuen), 1980.

28  Ibid., 129.

29  See Farley-Hills, 'The "Bad" Quarto of *Romeo and Juliet*', 43–4, 27.
30  Bloom, *The Western Canon*, 52.
31  See Julia Reinhard Lupton, *Citizen-Saints: Shakespeare and Political Theology* (Chicago: The University of Chicago Press, 2005), 177–8, 3–4, 210.
32  See Alain Badiou, *Ethics: An Essay on the Understanding of Evil*, trans. Peter Hallward (London: Verso, 2001), 30–4, 38; and Immanuel Wallerstein, *World-Systems Analysis: An Introduction* (Durham, NC: Duke University Press, 2004), 41. For an account of this universalist–anti-universalist symbiosis from the perspective of victimization, see Rastko Močnik, 'Regulation of the Particular and Its Socio-Political Effects', in *Conflict, Power, and the Landscape of Constitutionalism*, eds. Gilles Tarabout and Ranabir Samaddar (London: Routledge, 2008), 191–200.
33  Girard is interesting in this respect as well, as he explicitly gives arguments for having excluded *Romeo and Juliet* from his book *A Theatre of Envy: William Shakespeare* (see Girard, 'The Passionate Oxymoron in *Romeo and Juliet*', 42). As Philip Armstrong notes, today, the play is mostly read 'in the classroom, on the screen and on video' (Philip Armstrong, *Shakespeare in Psychoanalysis* (London: Routledge, 2001), 207).
34  Derrida, 'Aphorism Countertime', 423.
35  Ibid., 423–4.
36  Ibid., 426.
37  Critics for whom the families' reconciliation prolongs their feud, rather than suspending it, include Susan Snyder ('Ideology and the Feud in *Romeo and Juliet*', *Shakespeare Survey* 49 (1996): 96); Marjorie Garber ('*Romeo and Juliet*: Patterns and Paradigms', in *Romeo and Juliet: Critical Essays*, ed. John F. Andrews (New York: Garland Publishing, 1993), 131); Leggatt (*Shakespeare's Tragedies*, 53); Bloom (*Shakespeare*, 103); Armstrong (*Shakespeare in Psychoanalysis*, 194–5); and Thomas Betteridge (*Shakespearean Fantasy and Politics* (Hatfield: University of Hertfordshire Press, 2005), 23–4, 29). For contradictions inherent in the endings of Shakespeare's plays in general, see Robert Weimann, 'Thresholds to Memory and Commodity in Shakespeare's Endings', *Representations* 53 (1996): 1–20; and David Margolies, *Shakespeare's Irrational Endings* (Basingstoke: Palgrave Macmillan, 2012).
38  Here is Lacan on the analyst: 'There is no better way of placing him objectively than in relation to what was in the past called: being a saint. … A saint's business, to put it clearly, is not *caritas* [*charité*]. Rather, he acts as trash [*déchet*]; his business being *trashitas* [*il décharite*]. So as to embody what the structure entails, namely allowing the subject, the subject of the unconscious, to take him as the

39  Far from betraying class or sexual chauvinism, a reading of the Nurse as the agent of the superego can counter, for example, Stanley Wells's judgement that her speech is logically inconsequential, characteristic of a well-meaning simpleton and irrelevant to the plot (see Stanley Wells, 'Juliet's Nurse: The Uses of Inconsequentiality', in *Shakespeare's Styles*, eds. Philip Edwards, Inga-Stina Ewbank and G. K. Hunter (Cambridge: Cambridge University Press, 1980), 51–66)).

40  Two of Lacan's numerous iconic condensations are juxtaposed here, *entendre* and *Jouis!/J'ouïs!* For the former, see Lacan's *Le Séminaire. Livre XVII : L'envers de la psychanalyse: 1969–1970*, ed. Jacques-Alain Miller (Paris: Seuil, 1991), 211, 214 (and the English translation in *The Other Side of Psychoanalysis: The Seminar of Jacques Lacan, Book XVII*, ed. Jacques-Alain Miller, trans. Russell Grigg (New York: Norton, 2007), 182, 185); for the latter, see Lacan's 'Remarks on Daniel Lagache's Presentation: "Psychoanalysis and Personality Structure"', in Lacan, *Écrits*, 555–7; and 'The Subversion of the Subject and the Dialectic of Desire in the Freudian Unconscious', 696.

41  In his 2004 Yale edition, Burton Raffel even feels the need to add the annotation 'Romeo is still talking, quietly, to himself only'. Similarly, Raffel provides Romeo's line in the aubade scene 'How is't, my soul? Let's talk, it is not day' (3.5.25) with 'my soul = Juliet'.

42  'I gave thee mine before thou didst request it' (2.2.128).

43  'Do not swear at all' (2.2.112).

44  'The more I give to thee/The more I have, for both are infinite' (2.2.134–5).

45  See Derrida, 'Aphorism Countertime', 426.

46  '*Che vuoi?*', 'What do you want?' in Italian, the direct ancestor of the language spoken by Juliet's fictional mother, but also by the protagonist of Wolfgang Amadeus Mozart's *Don Giovanni*, whose '*Che vuoi?*' is used by Lacan to designate the leftover of the subject's anxiety regarding its symbolic mandate after it has already been interpellated by the Other (see Lacan, 'The Subversion of the Subject and the Dialectic of Desire in the Freudian Unconscious', 690).

47  For this formalization of Freud's ideal ego and ego-ideal, see Lacan, 'The Subversion of the Subject and the Dialectic of Desire in the Freudian Unconscious'.

48  Characterizing Juliet's spontaneous philosophy of language as nominalistic neglect of names, and her spontaneous practice as inevitably dependent on names, James L. Calderwood says of the balcony scene: 'Seeking an ideal

communion of love at a level beyond idle breath, Juliet would purify words quite out of existence and reduce dialogue to an exchange of intuition and sheer feeling – a marriage of true minds accomplished without the connective medium of language' (James L. Calderwood, *Shakespearean Metadrama* (Minneapolis: University of Minnesota Press, 1971), 91). This comes very close to the idea of the balcony scene as a monologue, but misses the tension between nominalism and realism inherent in the monologue.

49 'As soon as the subject who is supposed to know exists somewhere … there is transference' (Lacan, *The Four Fundamental Concepts of Psychoanalysis*, 232).

50 Juliet will use double entendre to stay faithful to her husband in her exchange with Paris as well (4.1.18–36).

51 See Lupton, *Citizen-Saints*, 21.

52 Due to this contradiction of the social structure, Capulet's servant can parody the list of invited suitors of Juliet even though he is illiterate. Overdetermined as he is by class struggle, he is able not only to guess that Capulet has invited only those who are allowed in advance 'within her scope of choice' (1.2.18) but also to reflect on this reproduction of the relations of production, to carnivalize in his prose the relation of the labour force to the means of production (1.2.38–44). Needless to say, the fact that 'the learnèd' (1.2.43), Romeo, stores his means of production inside his head does not make this relation any more symmetrical in his case: all he can read is, in his own words, 'mine own fortune in my misery' (1.2.58).

53 'Shakespeare has provided us with the opportunity', writes Marjorie Garber, 'to realize that his play, rather than the golden statues, is the fit monument by which Romeo and Juliet will be remembered, and their tragedy understood' (Garber, '*Romeo and Juliet*: Patterns and Paradigms', 131).

# Chapter 3

1 Harish Trivedi, 'Translating Culture vs. Cultural Translation', *91st Meridian*, May 2005. Available online: iwp.uiowa.edu/91st/vol4-num1/translating-culture-vs-cultural-translation (Trivedi made no alterations to his assessments for the 2007 republication in the collective volume *In Translation – Reflections, Refractions, Transformations*, eds. Paul St-Pierre and Partulla C. Kar (Amsterdam: John Benjamins, 2007), 277–87). And Hito Steyerl, 'Beyond Culture: The Politics of Translation', *Translate*, 2006. Available online: translate.eipcp.net/concept/steyerl-concept-en (both accessed 1 April 2019).

2   Anthony Pym, *Exploring Translation Theories*, 2nd edn (London: Routledge, 2014), 158.
3   See Boris Buden, 'Public Space as Translatión Process', *Transversal*, December 2003. Available online: eipcp.net/transversal/1203/buden/en (accessed 1 April 2019).
4   See Jürgen Habermas, *Knowledge and Human Interests*, trans. Jeremy J. Shapiro (Boston: Beacon Press, 1971), 214–45.
5   See Buden, 'Public Space as Translation Process'.
6   See Judith Butler, *Excitable Speech: A Politics of the Performative* (New York: Routledge, 1997), 86–95; and Homi Bhabha, *The Location of Culture* (London: Routledge, 1994), 226–9.
7   See Butler, *Excitable Speech*, 86–8; and Bhabha, *The Location of Culture*, 239–41.
8   Kate Sturge, 'Cultural Translation', in *The Routledge Encyclopedia of Translation Studies*, 2nd edn, eds. Mona Baker and Gabriela Saldanha (London: Routledge, 2009), 69.
9   Buden, 'Public Space as Translation Process'.
10  Boris Buden, 'Strategic Universalism: Dead Concept Walking', trans. Aileen Derieg, *Transversal*, February 2002. Available online: eipcp.net/transversal/0607/buden/en (accessed 1 April 2019).
11  See Judith Butler, 'Restaging the Universal: Hegemony and the Limits of Formalism', in Judith Butler, Ernesto Laclau and Slavoj Žižek, *Contingency, Hegemony, Universality: Contemporary Dialogues on the Left* (London: Verso, 2000), 20–1, 24–5, 35; see also Judith Butler, 'Competing Universalities', in Butler, Laclau and Žižek, *Contingency, Hegemony, Universality*, 172.
12  Cited in Herbert Robinson Marbury, *Pillars of Cloud and Fire: The Politics of Exodus in African American Biblical Interpretation* (New York: NYU Press, 2015), 228, n. 35.
13  'For Martin Luther King, racism was not a problem of tolerance. He does not ask the whites to tolerate the blacks. That would be ridiculous. For him racism was a problem of equality, economic justice, legal rights, and so on. Today we perceive racism as a problem of tolerance, which means we perceive it as a problem of cultural differences, cultural intolerance, which is really a mystification. The whole field of economy, public space, and so on disappears.' (Slavoj Žižek, 'Ecology', in *Examined Life: Excursions with Contemporary Thinkers*, ed. Astra Taylor (New York: The New Press, 2009), 157.)
14  The show, an episode of *Def Comedy Jam*, aired on the HBO television network in 1992.
15  Derrida, 'Signature Event Context', 16–17.

16 Butler, *Excitable Speech*, 150–1. Bracketed numbers 15 and 17 refer to Derrida, 'Signature Event Context'.

17 See also James Loxley, '*Performatives and Performativity*: Ben Jonson Makes His Excuses', *Renaissance Drama*, New Series, 33 (2004): 81–2, for Butler's 'insistence that the "breaking force" that Derrida identifies with iterability in his initial encounter with Austin is the same as "the force of the performative" in its productive, proper sense'. According to Loxley, 'to make this equation is to transform the aporia of the iterable into a structural account of performativity, the determination of an event of force by positive conditions of possibility'. This misreading, Loxley argues, 'allows Butler to speak of a "logic of iterability that governs the possibility of social transformation" and can be "enact[ed]"'. Loxley's citations are from Derrida, 'Signature Event Context', 9; and Butler, *Excitable Speech*, 147, 148.

18 Butler, *Excitable Speech*, 99.

19 Ibid., 84.

20 Ibid., 89–90.

21 Ibid., 91.

22 Ibid., 89.

23 Butler, 'Restaging the Universal', 20; see also ibid., 21, 24–5, 35; and Butler, *Excitable Speech*, 86–95.

24 Jure Simoniti, 'Nelagodje ob določnosti', in Axel Honneth, *Trpeti zaradi nedoločnosti* (Ljubljana: Krtina, 2007), 110 (my translation). Simoniti comments here on Axel Honneth, a proponent, like Butler, of the Hegel of recognition, who explicitly rejects Hegel's institutional view on *Sittlichkeit*. See also Ernesto Laclau's objection to Butler's appropriation of Hegel's dialectics of *Sittlichkeit*: Ernesto Laclau, 'Constructing Universality', in Butler, Laclau and Žižek, *Contingency, Hegemony, Universality*, 296; for a critique of Butler's neglect of dialectics in general, see Marcel Stoetzler, 'Subject Trouble: Judith Butler and Dialectics', *Philosophy & Social Criticism* 31, no. 3 (2005): 358–61, 350–4.

25 A critique of Butler's anti-statism is developed, for example, in Moya Lloyd, 'Butler, Antigone and the State', *Contemporary Political Theory* 4, no. 4 (2005): 460–6. A broader demonstration of the neoliberal turn in the second-wave feminism's anti-statism is given by Nancy Fraser in 'Feminism, Capitalism and the Cunning of History', *New Left Review*, 2nd Series, 56 (2009): 107–13. But see, for a critique of both Butler's culturalism and Fraser's economism, Anna Marie Smith, 'Missing Poststructuralism, Missing Foucault: Butler and Fraser on Capitalism and the Regulation of Sexuality', in *Judith Butler's Precarious Politics*,

eds. Terrell Carver and Samuel A. Chambers (Abingdon: Routledge, 2008), 79–91.
26  See Butler, *Excitable Speech*, 64, 75, 73.
27  In his critique of the theory of cultural translation and its belief that the law functions by way of excluding identities from its domain and can as such be universalized in these identities' struggle for recognition, Močnik writes: 'The universal is articulated in juridical terms, it is abstract and formal. The content from which it is abstracted is not this or that identity – it is the relations of production and exploitation' (Močnik, 'Regulation of the Particular and Its Socio-Political Effects', 206, n. 32).
28  See Butler, *Excitable Speech*, 62.
29  Ibid., 92–3, 96–7.
30  Ibid., 11–12, 15, 40, 41, 101–2, 125–6.
31  Ibid., 69.
32  'Suppose we try first to state schematically … some at least of the things which are necessary for the smooth or "happy" functioning of a performative …

(A. I) There must exist an accepted conventional procedure having a certain conventional effect, that procedure to include the uttering of certain words by certain persons in certain circumstances, and further,

(A. 2) the particular persons and circumstances in a given case must be appropriate for the invocation of the particular procedure invoked.

(B. I) The procedure must be executed by all participants both correctly and

(B. 2) completely.

(Γ. I) Where, as often, the procedure is designed for use by persons having certain thoughts or feelings, or for the inauguration of certain consequential conduct on the part of any participant, then a person participating in and so invoking the procedure must in fact have those thoughts or feelings, and the participants must intend so to conduct themselves, and further

(Γ. 2) must actually so conduct themselves subsequently' (Austin, *How to Do Things with Words*, 14–15).
33  Benveniste, 'Delocutive Verbs', 242.
34  For the distinction between the conventionalist and the intentionalist felicity conditions, see Aldo Milohnić, 'Performative Theatre', trans. Suzana Stančič, in *Along the Margins of Humanities: Seminar in Epistemology of Humanities*, eds. Aldo Milohnić and Rastko Močnik, trans. Paule Ečimović et al. (Ljubljana: ISH, 1996), 245.
35  Austin, *How to Do Things with Words*, 16.
36  See Butler, *Excitable Speech*, 39.

37  Ibid., 150–2.
38  Ibid., 23–4, 41, 125–6, 69.
39  Ibid., 162.
40  Butler's underestimation of the institutional dimension of gender performativity has been noted, for example, in Kathi Weeks, 'Subject for a Feminist Standpoint', in *Marxism beyond Marxism*, eds. Saree Makdisi, Cesare Casarino and Rebecca E. Karl (New York: Routledge, 1996), 89–118; Cinzia Arruzza, 'Gender as Social Temporality: Butler (and Marx)', *Historical Materialism* 23, no. 1 (2015): 35, 41–7; Kevin Floyd, *The Reification of Desire: Toward a Queer Marxism* (Minneapolis: University of Minnesota Press, 2009), 115–9; and Geoff Boucher, 'The Politics of Performativity: A Critique of Judith Butler', *Parrhesia* 1 (2006): 130–7. Available online: www.parrhesiajournal.org/parrhesia01/parrhesia01_boucher.pdf (accessed 1 April 2019).
41  Judith Butler, *Frames of War: When is Life Grievable?* (London: Verso, 2009), 26.
42  See Butler, *Excitable Speech*, 3, 82, n. 32.
43  Ibid., 13–14, 38.
44  Butler, 'Competing Universalities', 158.
45  See ibid., 157–8.
46  See Butler, *Excitable Speech*, 19, 69.
47  See Butler, 'Restaging the Universal', 27–9.
48  For a critique of a similar conflation of matter with materiality in Butler's seminal book *Bodies that Matter*, see Peter Hitchcock, *Oscillate Wildly: Space, Body, and Spirit of Millenial Materialism* (Minneapolis: University of Minnesota Press, 1999), 73–4; see also Toril Moi, *What is a Woman? And Other Essays* (Oxford: Oxford University Press, 1999), 47–51.
49  See Butler, 'Restaging the Universal', 25–7.
50  See, respectively, Eve Kosofsky Sedgwick, *Touching Feeling: Affect, Pedagogy, Performativity* (Durham, NC: Duke University Press, 2003), 3–9; Felman, *The Scandal of the Speaking Body*, ix–x; J. Hillis Miller, 'Performativity as Performance / Performativity as Speech Act', *South Atlantic Quarterly* 106, no. 2 (2007): 224–9; and Erika Fischer-Lichte, *The Transformative Power of Performance*, trans. Saskya Iris Jain (London: Routledge, 2008), 26–36.

## *Ad 3*: Butler's poetry of parasites in *We Are All Jews and Germans*

1  See Marbury, *Pillars of Cloud and Fire*, 228, n. 35.

2   Martin Luther King, Jr., *A Call to Conscience: The Landmark Speeches of Dr. Martin Luther King, Jr.*, eds. Clayborne Carson and Kris Shepard (New York: Warner Books, 2001), 185. The words in brackets and italics are used, in this edition of King's speeches, to capture the reaction of King's audience.

3   See, respectively, the television special titled *The Chocolate Sundaes Comedy Show*, dir. Scott L. Montoya (Entertainment One, 2013), and the music video for the song, by David Andrew Burd a.k.a. Lil Dicky featuring Chris Brown, *Freaky Friday*, dir. Tony Yacenda (Libby de Leon et al., 2018).

4   Cited in Olivier Marchesi, *Lyon en Mai 68* (Lyon: I.E.P. Lyon, 1998). Available online: doc.sciencespo-lyon.fr/Ressources/Documents/Etudiants/Memoires/Cyberdocs/MFE1998/marchesio/these_body.html (accessed 1 April 2019) (my translation).

5   As Messner says for a recent German documentary dedicated to his career: 'It was anarchy, the life we led in the mountains: no power for anyone. Images of the protest movement were already instilled in us. We stopped with the "Bergheil" greeting, we stopped with the flag waving; climbing no longer had any nationalist dimension. I was one of the first climbers to fully reject the heroic, or victorious, manner of climbing. And I was, of course, very much criticised by older climbers, the edelweiss-climbers, the Gamsbart-hat-climbers. But that didn't concern or interest me at all' (*Messner*, dir. Andreas Nickel (Explorermedia, 2012) (my translation)).

6   *Minute*, 2 May 1968, 1 (my translation).

7   Georges Marchais, 'De faux révolutionnaires à démasquer', *l'Humanité*, 3 May 1968, 1 (my translation).

8   The lack of confidence on Cohn-Bendit's face is mostly likely what makes Caron's photo a particularly fitting cover image of Jacques-Alain Miller's edition of Lacan's 1969–70 seminar, published by Seuil in 1991, especially given Lacan's reservations about the student revolt (of which more later).

9   Liam Considine, 'Screen Politics: Pop Art and the Atelier Populaire', *Tate Papers* 24 (2015). Available online: www.tate.org.uk/research/publications/tate-papers/24/screen-politics-pop-art-and-the-atelier-populaire (accessed 1 April 2019).

10  Ibid.

11  Ibid. Rancière is cited from Jacques Rancière, 'The Cause of the Other', trans. David Macey, *Parallax* 4, no. 2 (1998): 30.

12  Jacques Rancière and Davide Panagia, 'Dissenting Words: A Conversation with Jacques Rancière', trans. Davide Panagia, *Diacritics* 30, no. 2 (2000): 114.

13  Rancière, 'The Cause of the Other', 30. See also Rancière's books *Aux bords du politique* (Paris: La Fabrique, 1998), 89–92, 157; and *Disagreement: Politics and*

*Philosophy*, trans. Julie Rose (Minneapolis: University of Minnesota Press, 1999), 126–7, 59.

14 'Oui, Marie-George, je sais : je suis un juif allemand' ('Yes, Marie-George, I know: I'm a German Jew'). Cited in Alain Auffray, 'Ich liebe dich, moi non plus …', *Libération*, 1 July 2005. Available online: www.liberation.fr/grand-angle/2005/07/01/ich-liebe-dich-moi-non-plus_525342 (accessed 1 April 2019) (my translation).

15 Rastko Močnik, 'Ideological Interpellation: Identification and Subjectivation', in *Encountering Althusser: Politics and Materialism in Contemporary Radical Thought*, ed. Katja Diefenbach et al. (London: Bloomsbury, 2013), 315.

16 See ibid., 321, n. 35.

17 See James Irwin and Helena Motoh, *Žižek and His Contemporaries: On the Emergence of the Slovenian Lacan* (London: Bloomsbury, 2014), 13–38, for a presentation of the Ljubljana school of Lacanian psychoanalysis that relies heavily on Močnik's own analysis of the school's development and even cites the following statement from 1992 in which Močnik situates his critique of Derrida in this development: 'Derrida falls short of his critique of Husserl; he is unable to valorize the formalistic dimensions of phenomenology; in this way, his anti-metaphysical verve makes him overlook the very non-metaphysical moments in Husserl; Derrida falls victim to his own "activism" – we could call it "theoretical leftism"' (ibid., 34).

This is an early and relatively unknown example of showing, in an immanently Lacanian fashion, that the subject who is supposed to know knows only that which the object of analysis itself knows as the only true subject in the relation. A more recent and probably most well-known example, and one that brings together figures as important to our argument as Judith Butler and so-called pre-theoretic people, was given, rather expectedly, by Žižek in a talk documented in the film titled simply *Žižek!*: 'Look how it functions, deconstructionism, in its standard version, already at the texture of style. Like, you cannot find one text of Derrida without, A, all of the quotation marks, and, B, all of these rhetorical … distanciations. … To take an ironic example: if somebody like Judith Butler were to be asked: "What is this?", she would never have said: "This is a bottle of tea." She would have said something like: "If we accept the metaphysical notion of language identifying clearly objects, and taking all this into account, then may we not", she likes to put it in this rhetorical way, "risk the hypothesis that, in the condition of our language game, this can be said to be a bottle of tea?" – and so on, and so on. So it's always this need to distanciate. It goes even for love, like, nobody almost dares to say today: "I love you." It has to be: "As a poet would have put it: 'I love you'", or some kind of a distance. But what's the problem here? … Why this fear? Because I claim that, when the Ancients directly said: "I love you", they meant exactly the same: all these distanciations were included. So it's we today who are afraid that, if we were to put it directly, "I love you", that it would mean too much. *We believe in it*' (*Žižek!*, dir. Astra Taylor (The Documentary Campaign, 2006)).

18 In the 'Preface' to his 1974 critique of Althusser, Rancière took as his starting point 'an experience that', as he writes, 'a great many intellectuals of my generation lived through in 1968: the Marxism we had learned at Althusser's school was a philosophy of order whose every principle served to distance us from the uprisings which were then shaking the bourgeois order to its core' (Jacques Rancière, *Althusser's Lesson*, trans. Emiliano Battista (London: Bloomsbury, 2011), xix). And in the 'Foreword to the English Edition' from 2010, Rancière wrote that 'the book's undertaking coincided … with Althusser's own attempts to glue the pieces of Althusserianism back together, and thus to seal up the breach that had been opened up by the event', that is, by May '68, when Althusserianism in effect 'underwrote the condemnation of the student uprisings as a petit-bourgeois movement, one whose actors were in fact the victims of the bourgeois ideology they imbibed without knowing'; victims, that is, 'who had to be re-educated by the authority of Science and the Party' (Ibid., xiv).

19 'To broach my central thesis on the structure and functioning of ideology, I shall first present two theses, one negative, the other positive. The first concerns the object "represented" in the imaginary form of ideology. The second concerns the materiality of ideology.

   THESIS I: Ideology represents individuals' imaginary relation to their real conditions of existence.

   …

   THESIS II: Ideology has a material existence.

   As a first formulation, I would suggest: *all ideology hails or interpellates concrete individuals as concrete subjects* …

   *… The existence of ideology and the hailing or interpellation of individuals as subjects are one and the same thing*' (Louis Althusser, *On the Reproduction of Capitalism*, trans. G. M. Goshgarian (London: Verso, 2014), 181, 184, 190, 191).

20 Močnik, 'Ideological Interpellation', 308.
21 Ibid., 309.
22 *The Occupation Cookbook*, trans. Drago Markiša (London: Minor Compositions, 2011), 17. Available online: www.minorcompositions.info/wp-content/uploads/2011/03/occupationcookbook-web.pdf (accessed 1 April 2019).
23 Močnik, 'Ideological Interpellation', 312.

24  Ibid., 313.
25  Ibid., 313–4.
26  Ibid., 314.
27  Ibid., 316.
28  Ibid., 314–5.
29  Ibid., 315.
30  Ibid.
31  See the frontispiece of *The Occupation Cookbook* with Boris Kovačev's photograph of the occupied building of the Faculty of Humanities and Social Sciences in Zagreb.
32  Močnik, 'Ideological Interpellation', 315.
33  Ibid., 315–6.
34  'We who have participated in the actions attributed to a so-called *pègre*, we affirm that we are all rioters, we are all "*la pègre*"' (cited in, and translated in English by, Kristin Ross, *May '68 and Its Afterlives* (Chicago: The University of Chicago Press, 2002), 108).
35  Éric Hazan, *The Invention of Paris: A History in Footsteps*, trans. David Fernbach (London: Verso, 2010), 310. This cartoon commonplace – as well as its obverse: a character waving at the driver who just stole his car before noticing what is going on – is used by Žižek to illustrate the disintegration of any political system (see Slavoj Žižek, *The Parallax View* (Cambridge, MA: The MIT Press, 2006), 201).
36  Ross, *May '68 and Its Afterlives*, 79.
37  Sarah Hammerschlag, *The Figural Jew: Politics and Identity in Postwar French Thought* (Chicago: The University of Chicago Press, 2010), 3.
38  Mladen Dolar, 'Who Is the Victim?', in *The Final Countdown: Europe, Refugees and the Left*, ed. Jela Krečič (Ljubljana: Irwin; Vienna: Wiener Festwochen, 2017), 74.
39  'What you aspire to as revolutionaries is a master. You will get one' (Jacques Lacan, *The Other Side of Psychoanalysis*, 207).
40  Joan Copjec, 'May '68, the Emotional Month', in *Lacan: The Silent Partners*, ed. Slavoj Žižek (London: Verso, 2006), 90.
41  Cited in, and translated in English by, Ross, *May '68 and Its Afterlives*, 66.
42  See Mark Robson, '"A literary animal": Rancière, Derrida, and the Literature of Democracy', *Parallax* 15, no. 3 (2009): 95. 'A hierarchy is explicit in the Aristotelian emphasis on the difference between noble action and base life, in which all forms of art … bear a mimetic relation to that which is represented. … Such representational strategies, suggests Rancière, are based upon a specific sense of writing as speaking, and thus on a particular notion of the speech act,

of doing art with words. Here, perhaps, in this echo of J. L. Austin's influential concept, is where we begin to see one of the ways in which we might link Rancière's work to Derrida's conception of literature, since for both thinkers there is always an at least implicit sense of writing as a form of action or event, as in some sense performative.' See also Robson's text 'Introduction: Hearing Voices', *Paragraph* 28, no. 1 (2005): 8, 9, n. 3.

43  See Andrew Parker, 'Impossible Speech Acts', in *The Politics of Deconstruction: Jacques Derrida and the Other of Philosophy*, ed. Martin McQuillan (London: Pluto Press, 2007), 70–7.

44  See Šumič-Riha: 'If the elementary gesture of emancipatory politics consists in de-totalizing all totalization, it becomes apparent that emancipatory politics, as Rancière sees it, precisely because it depends upon the master's closure, is only possible in a world in which the Other exists. If, however, the subversion of the master's closure is not sufficient to account for an emancipatory politics that would be more attuned to the deadlocks of globalized capitalism, this is because the latter is articulated to the non-existence of the Other and has as its structural principle the "generalized metonymysation", which excludes from the outset the possibility of closure capable of rendering a given situation "legible"' (Jelica Sumic, 'Politics in the Era of the Inexistent Other', *Política común* 1, no. 2 (2012). Available online: dx.doi.org/10.3998/pc.12322227.0002.004 (accessed 1 April 2019)).

And Žižek: 'Rancière fetishizes the order of police, failing to recognize how this order itself relies on the excessive gesture of the Master, which is a stand-in for the political Lack – the "gentrification", the positivization, of the properly political excess. In short, we do not have the full positivity of the police order perturbed from time to time by the heterogeneous intervention of political subjectivity: this positivity itself always-already relies on the (disavowal of some) excessive gesture of the Master. ... Politics is not a *consequence* of the (pre-political) ... non-coincidence of the social subject with itself: the fact that the social subject is never complete and self-identical means that the social being itself is always-already *based on* a (disavowed) gesture of politicization and, as such, thoroughly political' (Slavoj Žižek, *The Ticklish Subject: The Absent Centre of Political Ontology* (London: Verso, 1999), 169, n. 27).

45  See Rancière, *Disagreement*, 81–93.

46  Jacques Rancière, *Aesthetics and Its Discontents*, trans. Steven Corcoran (Cambridge: Polity, 2009), 99.

47  'If there is anything revolutionary in Freud ... it is so to the extent that he brought to the fore a function that Marx has foregrounded as well – and which,

besides, is also the only element that they have in common – namely to know, to consider a certain number of facts as symptoms. ...

... I indicated several times, and a reading can easily spot, regarding the notion of the symptom that the one who is responsible for it is Marx' (Jacques Lacan, *Le Séminaire. Livre XVIII: D'un discours qui ne serait pas du semblant: 1970–1971*, ed. Jacques-Alain Miller (Paris: Seuil, 2007), 24, 164 (my translation)).

48  Dolar, 'Who Is the Victim?', 72, 73.
49  See Ross, *May '68 and Its Afterlives*, 57–8.
50  See ibid., 75–9.
51  Ronald Guillaumont, 'Nous sommes tous Gilets Jaunes !!!', *Profession gendarme*, 27 November 2018. Available online: www.profession-gendarme.com/nous-sommes-tous-gilets-jaunes/ (accessed 1 April 2019) (my translation).
52  'Communiqué des sociétés de journalistes: "Nous sommes tous des Charlie"', *Le Monde*, 7 April 2016. Available online: www.lemonde.fr/actualite-medias/article/2015/01/08/communique-des-societes-des-journalistes-nous-sommes-tous-des-charlie_4551306_3236.html (accessed 1 April 2019).
53  'Attentats à Paris: "Nous sommes Paris", proclament les Ultras marseillais', *Le Parisien*, 15 November 2015. Available online: www.leparisien.fr/faits-divers/attentats-a-paris-nous-sommes-paris-le-message-fort-des-ultras-marseillais-15-11-2015-5279467.php (accessed 1 April 2019).

## Conclusion: Literature and political disagreement from Austin to Rancière to Ducrot

1  Alain Badiou, *The Century*, trans. Alberto Toscano (Cambridge: Polity, 2007), 148.
2  See ibid., 149.
3  Ibid., 11, 88, 6, 69.
4  Ibid., 149, 88.
5  Emily Apter and Bruno Bosteels, 'Introduction', in Alain Badiou, *The Age of the Poets, and Other Writings on Twentieth-Century Poetry and Prose*, ed. and trans. Bruno Bosteels (London: Verso, 2014), xviii.
6  Rancière, *Aesthetics and Its Discontents*, 42; see also ibid., 28–44, 64–6.
7  See Rancière's article 'The Politics of Literature', *SubStance* 33, no. 1 (2004): 13–16, and his book *The Politics of Literature*, trans. Julie Rose (Cambridge: Polity, 2011), 12–13.

8 Jacques Rancière, *Mute Speech: Literature, Critical Theory, and Politics*, trans. James Swenson (New York: Columbia University Press, 2011), 66, 67, 117, 147, 170.
9 See Rancière, *Aux bords du politique*, 129–32. For the English translation of the first, 1992 edition of this book, see Jacques Rancière, *On the Shores of Politics*, trans. Liz Heron (London: Verso, 1995).
10 As in, for example, Robson, '"A literary animal": Rancière, Derrida, and the Literature of Democracy', 95–8; and Parker, 'Impossible Speech Acts', 71, 74, 75. See also Elie During, 'Politiques de l'accent: Rancière entre Deleuze et Derrida', in *Jacques Rancière: politique de l'esthétique*, eds. Jérôme Game and Aliocha Wald Lasowski (Paris: Éditions des archives contemporaines, 2009), 90–2.
11 See Rancière, *Aesthetics and Its Discontents*, 66–7, 100–2, 32.
12 Rok Benčin, 'Životarjenje boga pesnikov ali ontologizacije umetnosti', *Filozofski vestnik* 31, no. 3 (2010): 84 (my translation).
13 See Rancière, *The Politics of Literature*, 41–5.
14 See Macherey, *A Theory of Literary Production*, 62–4.
15 Derrida, 'Signature Event Context', 16–17.
16 Butler, *Excitable Speech*, 151.
17 Ibid., 99.
18 Ibid., 90.
19 See ibid.
20 See Jacques Rancière, 'Should Democracy Come? Ethics and Politics in Derrida', in *Derrida and the Time of the Political*, eds. Pheng Cheah and Suzanne Guerlac (Durham, NC: Duke University Press, 2009), 275–8; see also Jacques Rancière, *Dissensus: On Politics and Aesthetics*, ed. and trans. Steven Corcoran (London: Bloomsbury, 2010), 52–3, 59–60.
21 Oswald Ducrot, 'Enunciative Polyphony', trans. Johannes Angermuller, Dominique Maingueneau and Ruth Wodak, in *The Discourse Studies Reader: Main Currents in Theory and Analysis*, eds. Johannes Angermuller, Dominique Maingueneau and Ruth Wodak, trans. Johannes Angermuller et al. (Amsterdam: John Benjamins, 2014), 167.

For the crucial role of Ducrot's *Le dire et le dit* in bringing speech act theory to the level of Lacan's theory of the signifier, see Renata Salecl, *The Spoils of Freedom: Psychoanalysis and Feminism After the Fall of Socialism* (London: Routledge, 1994), 31–5. For the relevance of Ducrot's semantics in general for a Lacanian theory of ideology, see two further members of the Ljubljana school of Lacanian psychoanalysis, namely Rastko Močnik ('Regulation of the Particular and Its Socio-Political Effects', 184–8) and Slavoj Žižek ('The Spectre of Ideology', in *Mapping Ideology*, ed. Slavoj Žižek (London: Verso, 1997), 11). As co-founders of the Ljubljana Lacanian School, Močnik and Žižek have also contributed to the most productive reception of Ducrot's work outside France (and perhaps Spain), which includes Ducrot's *Slovenian Lectures*, his only book available in English besides the classic encyclopaedic dictionary of linguistics that he co-wrote with Tzvetan Todorov.

22  Patrick Dendale, 'Three Linguistic Theories of Polyphony/Dialogism', in *Sproglig polyfoni*, eds. Nina Møller Andersen, Henning Nølke and Rita Therkelsen (Roskilde: Institut for Sprog og Kultur, Roskilde Universitetscenter, 2006), 3.
23  See Oswald Ducrot, 'K slovenski izdaji', in Ducrot, *Izrekanje in izrečeno*, trans. Jelica Šumič-Riha (Ljubljana: ŠKUC and Filozofska fakulteta, 1988), 238; and Ducrot, *Slovenian Lectures*, 13.
24  See ibid., 11, 29.
25  See Močnik, 'Regulation of the Particular and Its Socio-Political Effects', 196–7, for a formalization of Lacanian subjectivation as unconditional identification (with the subject who is supposed to know) without any conditional identification (with a subject who is supposed to believe) – identification, that is, that disavows alternative identifications due to an ideological interpellation institutionally enforced as the only possible alternative and as the rational pole of an alienating forced choice.
26  Ducrot, 'Enunciative Polyphony', 167.
27  Ducrot, *Slovenian Lectures*, 38.
28  Lacan, *The Four Fundamental Concepts of Psychoanalysis*, 138–42.
29  See Umberto Eco, *Postscript to* The Name of the Rose, trans. William Weaver (San Diego: Harcourt Brace Jovanovich, 1984), 67–8.
30  See Lacan, *The Four Fundamental Concepts of Psychoanalysis*, 138–9, 37–8.
31  Henry James, *The Portrait of a Lady* (Harmondsworth: Penguin, 1984), 385.
32  In this novel, however, there is an utterance that is even more pertinent to our problematic, namely Ralph's quip: 'There's no more usual basis of union than a mutual misunderstanding' (James, *The Portrait of a Lady*, 198). This is an uncannily literal glossing of Lacan's concept of communication as a double, successful misunderstanding.
33  Lewis Carroll, 'Alice's Adventures in Wonderland', 32.
34  Ducrot, *Le dire et le dit*, 222–3 (my translation).
35  See ibid., 222.
36  Ibid., 223–4.
37  Ibid., 211, 212, 223.

38  Ibid., 211–2: 'In an expensive restaurant, a guest takes a table with his dog, a small dachshund. The proprietor starts a conversation by bragging about his establishment: "You know, sir, our chef used to cook for King Farouk." "You don't say", replies the guest. Without losing his courage, the proprietor goes on: "And our sommelier is the former sommelier at the English court … and our pastry chef, we got him from Emperor Bao Dai." Noticing the guest's silence, the proprietor changes the topic: "You have a very nice dachshund, sir." To which the guest responds: "My dachshund, sir, used to be a St Bernard."'

39  Ibid., 211.

40  For Lacan's analysis of 'Je crains qu'il ne vienne', see his *écrits* 'Remarks on Daniel Lagache's Presentation', 555–7, 'The Subversion of the Subject and the Dialectic of Desire in the Freudian Unconscious', 677, and his seminar *The Ethics of Psychoanalysis*, 64, 305–30. See also his seminar *The Four Fundamental Concepts of Psychoanalysis*, 56–7.

41  René Descartes, 'Discours de la méthode', in Descartes, *Œuvres de Descartes*, vol. 6, eds. Adam Charles and Paul Tannery (Paris: Léopold Cerf, 1902), 35; the *ne explétif* is 'n"' in 'n'en'. And here is John Veitch's translation: 'Besides, I had ideas of many corporeal things; for although I might suppose that I was dreaming, and that all which I saw or imagined was false, I could not, nevertheless, deny that the ideas were in reality in my thoughts' (René Descartes, *Discourse on Method* (Edinburgh: Sutherland and Knox, 1850), 78).

42  For this, see Chapter *Ad* 1 and its references to Lacan, *The Four Fundamental Concepts of Psychoanalysis*, 222–7.

43  Derrida, *Voice and Phenomenon*, 10.

44  See Lacan, 'The Subversion of the Subject and the Dialectic of Desire in the Freudian Unconscious', 689–702.

45  For the constitutional role of the thinking/being alternative in the history of modern science, and for the signifying chain and non-being as the material existence of thinking and being respectively, let us recall Lacan's pun from Chapter 1 – '*I am thinking: "therefore I am"*' – and Lacan's introduction of the alienating *vel* in *The Four Fundamental Concepts of Psychoanalysis*, 209–31. See also Mladen Dolar, 'Cogito as the Subject of the Unconscious', in *Cogito and the Unconscious*, ed. Slavoj Žižek (Durham, NC: Duke University Press, 1998), 18–25; and Jean-Claude Milner, 'The Doctrine of Science', trans. Oliver Feltham, *Umbr(a): A Journal of the Unconscious* 5 (2000): 33–63.

46  "'*L'homme c'est rien – l'œuvre c'est tout*," as Gustave Flaubert wrote to George Sand', says Holmes to Watson as he solves the case of 'The Red-headed League'; 'Man is nothing – the work is all' – but to convey that, Holmes nonetheless

refers, not to one, but to two authorities, if only so as to be intelligible to Watson (Sir Arthur Conan Doyle, 'The Red-headed League', in Conan Doyle, *Sherlock Holmes: The Complete Novels and Stories*, vol. 1 (New York: Bantam Dell, 1986), 287).

47  Phillip E. Wegner, 'Lacan avec Greimas: Formalization, Theory, and the "Other Side" of the Study of Culture', *The Minnesota Review* 77 (2011): 68.

48  Jean-François Lyotard, *The Postmodern Condition*, trans. Geoff Bennington and Brian Massumi (Minneapolis: University of Minnesota Press, 1984), xxiv.

49  Lacan, *Le Séminaire. Livre XVII*, 92 (for the English translation, see Lacan's *The Other Side of Psychoanalysis*, 81).

50  See Althusser, *On the Reproduction of Capitalism*, 142–7.

51  Juliet Flower MacCannell, 'Surplus Knowledge; or, Can We Teach Today?', *Polygraph* 21 (2009): 30.

52  See Rastko Močnik's 'La nouvelle chair à canon', *Rue Descartes* 62 (2008): 90.

53  'Giving what you don't have' is Lacan's definition of transference love fulfilled in the separation from the lack in the Other (Jacques Lacan, 'The Direction of the Treatment and the Principles of Its Power', in Lacan, *Écrits*, 516; see also Jacques Lacan, 'The Signification of the Phallus', in Lacan, *Écrits*, 580). As such, Z's irony is indeed an Ecoian postmodern declaration of love – and Lacan is indeed its critic.

54  For successful communication as the return of the subject's message to the Other back to the subject in its inverted form, which betrays the subject's unconscious desire, see Lacan, *The Four Fundamental Concepts of Psychoanalysis*, 139–40.

55  See Lacan's *The Other Side of Psychoanalysis*, 39–53.

56  See respectively Mikhail Bakhtin, *Problems of Dostoevsky's Poetics*, trans. Caryl Emerson (Minneapolis: University of Minnesota Press, 1984), 193–204; and Valentin N. Vološinov, *Marxism and the Philosophy of Language*, trans. Ladislav Matejka and I. R. Titunik (New York: Seminar Press, 1973), 23. Both active in the Bakhtin Circle, Bakhtin and Vološinov have used the same term ('raznonapravlennoe') to theorize 'varidirectional' and 'differently oriented' social positions respectively: see M. M. Bahtin, 'Problemy poetiki Dostoevskogo', in Bahtin, *Sobranie sochinenii v semi tomakh*, vol. 6, eds. S. G. Bocharov and L. A. Gogotishvili (Moscow: Russkie slovari, 2002), 222, 226; and V. N. Voloshinov, 'Marksizm i filosofija jazyka', in M. M. Bahtin, *Pod maskoj*, ed. I. V. Peshkov (Moscow: Labirint, 2000), 366.

For a recent return to Bakhtin and Vološinov with the aim of critically engaging with Derrida's reading of Austin, see Constantine V. Nakassis's two-part essay 'Para-s/cite', *Semiotic Review* 1 (2013). Available online: semioticreview.com/ojs/index.php/sr/article/view/33 and semioticreview.com/ojs/index.php/sr/article/view/34 (both accessed 1 April 2019).

57  See Lacan, *The Ethics of Psychoanalysis*, 182–4.

58  For Lacan's condensation of *publication* and *poubelle* ('dustbin'), see, for example, his 'Postface' in Lacan, *Le Séminaire. Livre XI*, 252 (and the English rendition in Jacques Lacan, 'Postface to the French Edition of *Seminar XI*', trans. Adrian Price, *Hurly-Burly* 7 (2012): 18); his *écrit* 'On a Purpose', in Lacan, *Écrits*, 304; his book *Le Séminaire. Livre XX: Encore: 1972–1973*, ed. Jacques-Alain Miller (Paris: Seuil, 1975), 29 (and Jacques Lacan, *On Feminine Sexuality, The Limits of Love and Knowledge: The Seminar of Jacques Lacan, Book XX*, ed. Jacques-Alain Miller, trans. Bruce Fink (New York: Norton, 1998), 26); and his paper 'Du discours psychanalytique', in *Lacan in Italia 1953–1978 / Lacan en Italie 1953–1978*, ed. Giacomo B. Contri (Milan: La Salamandra, 1978), 34.

# Index

Adorno, Theodor W.   113
Althusser, Louis   6, 25, 116–18, 128–9, 143, 172 n.18
Apter, Emily   175 n.5
Aristotle   3, 8, 11
Armstrong, Philip   163 n.33
Austin, John L.   1–5, 7–19, 21–2, 24–8, 30–1, 44, 47, 49–52, 61–2, 65, 67–9, 91, 94–8, 104–5, 107, 109–10, 123, 127, 130–2, 134, 147 n.1, 147 n.3, 148 n.12, 149 n.27, 157 n.52, 159 n.25, 160 n.35, 179 n.56

Badiou, Alain   75, 128–9
Bakhtin, Mikhail M.   25, 135, 145, 179 n.56
Beethoven, Ludwig van   37
Benveniste, Émile   24, 29, 104
Bhabha, Homi   92–3, 95, 99, 111
Blanchot, Maurice   121
Bloom, Harold   19–21, 73–5, 157 n.53
Bosteels, Bruno   175 n.5
Boucher, Geoff   3, 159 n.25, 169 n.40
Bourdieu, Pierre   98
Brown, Chris   170 n.3
Buden, Boris   92–3
Buffet, Marie-George   115
Burd, David Andrew   170 n.3
Butler, Judith   1–5, 7–8, 49, 91–5, 97–111, 114–15, 127, 130, 132–3, 167 n.17, 167 n.24, 167 n.25, 169 n.40, 169 n.48, 171 n.17

Calderwood, James L.   164 n.48
Caron, Gilles   113, 170 n.8
Carroll, Lewis   13–14, 17, 149 n.27
Cavell, Stanley   8, 10, 147 n.3
Cclan, Paul   73, 128
Chappelle, Dave   95, 111
Chaucer, Geoffrey   146
Cohn-Bendit, Daniel   5, 112–16, 120–1, 170 n.8
Conan Doyle, Arthur   178 n.46

Considine, Liam   170 n.9
Copjec, Joan   122

de Gaulle, Charles   113, 122
de Man, Paul   73, 147 n.3
Descartes, René   34, 63, 140
Dolar, Mladen   34, 122, 124, 153 n.20
Dollimore, Jonathan   162 n.22
Ducrot, Oswald   1–2, 5–6, 15, 18, 24–6, 28–31, 47–8, 60, 127, 134–7, 139–40, 142–3, 145, 151 n.63, 158 n.14, 176 n.21
Duras, Marguerite   121

Eco, Umberto   136
Emerson, Ralph Waldo   20

Fanon, Frantz   122
Farley-Hills, David   75
Felman, Shoshana   30, 110
Fischer-Lichte, Erika   110
Fish, Stanley   148 n.25
Fouchet, Christian   121
Fraser, Nancy   167 n.25
Freud, Sigmund   3, 33–4, 41, 46, 128, 152 n.8, 162 n.24, 164 n.47
Frye, Northrop   74

Garber, Marjorie   165 n.53
Geisel, Theodor Seuss   157 n.52
Gibbons, Brian   74–5
Girard, René   74, 163 n.33
Giroux, Henry A.   35, 38, 157 n.53
Goldman, Pierre   122
Gorman, David   8
Graff, Gerald   49
Guillaumont, Ronald   125

Habermas, Jürgen   92–3, 99–100
Haillot, Jacques   113
Hammerschlag, Sarah   122
Hartman, Geoffrey   73

Hazan, Éric   121–2
Hegel, G. W. F.   100–1, 158 n.3, 167 n.24
Heidegger, Martin   160 n.32
Herrick, Robert   32–4, 41
Hitchcock, Peter   169 n.48
Honneth, Axel   167 n.24
Husserl, Edmund   4, 51–5, 57, 61–4, 67, 116

Irwin, James   171 n.17

Jakobson, Roman O.   11–12, 22, 150 n.49
James, Henry   177 n.32
Johnson, Barbara   69, 71, 158 n.13

Kant, Immanuel   100, 156 n.41
King, Martin Luther, Jr.   94–5, 111–13, 124, 170 n.2
Kleinbaum, N. H.   31, 157 n.51
Krishna, Nakul   148 n.19
Kristeva, Julia   162 n.22
Kržan, Marko   158 n.14

Lacan, Jacques   2–4, 11, 23, 29, 33, 36–7, 44, 61, 69–72, 77–8, 82, 113, 117, 122–4, 128, 136, 140–3, 145, 147 n.11, 151 n.51, 152 n.10, 153 n.11, 153 n.12, 154 n.27, 155 n.41, 156 n.45, 156 n.48, 158 n.13, 159 n.25, 163 n.38, 164 n.40, 164 n.46, 164 n.47, 165 n.49, 170 n.8, 173 n.39, 174 n.47, 176 n.21, 177 n.32, 178 n.40, 178 n.45, 179 n.53, 179 n.54, 180 n.58
Laclau, Ernesto   167 n.24
Lakoff, Robin Tolmach   14
Lenin, Vladimir I.   128
Lessing, Gotthold Ephraim   45
Lévi-Strauss, Claude   17
Lloyd, Moya   167 n.25
Loxley, James   167 n.17
Lupton, Julia Reinhard   75, 88
Lyotard, Jean-François   143

MacCannell, Juliet Flower   143, 153 n.20
Macherey, Pierre   25, 131–2
Mandelshtam, Osip E.   128
Mannoni, Octave   67, 108
Marbury, Herbert Robinson   169 n.1
Marchais, Georges   170 n.7

Marchesi, Olivier   170 n.4
Marsh, Jack E., Jr   159 n.15
Marx, Karl   117, 123–4, 129, 162 n.24
Mauss, Marcel   17
Medvedev, Pavel N.   25
Messner, Reinhold   112, 170 n.5
Miller, Jacques-Alain   40, 155 n.41, 170 n.8
Miller, J. Hillis   9, 73, 110
Miller, William Ian   152 n.8
Milner, Jean-Claude   14, 19, 58–9, 71, 149 n.33
Milohnić, Aldo   168 n.34
Moati, Raoul   3, 159 n.25, 160 n.35
Močnik, Rastko   11–12, 45, 64, 116–20, 134, 143, 163 n.32, 168 n.27, 171 n.17, 176 n.21, 177 n.25
Moi, Toril   3, 147 n.3
Montoya, Scott L.   170 n.3
Moretti, Franco   20
Motoh, Helena   171 n.17
Mozart, Wolfgang Amadeus   164 n.46
Mulligan, Kevin   159 n.15

Nakassis, Constantine V.   3, 158 n.11, 179 n.56

Ohmann, Richard   49

Parker, Andrew   123
Perrine, Laurence   153 n.13
Perse, Saint-John   128
Plato   73, 130
Poe, Edgar Allan   4, 70–2, 78, 158 n.13
Pratt, Mary Louise   49

Raffel, Burton   164 n.41
Rancière, Jacques   1–2, 5, 114–17, 123–4, 127–34, 172 n.18
Rancillac, Bernard   113–14
Ricoeur, Paul   160 n.32
Robson, Mark   123, 173 n.42
Ross, Kristin   122, 124
Royle, Nicholas   70, 72

Sade, D. A. F. de   155 n.41
Salecl, Renata   176 n.21
Saussure, Ferdinand de   158 n.14
Schulman, Tom   157 n.51
Searle, John R.   3, 16, 49, 51–4, 56, 60–2, 130, 158 n.9, 159 n.25

Sedgwick, Eve Kosofsky   110
Shakespeare, William   4, 46, 69, 72–5, 86, 89, 162 n.22, 162 n.24, 163 n.37
Simoniti, Jure   167 n.24
Smith, Anna Marie   167 n.25
Steyerl, Hito   92
Sturge, Kate   166 n.8
Šumič-Riha, Jelica   123, 174 n.44

Taylor, Michael   162 n.24
Todorov, Tzvetan   176 n.21
Trivedi, Harish   92

Vico, Giambattista   7, 34, 45
Vološinov, Valentin N.   145, 179 n.56

Wallerstein, Immanuel   75
Weber, Samuel   49
Wegner, Phillip E.   142
Weir, Peter   3, 31, 48
Wells, Stanley   164 n.39
White, R. S.   162 n.24
Whitman, Walt   3, 15–17, 19–21, 26, 32, 34, 36–7, 41–2, 44, 46, 149 n.27, 154 n.27, 157 n.53

Žagar, Igor Ž.   27–8, 30
Žižek, Slavoj   71, 123, 156 n.49, 166 n.13, 171 n.17, 173 n.35, 174 n.44, 176 n.21
Zupančič, Alenka   3, 40, 155 n.41

www.ingramcontent.com/pod-product-compliance
Lightning Source LLC
Chambersburg PA
CBHW052046300426
44117CB00012B/2001